A History of Canadian Cricket:
An Immigrant's Game?

by

Patrick Adams

This book is dedicated to:
Cate and Jennie
Our two demi-canucks

Acknowledgements: An apology
I am truly sorry that this book has no specific acknowledgements. My
record keeping and memory are simply not reliable enough to compile
a list that would not omit someone important. I thank everyone who has
given me encouragement, carried out proof reading, shared information
(in one specific case, allowed me to view his own extensive private
library), lent me books and provided me with pictures and photocopies
free of charge, posted at their own expense. I only hope that somehow,
one day, I can return the many favours that I owe.

*If we knew what we were doing, it would not be called research, would
it?*
Albert Einstein

Published by www.lulu.com

ISBN:978-1-4466-9652-1

Contents

Chapter 1: Introduction

It's a funny kind of month, October. For the keen cricket fan it's when you realise your wife left you in May.
Denis Norden

There are two great loves in my life: cricket and Holly, my Canadian wife. This book combines the two in a labour of loves.

Both my parents have Canadian heritage and I expect this influenced their decision to move to Canada after they got married, although they vowed to their family and friends that they would return. My parents are of the generation that did not cohabit before marriage, and so their Canadian adventure gave them the opportunity to strike out on their own and get to know each other before returning to Britain to settle down and start a family. When my father's boss in Montréal got wind of my parents' plan to return home he advised that they try the $1,000 cure. This involved spending what then must have been an exorbitant sum on a short holiday to Britain to cure immigrants of any nostalgia they had for the Old Country and realise that their future was in Canada. Apparently it was a practice that successful husbands imposed on their wives, but in my parents' case neither of them tried the $1,000 cure and my future as an Englishman was assured.

At my school it was football that was king, even in the summer months. Some of us did try and play cricket during break-time but the chalked outline of a set of stumps on the back of the brick bike shed caused endless disputes as anything striking the wall within a yard of this two dimensional target would be claimed by the bowler and all the other boys waiting to bat. The most likely outcome was a compromise such as playing out a number of deliveries with the bat turned upside-down, known as "candlesticks", but this depended more on your ability to argue, than the facts of the case. The proximity of the wall to the fence was also unsatisfactory; a rule had been introduced somewhere in the mists of time when one lost ball too many had convinced the playground leaders of the day to decide that anything striking this fence was out. This sacred law was passed down from each year to the next without question. The purists would no doubt approve of the fact that any firm leg-side strike led to instant dismissal, but it limited the enjoyment of the game, as well as giving an unfair advantage to left-handers, so most of us played football instead.

Fate played its hand during one particularly wet April. Leaves, twigs and crisp packets blocked the drain on the playground, giving the kids a great big puddle to play in. To keep the drain clear the inventive caretaker found an old spring-loaded set of stumps with a square base and placed it on the drain cover. This blocked any detritus, but allowed the rainwater to flow away. More importantly it gave us our first opportunity to play a game of cricket with three-dimensional stumps and no restrictions on where we could play our shots. We played with a tennis ball, but the headmaster responded to our interest by adding cricket to the sporting curriculum with a hard ball and real protective equipment. Before long cricket thrived at the school and a single-wicket competition was organised. Ironically the final was contested by an American and a Canadian, much to the astonishment of the headmaster.

During my formative years there was a dispute between the teachers and the Government regarding overtime, which meant that a generation of state school children was deprived of inter-school sports matches. It was also at around this time that the non-competitive sport initiative took hold in many schools and as a result children such as I had to look elsewhere to play meaningful competitive cricket. I was fortunate that the next village from where we lived had a thriving junior movement. Stapleford Cricket Club ensured that my youthful enthusiasm was not lost and in the fullness of time I would become Secretary of this Club. It is to my lasting regret that after over 70 summers the Club has folded due to a lack of players.

Neither of my parents is particularly interested in cricket, although they were keen to nurture the interest and ability of their two sons. My mother tried to understand the game, particularly when one of us had done well, but when she made it clear that she thought that the two batsmen were on opposing teams we realised that any interest was feigned. She once told me that if I ever played first-class cricket she would learn the rules. Sadly she knows no more about the game now than she did then.

My father at least understood the rules as both his father and his uncle were keen players. I suppose that the cricket gene has simply skipped a generation, which condemned my father to what for him must have been many tedious hours in the sun as both man and boy for the benefit of either his father and uncle or his sons. I only realised this recently when I invited him to a county game. He appears to be enjoying his retirement and I hope his polite refusal was an indication that he's finally finding the time to do things that he wants to do.

Every summer I would spend a week with my paternal grandparents down in Dorset, where many hours would be spent in front of a flickering television image showing the latest Test match. Grandad had no problem encouraging my interest in the game, although he never managed to convince me to appreciate skilful play by the opposing team or have the patience to continue watching a game which appeared to be a foregone conclusion; I suppose only time and experience can do that. I went up to my room during the closing stages of the 1985 Edgbaston Test against Australia, as I was convinced it would be a draw. Granny and Grandad called me down just in time to see the replay showing David Gower catching out Greg Ritchie off the boot of Allan Lamb. I'd missed the turning point of that Test and arguably the series, which England won 3-1. I wonder if Grandad was smiling down on me when I did exactly the same thing 20 years later during the 2005 Edgbaston Test and missed that crucial delivery of Harmison's to Kasprowicz, which won the match and turned the series England's way.

I shared a love of cricket as well as my name with my Great Uncle Pat. He was a member of the MCC and it is to my shame that I behaved like the sullen teenager that I probably was at the time and refused his invitation to see a Test match with him in 1993. My brother went instead and we all saw England win against Australia, although I viewed it on my bedroom television. My memory says that the game was at Lord's, but the records show it to have been at the Oval.

My parents' first years of marriage ensured that I grew up in a home with an Eskimo carving on the mantelpiece, a picture of a kayaker on the wall and the sound of Gordon Lightfoot on the record player. This gave me a way of breaking the ice when my boss introduced me to my new co-worker, a beautiful Canadian from Winnipeg called Holly. She taught me that Canadian music had changed in the last 30 years or so and that the term Eskimo meant "eater of raw fish" and was no longer used in polite society. In turn I tried to convince Holly that cricket wasn't just an insect and provided her with updates on her country's progress in the 2003 World Cup, where they defeated a Test playing nation (Bangladesh) in a competitive match for the first time in their history[1].

Whilst my knowledge of Canada grew, so did my knowledge of Canadian cricket. I learned that the first cricket international was played in 1844 between Canada and the United States and this contest had become an annual match. I discovered that the first cricket tour took place in 1859 when George Parr's professionals had toured first Canada and then the United States. The great WG Grace had toured Canada in 1872 and according to his biographer Simon Rae this had been his happiest tour. I wondered why cricket had not developed in Canada as it had in other Commonwealth countries and this sowed the seeds for a lengthy research project.

---

[1] But it wasn't the first time they beat Bangladesh (see chapter 10).

I was keen to make my first trip to Canada, partly to see the places that had only been described to me, but mostly to meet Holly's family, which I felt in all decency I had to do before I proposed to her. Both Holly's parents are retired teachers and as we sat in the Ichiban restaurant following the Blue Bombers victory against the Edmonton Eskimos (apparently this is an acceptable name for a football team, but not an Inuit carving) I tried to impress them with my knowledge of Gordon Lightfoot songs and then by announcing my intention to write a book. My future father-in-law's only advice was that I should write on a subject that had not already been extensively covered. A few quick Google searches later and the planned book on Captain Scott was shelved in favour of Canadian cricket.

Chapter 2: The First Clubs

If a man will begin with certainties, he shall end in doubts, but if he will be content to begin with doubts, he shall end in certainties.
Francis Bacon

A MATCH AT IGLOOLIE, BETWEEN H.M. SHIPS "FURY" AND "HECLA."

Wherever Britons travelled, they brought their games with them, even on the ice of Igloolik in 1823.

Unfortunately most public debates degenerate into unseemly contests between protagonists attempting to win the argument instead of objectively trying to find the truth. Any discussion on the origins of cricket will inevitably follow this pattern as the evidence is so sparse it is impossible to find an accepted truth. Any new discoveries or alternative views can too easily be contested or even derided. For example, much ink has been spilt on the thirteenth century reference to creagh, but even if there is some distant link between creagh and the modern game we will never know what the game creagh entailed or indeed anything significant about any of the games mentioned in the earliest references. Before attempts were made to try and standardise the rules it is impossible to know exactly what constituted early cricket.

If I were writing a book on the history of cricket I would dismiss the pre-eighteenth century material in a few paragraphs. My book is on Canadian cricket and so I've dismissed it in one. I will however assign a few paragraphs to the earliest references to cricket in Canada, which are just as scarce as the early references to British cricket.

Most books on the history of cricket make insufficient reference to the rules and their subsequent changes. Rule changes hardly feature at all in this book because generally the game in Canada followed the rules agreed in Britain. Indeed nineteenth century editions of the Toronto based *Globe* newspaper had adverts for copies of the rules as determined by the MCC and the 1858 Canadian Cricketers' Guide listed these rules within its pages. Any differences between the Canadian and British games tended to be in conventions, such as the late adoption of boundaries in Canada, which until surprisingly recently were not referred to at all in the rules and the preparation of pitches, with matting wickets being preferred in Canada for most of the twentieth century. The number of balls delivered in an over was also a difference.

As a schoolboy I was told that pre-history ended and history began when man first wrote something down. I believe that cricket history only truly began when the rules were written down; before the early attempts to standardise the rules it is impossible to know what was being played. Canadian cricket pre-history is represented by the obscure references to games being played by soldiers in garrison towns, or sailors in the frozen north or by civilians in scratch games. It is impossible to know the significance of these games, but the scarcity of the references suggests that they had little influence on the social development of the country. Canadian cricket history begins with the formation of the first clubs.

A glance at the countries that play cricket shows that wherever the British went they took their favourite summer pastime with them. In September 1759 the British forces under General Wolfe defeated the French on the Plains of Abraham. This is a landmark in Canadian history as it marked the culmination of the end of the Seven Years War and the beginning of the end of French involvement in what became British North America. It also sowed the seeds of the second round of the war between the French and the British, which is now known as the American War of Independence. Intriguingly, both the French and the US are keen to downplay the key involvement of France in this conflict.

Legend has it that following the battle an impromptu cricket match broke out between the English and their French captives. It is hard to imagine the British scaling the cliffs outside Québec with cricket bats instead of cold steel on their backs and the very real threat of a French counter-attack from the French General Lévis suggests that storytellers have been exaggerating the English reputation for eccentricity. Following the death of Wolfe on the battlefield, command passed to General James Murray, who being a tough practical Scot would no doubt have disapproved of his soldiers playing this English game. The British had been bombarding the city for the best part of the year and now found themselves unprepared for the onset of winter amongst the devastation they had wrought. These are not conditions conducive to the playing of ball games. However, according to *Le Soleil* of Wednesday 15 July 1908, cricket was played on the Plains of Abraham between the Club de Québec and the Royal Canadian Dragoons. Cricket was played on the Plains of Abraham, not immediately after the Battle, but 150 years later between the British Army and a civilian team with a French Canadian name.

Wherever the British travelled they took their games with them, which is why cricket now flourishes in most Commonwealth countries. Naturally in any conquest the first people to establish themselves in a new land will be the soldiers and many British regiments have a proud cricketing tradition. For example the Honourable Artillery Company, the oldest British regiment, was involved in one of the earliest recorded cricket games at the Artillery Ground, which was a prominent cricket ground in London until the 1830s. So therefore it can be assumed that after the war with France was concluded with the Treaty of Paris in 1763, the British soldiers garrisoned in Québec and Montréal would have played the same games they had enjoyed at home. The equipment may have been improvised but nonetheless it is probable that some form of cricket was played for the first time in Canada around this period.

The earliest accepted reference to Cricket in Canada is of a game that was played on the Ile-Sainte-Hélène in 1785[2] involving two garrison teams. This island is part of modern day Montréal and was the site of Expo 67. Coincidentally the cricket historian Rowland Bowen states in his book *Cricket: A History of its Growth and Development throughout the World* that the earliest record of cricket in Canada was also in 1785 and also in Montréal, but he refers to a game between French Canadians on a Sunday after Mass. By all accounts cricket has failed to make any lasting impact on French Canadians and so Bowen's reference serves as a warning against relying on a single surviving record to define a whole era.

The records are sparse in the late eighteenth century and there would be a gap of almost 50 years before the first known clubs were formed. As we shall see later in this chapter the claim to being the first cricket club in Canada is disputed.

What is not in dispute is that British soldiers played an essential part in the settling of Canada, with garrisons based in every town. In 1841 it was determined that every army barracks was to have a cricket ground, by order of the Duke of Wellington, who was then commander-in-chief of the British army. This ensured that the presence of British soldiers continued to greatly assist the development of cricket in Canada throughout the nineteenth century. Soldiers provided domestic teams with talented opposition to play against and inevitably provided some of the best players for representative teams selected to play against touring sides or against the United States. In the 1870s many of the soldiers garrisoned in Canada were posted elsewhere throughout the Empire and their influence on cricket in the country declined.

The British Navy has also played an important role in Canada's cricket history. On his second Arctic expedition Captain Edward Parry and his crew played cricket on the shoreline in March 1823 at Igloolik, as well as football and quoits. These British sailors were wintering with Inuit at the time, although disappointingly there is no written evidence that any of the native Canadians participated in these sports.

Whilst garrisons provided opposition for civilian cricket teams, the navy provided transient opponents for teams residing in the nation's ports. Many games were played in Halifax, Vancouver and St Johns, Newfoundland against teams made up from the crews of visiting ships. These teams were inevitably of a variable standard thus providing civilian teams with an opportunity to beat touring teams that represented the Empire.

---

[2] The *Montreal Gazette* of 7 May 1927 concurs that the first cricket played in Montréal was played on St Helen's Island between two garrison teams, but in 1843 not 1785.

Cricket in Newfoundland

Newfoundland became Canada's 10th province in 1949, thus creating a headache for historians of Canadian history: should events in Newfoundland that occurred before 1949 be included as part of Canada's history? I am including references to cricket in Canada before confederation in 1867 so I shall include references to cricket in other provinces before they joined Canada. So my book includes cricket in what would become Manitoba before 1870, cricket in British Columbia before 1871 and cricket in Newfoundland before 1949. This is hardly a momentous decision as I have found few references to cricket in Newfoundland. It can be assumed that cricket was played in Newfoundland from the formation of the first club in 1828 up to the First World War, although much of it has gone unrecorded. PJ Myler's book *Recollections of Cricket* details the cricket played in the 1890s by Newfoundlanders of British descent living in the St Johns area. It mentions the games they played against each other and against visiting British sailors. In the short period covered by the book, teams were coming in and out of existence and the impression given is of a game with an uncertain future and cricket declined from what was a low base after the First World War. It is probable that many of its cricketers crossed the Atlantic never to return, but this is covered in another chapter. However, cricket did not disappear entirely. JW Cole, the Chairman of the Canadian Cricket Association, refers to cricket being played in Canada from Newfoundland to British Columbia in a letter printed in November's Playfair Cricket Monthly in 1972. More recently Newfoundland managed to send a team over to the mainland to compete in the 2010 Maritime Twenty20 tournament.

Cricket in the Maritimes

Many of the loyalists who were forced to flee America following the War of Independence settled in the Maritimes and it is probable that many of them would have been cricket players, although I have failed to find any evidence of this.

The cricket in the Maritimes was sustained by the British soldiers and sailors. In 1871, nearly a hundred years after the American Revolution, Colonel NW Wallace arrived in Halifax where he was critical of the ground, which he stated had the appearance of a ploughed field, and he was critical of the standard of civilian cricket compared to that of the British servicemen or the civilian players of Upper Canada[i]. Wallace was instrumental in setting up the Halifax Cricket Tournament in 1874, which attracted a team from Philadelphia, who beat Canada and a side made up of British Officers to win the competition. Wallace played for the British Officers and top scored with 68 in an exhibition game for Halifax who took on "All-comers" a team made up of Canadian and Philadelphians. Halifax won by 5 wickets. A return tournament was held in Philadelphia in 1875 and won by the hosts. When a domestic competition was set up for teams in and around the Philadelphia area it was called the Halifax Cup and was contested from 1880 to 1926.

Following the recall of the British Army and Navy to Europe in the mid-to-late nineteenth century, cricket in Halifax went into decline, although matches between civilians and servicemen continued to be played. On 18 July 1889 FA Kaiser and FAW Taylor scored an unbeaten partnership of 252 for Halifax Wanderers v Navy; a Canadian record.

Cricket in Québec
Early cricket in Québec centred round Montréal and its garrison. It was played amongst the English settlers but has never established any roots in the French speaking population. The cricketing rivalry between Montréal and Toronto is discussed in later chapters.

Cricket in Manitoba
JJ Hargrave's book *Red River* states that a considerable quantity of cricket equipment was imported into the Red River Settlement preceding the setting up of the North West Cricket Club, by William Coldwell, a local journalist and businessman, on Saturday 24 September 1864, with the Governor as President[ii]. Hargrave states that the bats were imported from the United States, which was the only realistic route for goods to be imported. He describes a merry game following the donation of a gallon of sherry by Chief F Sinclair. Apparently this was Manitoba's first organised sports club, but it declined as old members left and the newer members appeared indifferent by comparison. It appears that the history of the North West Cricket Club was a short one, but reports in the *Winnipeg Free Press* of the 1870s show that from these stuttering starts cricket became a major sport in Manitoba in the latter part of the nineteenth century.

Cricket in Saskatchewan
The Regina Cricket Club was formed in 1883 and the North West Mounted Police team played at the around the same time.

Cricket was played at the faintly ridiculous Cannington Manor a settlement formed by the eccentric British aristocrat Captain Edward Michell Pierce in 1882. For the princely sum of £100 British immigrants could pretend to live like country gentlemen at Cannington Manor. Pierce died in 1888 and the unsustainable Cannington Manor fell into decline. However, cricket did not cease entirely and in 1913 the village of Maryfield played against a team from Cannington Manor at Wawota.

Cricket in Alberta

Edmonton Cricket Club was founded in 1882 and Strathcona CC was set up a few years later. The Edmonton League was set up and in 1912 a cup was donated by the local newspapers. This trophy is still awarded to the League winners today. Calgary's St John's Zingari Cricket Club was formed in 1908.

Lloydminster was formed in 1903 by British immigrants, who intended to establish a utopian society. The cricket club was established in 1904 and the arrival of the railroad in 1905 made it easier for tours to take place. In 1911 Lloydminster managed to defeat Edmonton twice. Cricket declined rapidly after the First World War and by the 1920s cricket had died out in the settlement.

Cricket in British Columbia

Cricket took root quickly in what was to become British Columbia as it was the main sport to be played by the first British settlers. Captain William Colquhoun Grant is credited with bringing the first cricket equipment to Victoria in 1849. Naval teams competed against domestic sides in British Columbian ports; in 1858 Victoria Cricket Club beat the crew of the *HMS Satellite*. The Victorian Cricket League was established in 1877 and by the 1880s a great rivalry had developed between the Vancouver and Victoria clubs who played against each other annually from 1888 onwards.

There is a report of a Parsee team touring British Columbia, which unfortunately I have been unable to verify. There were about 2,000 Indians living in Canada in 1914, almost all of them were residing in British Columbia. So it is perfectly possible that a Parsee team toured British Columbia at this time.

Cricket in Ontario

Whilst cricket in the other provinces should not be forgotten there can be no doubt that the majority of cricket in Canada was and still is played in the province of Ontario and in and around Toronto in particular. It is to the credit of those who ran the game that they strove to include cricketers from the other provinces in selecting national teams and in organising domestic competitions, when it would have been far easier to have restricted these ventures to local cricketers.

The title for Canada's first cricket club is disputed. St Johns Cricket Club in Newfoundland was formed in 1828 and can claim to have been in existence six years before Toronto Cricket Club, which was created in 1834, but this is not the whole story. Toronto Cricket Club adopted its current name in 1834, but this was when the town changed its name from York to Toronto. The Club came into existence seven years before, as the York Cricket Club. In 1927 the Club celebrated its centennial year, but unfortunately papers proving its formation in 1827 were lost in a fire at the Club's premises in March 1952. So the first Canadian cricket club was the York Cricket Club, which was formed in 1827 and changed its name to Toronto Cricket Club in 1834.

It is fitting that Toronto Cricket Club is Canada's oldest club as it dominates the history of Canadian cricket along with the Upper Canada College Cricket Club. George Anthony Barber was heavily involved in the establishment of both. In 1829 Upper Canada College was founded. Three teachers: George Barber, Frederick Barron and John Kent, ensured that cricket became an essential part of the curriculum.

FW Barron was the principal of the Upper Canada College (UCC) from 1843-56, and he keenly promoted cricket. Like many cricketers he was also a member of the Royal Yacht Club. Cricket and yachting were the pastimes of the elite. John Kent played alongside Barber and Barron for both the UCC and Toronto. He died in Newfoundland in 1872.

It is George Anthony Barber who is most remembered. Through his efforts he became known as the Father of Canadian Cricket. He became the President of Toronto Cricket Club in 1852 and was a traditionalist who declared at the start of the 1855 season, when receiving a presentation, that he was "an Englishman by birth, a British subject by choice and a Canadian by adoption". His involvement as player, administrator, selector and umpire was unsurpassed, but when his influence waned towards the end of his life he did not go quietly.

The Toronto *Globe* of Wednesday 8 July 1868 published a letter from Barber in which he accused John Heward, the President of the Toronto Cricket Club, of deliberately arranging the Province versus Upper Canada College game on date that he could not attend and of threatening to cancel the fixture if the captain of the Province team chose Barber as their umpire. The lengthy letter alludes to an incident during the cricket week in London 1867 that led to falling-out between these two men. I can find no evidence of any public response from Heward to Barber's accusation of vindictiveness. Every man reacts differently to growing old and realising that he is no longer as competent as he used to be. Barber was in his mid to late sixties and it is probable that he was no longer as reliable an umpire as in the past. Perhaps Heward's actions can be explained in this light.

The dispute did not end there. The Toronto *Globe* of Saturday 17 September 1870 published another letter from Barber, which accused Heward of deliberately organising a match between Toronto Cricket Club and Cobourg in order to prevent a game between 15 of Ontario and Toronto, which Barber was organising, from going ahead. The Secretary of Toronto sent Barber a letter of explanation, to which Barber's response was "credat Judaeus!" At first I assumed that Barber was calling Heward a Judas, as Ian Botham would do to Peter Roebuck over 100 years later during the Somerset mutiny. Barber's comments actually translate to "tell that to the Jews", or a rather apolitically correct version of "tell that to the marines". Barber died four years later. This giant of the Canadian game got little more than a footnote of an obituary in the Press, suggesting that he had alienated those who had followed in his footsteps.

In 1836 the Upper Canada College Cricket Club was formed, although clearly cricket had been played at the College since its founding. The College's links to the ruling elite were enhanced when the Governor of Upper Canada, Francis Bond Head, became the Club's first patron. Popular historian Will Ferguson states that at the time diplomacy was required in the ruling of Canada, but appointing Bond Head was like setting a kangaroo loose in a minefield[iii]. This may be so, but Bond Head started a long running relationship between Governor-Generals and the game of cricket.

A glance at www.cricketarchive.com shows that many Canadian cricketers at this time played for more than one Club. In an age before eligibility criteria it is not surprising that loyalties were more flexible. In 1836 the Upper Canada College Cricket Club and the Toronto Cricket Club played their first match in what would become an annual fixture. The College team was open to "old boys" as well as current students, making many players eligible to play for both teams. In the first match George Barber and Frederick Barron, two long-standing members of Toronto Cricket Club, represented the College team, who won the game.

Other clubs in the area were also in existence at this time. In 1834 Toronto Cricket Club played against Guelph at Hamilton, in what was the first recorded match in Canada where the teams had to travel any real distance[3]. Hamilton was chosen as a neutral venue as it gave both teams an equal distance to travel. This also became a regular match and in 1840 the team of Toronto were about to embark on a journey to play their old foes Guelph when they received some unexpected visitors. This meeting would lead to the establishment of a far more important regular contest.

---

[3] According to the Montreal Gazette of 7 May 1927 Toronto first played against Montréal in 1846, where the visiting Torontonians won by seven wickets.

Chapter 3: Canada vs America: the Series from 1844-65

"Geography has made us neighbors. History has made us friends. Economics has made us partners. And necessity has made us allies. Those whom nature hath so joined together, let no man put asunder." President John F Kennedy in speech to Canadian Parliament

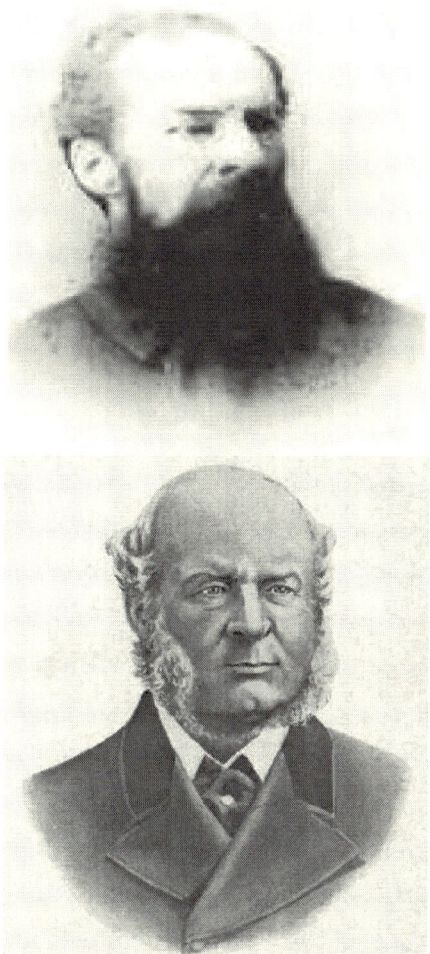

The Reverend TD Phillipps (top) was one of the few players to play in the Series before and after the 1865-79 gap and Mayor of Toronto John Beverley Robinson (bottom) played in the first International in 1844.

From an inauspicious beginning the International Series became the highlight of the cricket season for enthusiasts on both sides of the border. Planned as an annual contest, it was interrupted by disputes on the pitch and a civil war off it. Scorecards can be found on www.cricketarchive.com

The catalyst for a major event is often small and seemingly insignificant to those who witnessed and took part in it. It is the historians and statisticians who then bestow mythical status on the protagonists who competed and in many cases died in ignorance of the importance that enthusiasts would later place on their deeds. For example the first Test match between Australia and England was only so named after the event. The Australian press referred to the home side as a combination team of Victoria and New South Wales before the match, only calling them Australia after victory had been achieved. Mr Frank Allan pulled out of the "Australian" team a few days before to attend an agricultural show.[iv] I expect that it was many years before he truly regretted this.

In September 1840, 37 years before what became known as the first Test match and 42 years before the seven run defeat which would lead to the establishment of "the Ashes", St George's Cricket Club from New York arrived unexpectedly in Toronto to play the local team.

A month before, a man calling himself Mr GA Phillpotts of Toronto Cricket Club visited the St George's Club and proposed that the two sides play each other home and away, starting with a match at Toronto later that year. The hosts would pay the expenses of the visitors. "Mr Phillpotts" assured the New Yorkers that no further correspondence was necessary, other than the announcement of the date they intended to travel. Whether by design or by accident the contact given to the St George's Club was for a gentleman who was at that time absent from the city. Members of the Toronto Cricket Club read of the impending tour from an imported copy of the New York newspaper, *The Spirit of the Times*, however without any evidence to the contrary they assumed that the report was false. So when 18 members of the St George's Club arrived in Toronto on 2nd September, after travelling by land and lake for the best part of a week, the Canadians had not made any arrangements for their unexpected guests and were preparing to leave for a match against nearby Guelph. The man who had visited New York the previous month was an impostor, which was proven to the Americans when they met the real Mr Phillpotts, the Secretary of Toronto Cricket Club, in a dinner after the game.

The mystery regarding the impostor's identity and his motives remains. The cricket historian Rowland Bowen states that the embarrassing event "involved one individual without any authority at all who made arrangements with another who rarely cleared his pending tray!"[v] Bowen's account puts some of the blame on the Toronto Cricket Club's administration, which does not explain the reason for the impostor's duplicity. John Marder, author of *The International Series*, blames the scheming impostor who was identified "but never officially named"[vi], but he does not explain the impostor's motive; he appeared to have been from Toronto but his actions inconvenienced the players from New York. What is not in doubt is that he inadvertently cemented a friendship between the two clubs that would lead to the establishment of the longest-running international cricket series.

An impromptu committee meeting with representatives from both sides was hastily convened. It resolved that Toronto had no knowledge of the affair, but at the same time should apologise or at least "express regret" for it. Most importantly they also agreed that a game should be played for a sum of £50 and arrangements were made for an after match dinner. The St George's team were given two days to recover from their journey and duly won the game by 10 wickets. There were five run outs in Toronto's first innings, an astonishing occurrence in any era and one that suggests the St George's team were a more competitive side. It is also possible that the American cricketers also played baseball, whose fielders continue to be more skilled than those on a cricket field.

The haphazard nature of the match should not shroud its importance. It not only started a chain of events which would lead to the International Series, but it was an event in itself. Sir George Arthur, the Lieutenant Governor of Upper Canada, attended with his staff, which indicates that those who played cricket had sufficient social standing to ensure such notable spectators at very short notice.

It is tempting to see the Lieutenant Governor's presence in terms of international diplomacy, as this was a volatile time. After failing to form a Canadian republic with approximately 600 men in 1837, the radical newspaper publisher William Lyon McKenzie[4] fled south to carry out border raids into Upper Canada with American support. In response Canadian loyalists sank McKenzie's supply ship the *Caroline*, killing an American called Amos Durfee in the process. This led to much sabre-rattling in the United States, with the majority of American public opinion, but certainly not all, backing McKenzie's rebels. In the winter of 1838-39 a separate dispute broke out between lumberjacks from New Brunswick and Maine, resulting in a bloodless confrontation called the Aroostook War. Calmer heads ensured commitment to a diplomatic

---

[4] William Lyon McKenzie was given an amnesty and returned to Canada in 1849. He died in 1861, but his grandson, William Lyon McKenzie King, became Canada's tenth Prime Minister and served for a record 21 years (but not continuously), between 1921 and 1948.

solution in March 1839 with a formal treaty signed in 1842. Can the attendance of Sir George Arthur and his staff be explained by these events?

The answer is probably yes, but more as a rallying call to loyalists than as a diplomatic mission to improve relations with America. The cricket players in the 1840 match would have been united, not separated, by these border disputes. Unsurprisingly for an organisation of this name, the St George's Club had links to Britain. Whilst American public opinion was being swayed by the cry to "remember the *Caroline*" those present at the St George's Society annual meeting were toasting one Captain Drew, leader of the attack on the ship, whilst the flag of the *Caroline* hung as a war trophy behind the chair of the Society President[vii]. This Society was also toasted loudly at the after match dinner along with the Queen, the sports of England - "may they never be forgotten this side of the Atlantic" - and the sons of the British Patron Saints. It is clear where the loyalties of both teams lay and instead of fostering better relations between Canada and the United States, the Lieutenant Governor would have been showing the strength of the Family Compact, an elite group of Anglican Conservatives, which effectively ran Upper Canada until the Act of Union of 1841 joined Lower and Upper Canada under a single government. John Beverley Robinson, who played for Canada in the first International match, was a member of this Family Compact and was Attorney General and Tory Member of the Assembly. As a judge he sentenced two of the 1837 rebels to death.

The start of the International Series
The only truly "international" aspect of the 1840 match was the geographical location of the two teams. They continued to play against each other; in September 1843 Toronto beat St George's by four wickets, although apparently betting had been in favour of St George's after the first day's play. These contests were strictly between the two clubs and when the St George's Club attempted to include three Philadelphian players in their team for a match scheduled for 25 July 1844,[5] the Torontonians objected and the game was cancelled. However, those players from both sides of the border who wanted to develop the game beyond club loyalties would not be denied and the St George's/Philadelphian team played a side made up of five Guelph and six Upper Canada College players on 26 July. This match was merely a side-issue, played in the hope that the more important abandoned game would still take place; however the restrictive club boundaries

---

[5] Marder states this took place in 1843 on p.14 of The International Series. This is contradicted by Cricket Archive, which states the date given.

had been broken and what became known as the first international match would be played later the same year.

The St George's Club issued a challenge via a newspaper advert to the Toronto players, indicating how much money should be at stake and allowing selection of players beyond club boundaries. The Toronto Cricket Club replied with a letter sent to a New York newspaper, accepting the challenge for a match to commence on 24 September for a stake of $1,000. Given the communication failure four years previously it is surprising that the clubs felt obliged to liaise through a newspaper, instead of writing directly to the club's secretaries. Indeed there were some dissenting voices from the St George's Club, questioning the veracity of Toronto's acceptance as it had not been sent to them directly. The *New York Herald* of 14 September asserted that the Club should:

> *"consider how far it will go to maintain their character as cricketers and gentlemen, to refuse the acceptance of a challenge through the public press, when they themselves adopted the same means to give it."*

Fortunately Toronto's acceptance was acknowledged and the first ever cricket international match took place on 24-26 September, with no play on the 25th. The *Toronto Patriot* of 24 September 1844 referred to the names of the two clubs, not the two countries and the New York *Weekly Herald* referred to the *St George's Club* playing against the *Canadians*. However, the American team included the Ticknor brothers, John and Robert, who were members of the Philadelphia Cricket Club. If there were any rules regarding eligibility, they appeared to be based on residency in the early matches, although stricter guidelines would be brought in later. How rigidly these were followed is a matter of conjecture.

The official stake for the match was $1,000, but far more money was being gambled on the result. The *Weekly Herald* of 28 September estimated $50,000 to $100,000 had been bet on the result, a huge sum in today's money. The odds fluctuated throughout the match. At the end of the 1st day's play few punters were taking the 5 to 4 odds on a Canadian victory. In a possible attempt to minimise their losses the bookmakers were offering odds of 3 to 1 on an American win after the Canadian second innings.

It had been agreed beforehand that batsmen would have to run for everything, unless the umpire called lost ball. It would be decades before a set score for hitting the ball beyond a boundary would become accepted practice in the international matches.

The weather prevented any play on 25 September and so it was agreed that the two-day match should be extended to a third day to allow a result. The umpire R Waller was unable to officiate on 26 September and it is probable that his excuse of an appointment in Philadelphia was a genuine one. However, in America's first innings J Ticknor was incorrectly given out LBW, which according to the *Weekly Herald* "gave a great degree of dissatisfaction." It is impossible to discern which umpire gave the decision, but if it was Waller it could explain his absence for the rest of the match. Harry Russell of the St George's Club was persuaded to stand at short notice. He had umpired in a match three months before between St George's and the New York Cricket Club and so was a logical choice.

The press estimated 5,000 spectators for the first day's play and 4,000 for the second. Despite the significance of the match it started 40 minutes late and this was not the only example of tardiness. The American player George Wheatcroft did not bat in the second innings because he turned up to the ground 20 minutes after the game had ended. He had been absent the entire day under the mistaken belief that no play would be possible due to the weather. Given the importance of the match his behaviour does seem extraordinary. The amount of money riding on the game led the *Weekly Herald* of New York to report that "[s]ome ugly rumors were afloat to account for this gentleman's absence at such a crucial time". The first allegations of match fixing had hit international cricket in its inaugural contest.

The Canadians, who had allowed a substitute fielder throughout the day, refused the request to allow a substitute to bat in Wheatcroft's place. When the errant player finally arrived a new dispute flared up over whether the game should be restarted to allow Wheatcroft to bat. The rules agreed by the MCC in 1829 stated that a batsman must be ready to bat within two minutes of the fall of the wicket, although there was no specific "timed out" rule. In any event, the fact that the match had finished before he arrived at the ground meant that the Canadians were within their rights to refuse the request and pocket their considerable winnings. The Americans immediately instigated a "double or quits" attempt to recoup their losses by challenging the Canadians to a re-match the following day for any amount from $500 to $2,000. This fresh challenge was declined.

The victory margin was a relatively comfortable 23 runs or about a third of the average score for an innings in the match. It is doubtful then that the result would have been different had Wheatcroft been allowed to bat. Despite, or perhaps because of this experience, Wheatcroft would umpire in the seventh match in 1856.

The man of the match, had such a thing existed, would have been D Winckworth for top scoring in both Canadian innings and taking at least five wickets, in a scorecard where the wicket taker is unknown for three of the dismissals. He also took an impressive catch in the American second innings, reportedly jumping four feet in the air to dismiss Dudson. Sharpe also had a good game, joint top scoring with Winckworth in the first innings and taking at least six American wickets in their second innings. Naturally the reliance that Canada had on these two indicates that there were a number of players who contributed little to the victory. Incidentally, it is probable that the Sharpe in this game was George Sharpe, who played in the 1859 and 1860 games. A gap of 15 years between internationals may appear unlikely in a player's career, but AL Marsh of America also played in both games.

Eligibility for either team depended on a player's residency not his nationality, but in the history of the Series I can trace only two players who competed for both countries, which suggests that patriotism did influence selection. Most of the players in the first match were born in Britain; the aforementioned John Beverley Robinson was born in York, before it became Toronto, and he is the only one of the 22 who is known to have been born in North America. The St George's Club regularly played an internal match between those club members born in the south of England and those from the north, emulating the great North v South matches in the home country. The Series would never shake its reliance on players who were born overseas and the lack of second generation Canadians playing cricket has been a constant handicap to the game's development in Canada.

The Canadian players returned to Toronto in triumph. Alderman William Boulton had accompanied the cricketers to and from New York and had allegedly made thousands of dollars by betting on the outcome of the game. Such behaviour not only enhanced Boulton's reputation, it also launched his political career. When the Canadian team and their entourage arrived at Toronto, part of the waiting crowd starting calling for Boulton to be elected to the Legislative Assembly. There had been a dispute between the conservatives and reformers on who should stand in the forthcoming election, and in Boulton the powers that be found an acceptable third candidate. Boulton would be elected Mayor of Toronto by his fellow Councillors in 1845 until 1847 and then again in 1858. He was defeated in 1859 when the office of Mayor was elected directly by the electors for the first time.

1845 – Second and third matches
In 1840 a home and away match had been envisaged and in 1845 that is what happened, for the first and only time. Complete bowling

analyses exist only from the seventh match in 1857 onwards, so it is impossible to know with any certainty who was selected to play as a bowler for the first six games. It is a feature throughout the Series during this period that there were a large proportion of "thanks for coming" players who failed to contribute with either bat or ball. This suggests that selection in part had to be based on who was available to play, which included being able to travel to the ground. This is emphasised by the fact that the Americans only managed to field 10 players in the 1865 match at Toronto. It is also probable that social standing was a factor in selection.

In 1844 Montréal became the capital of Canada and this may have influenced the decision to hold the second match there on the McGill College Grounds on 30 and 31 July 1845. The majority of players resided in the Toronto area and the next time that Montréal was used as a venue was 1909; by then the Series was heading for a terminal decline. The selection process and the perceived bias towards Toronto players led to disputes with those from Montréal, culminating in a short-lived rival series in the late 1850s. Four of the players appearing for Canada in this match were from Montréal. The American press billed the game as a selected St George's Cricket Club team against All Canada.

Once again Sharpe and Winckworth were the key bowlers for Canada; they took all 19 of the wickets to fall to the bowlers in this match, with one run out, finishing with 8 and 11 wickets respectively. They showed their stamina by bowling unchanged in the second innings for a combined total of 39.3 six ball overs and were more accurate than their American counterparts. They conceded no extras in the American first innings and only five in the second, compared to 28 extras conceded in the two Canadian innings.

Sharpe proved his worth as an all-rounder by hitting 31 at number five in the Canadian second innings. Hornby top scored with 35 to help Canada to a total of 135. The Americans were set a victory target of 137 that was always going to be out of their reach and Canada won by the large margin of 61 runs.

The third match was played on 28 and 29 August 1845, at the ground of St George's Club in New York. There were approximately 3,000 spectators to witness the start of the match and this number increased to an estimated 5,000 as the game progressed. They saw Hornby, Sharpe and Winckworth repeat their feats of a month before and again produce performances that were instrumental in the Canadian win. The Canadians won the toss and elected to field first, which was clearly the right decision as the Americans were bowled out for 49, "recovering" from 11 for 6. Sharpe took two wickets whilst Winckworth took six in the first innings, including the dismissals of Turner, R Ticknor and G Wheatcroft all without scoring in five deliveries. In the American second innings their fortunes were reversed as Sharpe took six wickets and Winckworth had only one success. Hornby scored 28 in Canada's first innings total of 82, with Winckworth being the only other batsman to reach double figures with 12. Hornby would have scored many more had it not been agreed beforehand that only three runs would be awarded for hitting the ball beyond the boundary.

Needing just 60 to win, the Canadians made heavy weather of the chase. Sharpe was promoted up the order to 3 and he made 9, sharing a match winning 29 run partnership with Hornby who scored 10. Canada then appeared to suffer a mid-order panic before stumbling to victory by two wickets. When victory was declared by the scorers, then known as markers, a great cheer was heard from the Canadian tent. The close finish would have entertained the crowd and also shown that despite the easy wins in the first two matches, the two countries were evenly matched. There was every reason to suppose that this competitiveness would cement the international match as an annual fixture for many years to come, but an incident in the next game nearly killed off the Series for good.

27-28 August 1846 – Fourth Match

This match was played in New York and ended in a dispute that led to a cessation of the Series for seven years. All official records list this match as a draw, which is surprising as the Canadians had refused to continue and the Americans, who were in a winning position, claimed the game and their winnings from the bets made with their Canadian opponents.

Canada were bowled out for only 28 in their first innings, with the number 11 batsman John Connolly, who had been an umpire in the first match, top scoring with 4 not out. The United States made 57 and Connolly opened Canada's second innings 29 runs behind. It was not uncommon in Canadian cricket for the not out batsman in the first innings to open the batting in the second, even if he were a tail-ender. There could be no tactical advantage in this, so I can only assume that it was a convention to allow an unbeaten batsman to continue his innings.

With the score on 13-2 the Canadian opener, John Helliwell, struck the ball in the air and on seeing that he was likely to be caught out he ran into the American bowler Sam Dudson. Despite the collision Dudson completed the catch and then ran towards Helliwell and threw the ball at him, hitting him on the bounce, before being restrained by his teammates. Despite an apology from Dudson the Canadian batsmen refused to take the field and the game was abandoned with Canada 16 runs behind with 7 wickets in hand.

Marder suggests that Helliwell believed he was entitled to charge the bowler as the rules of 1744[6] state that either batsman may hinder the bowler from completing a catch if the bowler is within the "running ground" of the batsman. This is unlikely for a number of reasons. The rule was already a hundred years old; it prohibited striking the bowler or making contact with the hands and specifically restricted the batsman to his normal running ground. Deaths had occurred due to collisions between batsmen and fielders and the rules agreed at the Star and Garter in 1744 aimed to prevent players charging down their opponents. Helliwell had to run two feet out of his normal running ground[viii] to collide with Dudson, so he had a poor grasp of the rule that was later used to defend his behaviour. I cannot find anything from the sparse records of domestic Canadian cricket to suggest that the charging down of a bowler was an accepted part of their game so it is more likely that the rules were misleadingly quoted after the event in an attempt to legitimise Helliwell's violent conduct and the Canadian reaction to Dudson's retaliation.

George Barber was umpiring in this match and he was quoted in *Bells Life* as stating that Helliwell, a former pupil of his at the Upper Canada College, would have been given out obstructing the field had Dudson not completed the catch.

Due to the controversy the fact that D Winckworth became the first player to represent both teams has been largely overlooked. He had played for Canada in the first three matches but it was deemed permissible for him to represent the United States in this match as he had moved to Detroit. Despite the flexible qualification rules, only one other player has represented both sides. This was SFAF Bacchus, who played 18 Tests for the West Indies. He played for Canada in 1977 and for the US in 1994 and 1995.

No international matches were played for seven years, which is a long gap in a series of only four games, two of which had taken place in the same year. Despite this the game played in 1853 was linked with those that had been played in the 1840s in the public consciousness and by the fact that five players competed in both the 1846 match and the

---

[6] Marder incorrectly attributes this rule to 1702. Page 30 of the 1851 edition of Box details the rules as agreed in 1744 at the Star and Garter, including the reference to how a batsman may interfere with a catch referred to above. This reference is undated in Box but follows an explanation of block-hole cricket on page 29, which ends with the date 1702, hence the confusion.

game played in 1853. The great George Barber umpired in both matches, thus giving the contest legitimacy and linking it to the earlier games.

24-25 August 1853 – Fifth match

The *New York Times* of 30th July 1853 downplayed the amount of time since the previous international by stating that it had been "about three years" since the last game in what was called "the annual cricket match between the St George's Club and the best eleven of the Canadian Clubs." Despite equating the American team to that of the St George's Club the article goes on to state that the forthcoming contest was between all the players of Canada and all the players of the United States, suggesting that the Series was now a truly international contest. This is supported by the 1858 Canadian Cricketers' Guide, edited by the Reverend Thomas Phillipps, which mentions the accepted date of 1844 but asserts that the 1853 match was the first true international without elaborating.

The St George's Club had been responsible for the selection of the "American" team for the earlier contests, but by 1853 selection was determined by a committee which instigated a trial match which was open to all eligible players. Although only one player from outside New York played in this game[ix], the establishment of a selection committee and a trial match open to all American players represented an important development in the Series. The St George's Club had been instrumental in the setting up of the Series and no fewer than seven of the American players for this game were from that club. It appears likely that despite the trial match, selection was dependent on who could get to the venue, thus giving an advantage to players of St George's Club as the match was played on their ground. It should be noted that according to the *New York Times* of 15 August 1853, the venue for the match was chosen by the Canadian team. The number of players from St George's Club declined as more players were selected from other New York clubs. Following the Civil War the American team would become exclusively Philadelphian.

The Canadian team was and continued to be from a more varied background, although the vast majority were always from the Toronto area. In 1853 Bill Napier was from Montréal and three other players were from the army. Four players were members of Toronto cricket club and the rest were from nearby teams. In mid August the annual match between Old Country and Young Canada had been played at Toronto, which may have had an impact on selection for the international match. The Canadian team used an early form of bowling machine, described as a catapult, in order to prepare themselves for the fast American bowlers. This early contraption did not prevent an American victory which reports[x] attributed to superior bowling.

The result of this game was much gambled on, with the *New York Times*[xi] stating that the Canadians offered four to five on the result and evens on making the higher first innings score. However, the accuracy of the cricket reporting in the *New York Times* does need to be questioned. The 26 August 1853 edition states that Fletcher was caught off a shooter, which is hard to imagine. Comery is frequently misspelled as either Connery or Conery. Apparently fewer bets were made by the Canadians after a first innings deficit was conceded. Clearly to bet against one's team was not done and when the American team ended the first day with a lead of 65 and five wickets remaining there were few willing to bet on a Canadian victory. The *New York Times* reports that there were more spectators on the second day, but less betting, suggesting that although gambling was part of the game, many were content to attend without such a distraction, especially if the home team were winning.

Despite the importance of the match there were a number of players who did not contribute with either bat or ball. The five bowlers who took wickets for Canada all batted in the top six and the Americans Wilson and Burnett did not appear to bowl[7] and batted at 9 and 10 respectively. It is probable that, as already mentioned, selection had to be determined by who was willing and able to travel to the venue.

The Americans won the match by what was then considered to be a comfortable margin of 34 runs. They entertained their guests at the luxurious Delmonico's Restaurant, where they were entertained by the renowned comedian Charles Walcot. Clearly any bad feeling from the previous encounter had disappeared. The *Milwaukee Sentinel* concluded its match report of 30 August 1853 with the words "we have merely to say that this was, perhaps, the most severely contested match ever played on this Continent." Through a single match the International Series was back on track.

19-20 July 1854 – Sixth match
The *New York Times* described this as the second match, beginning an inconsistency that would continue throughout the nineteenth and early twentieth century, illustrated in the table below:

---

[7] Without a bowling analysis it is impossible to know for certain whether Wilson or Burnett bowled; if they did bowl they failed to take a wicket.

New York Times edition	Match number in paper	Actual match number
2 August 1859	6th	10th
7 August 1860	7th	11th
14 August 1883	12th	17th
16 September 1884	13th	18th
8 September 1897	25th	29th
30 August 1898	30th	30th
9 September 1901	29th	33rd
13 September 1902	30th	34th
10 July 1906	34th	38th
15 September 1908	40th	40th
27 August 1911	37th	42nd
8 September 1912	43rd	43rd

The *New York Times* of 13 August 1886 stated that the first international was played in 1844, but gives a brief history which does not include the games played in 1845, 1846 and 1865. The *New York Times* of 11 July 1904 also reported that the first match was played in 1844. They were also undecided on what to call the two teams. On 21 July 1854 the American side is called both a combined team and a national side. The team was described as New York clubs three days later following the Canadian victory, but then the side is called the US team the day following that.

The Americans won the toss and decided to bat. Unfortunately for them their innings was interrupted by a thunderstorm after an hour's play, which made the pitch difficult to bat on when the game resumed. They finished the first day on 32 for 9, a position from which they never recovered. J Bradbury took 9 wickets for 6 runs in the first American innings and would finish with 13 wickets overall, helping Canada to win the game by 10 wickets. Dexter, who had been unbeaten batting at 10 in the first innings, opened the second innings for Canada and was again unbeaten. George Barber umpired again for the Canadians and although one of his decisions was disputed by the American Waller, his speech on behalf of the Canadians at the end of the game, as President of Toronto Cricket Club, was well-received. The speeches and toasts were given at a joint dinner in honour of the American cricketers at the St Lawrence Hall, where the band of the Canadian Rifles played. The fee for non-guests was the princely sum of $5.

The perception that the match was one between nations is strengthened by the fact that the American team brought their national flag to the Toronto ground, whilst in the previous year's contest the only flags visible had been those of the clubs, including the St George's cross, displayed above the tents for their members. After the

Canadians had won the game comfortably, the Americans lowered their flag. In response Captain LH Denne from the Canadian side ordered that the Union Jack also be lowered, not to be raised until after the Stars and Stripes was re-hoisted and saluted. This pleasant little incident showed how far the contest had changed from 1840 when the after dinner toasts had been exclusively pro-British. The after dinner toasts in 1854 included three cheers for the Queen and the American President.

Marder suggests that the movement of troops due to the Crimean war prevented a match from being played in 1855. This is strengthened by a report of the *New York Times* of 6 September 1856 which stated that a number of the Canadian players had just returned from the Crimea. This would have included Captain Lansada who played in the 1856 match.

11-12 September 1856 – Seventh Match
The pitch at Hoboken New Jersey was described as poor by Marder and the heavy rain which delayed play on the first day would not have helped. Whatever the state of the wicket it did not prevent the Americans from scoring 111 in their first innings, thus achieving a decisive lead of 47. Gibbes top scored with 43. Wicket-keeper Captain Lansada's 23 for Canada was the second highest score of the match, but was not enough to prevent an American victory by 9 wickets. The Mayor of Toronto, John Beverley Robinson, was one of the 5,000 spectators on the second and final day. He had represented Canada in the first international in 1844.

A hospitality tent was supplied with Kendall's Allsop's Pale Ale and after the match Canadians retired to the Astor House. Unsurprisingly they were "well pleased with their trip."

19, 20 and 21 August 1857 – Eighth Match
More than half the Canadian team were playing in their first international. The match was played on a good wicket, which is proved by the runs scored on an outfield that had been drenched in heavy rain which meant that the batsmen did not get full value for their shots. According to the *New York Times*, shots that would have been worth 4-5 were yielding only 1-2, showing the impact the condition of the surrounding ground can have on a match without boundaries.

Three scores of over 30 by Heward, Bradbury and Parsons ensured a first innings score of 145 and a lead of 37 for Canada. This proved to be decisive with no American batsman scoring more than 30 runs in the match and Parsons completing an excellent all-round performance by taking four wickets in both innings. Canada were victorious by seven wickets[8]. There were 25 byes in the match, which were attributed to the long stops who were Barlow for the Americans and H Phillips for the Canadians.

2, 3 and 4 August 1858 – Ninth match

This was the first of the four international matches played by the Rev TD Phillipps. Rain delayed the start of the match by two hours, allowing the Canadian team to enjoy a hearty meal provided by their hosts as the players waited for the weather to clear. The Canadians could only manage 73-7 before the close of play, the weather causing more interruptions. An uncertain weather forecast did not prevent 2-3,000 people from attending the second day's play, who were probably encouraged to attend by the dominant position of the home side. Canada were dismissed for 81, leaving JO Heward stranded on 31 not out. The Americans then amassed 147 with the Honorary H Bingham top scoring with 34. The Canadian decision to play without a wicket-keeper undoubted contributed to the 34 extras in the American innings compared to only 16 in the Canadian innings, despite a similar number of deliveries being bowled by both teams.

The Americans were assisted by interference from the crowd with the Canadian fielder Foudrinier being prevented from catching Bingham when he was in single figures and a shot from JC Rykert which was estimated as being worth 6 coming back from the crowd and only being worth 2. The press[xii] were particularly critical of those responsible for policing the behaviour of the spectators and it is not difficult to discern why boundaries were introduced.

Canada began the final day on 26-4, needing to score 40 to make the United States bat again. Both Hardinge and Head hit double figure scores and Canada reached 101, leaving the Americans to require only 36 for victory. Hardinge, who had a tumour removed from his foot after arriving in New York, combined with Head again to take three wickets each before the United States scrambled home by 4 wickets.

There was a dispute at this time regarding the selection of the Canadian team. Pickering, secretary of the Eastern Clubs, had been selected to play in the 1858 match. He refused to play, due to a perceived bias in selection. He wanted "cricketers in the United States to fully understand that there is a stronger eleven to be got in Canada than the one present playing at Hoboken."[xiii] Montréal would participate

---

[8] The scorecard shown on page 54 of *The International Series* only has one not out batsman. This is inexplicable as Canada won the game by seven wickets and so would have had two not out batsmen at the time of victory.

in their own international matches against American opponents[9], which the press, if not posterity, would give equal prominence to the games of the International Series.

The Canadian captain, JO Heward, responded to Pickering's criticism in his after match speech. After presenting the ball to the victorious US captain and thanking the Americans for their hospitality, he explained that the captaincy had been offered to Mr Pickering of Montréal, along with the selection of two other players. No response had been received and Heward expressed that he was "greatly surprised" at hearing the protest of Mr Pickering. This suggests that the dispute was at least partly due to communication problems. However, the fact that the captain saw fit to mention it in his after match speech implies that this was a significant matter. Heward also advised players from New York to heal dissensions, suggesting that there was disquiet both sides of the border[xiv].

3-4 August 1859 – Tenth match
This match was played in the knowledge that Parr's professionals were due to arrive in Canada in just over a month on the first ever international cricket tour. The dispute regarding selection for the International Series influenced the venues for the tour matches. This is referred to in the following chapter. Marder describes this as a trial game for the forthcoming tour games and it is certainly true that a number of the players in this match would also play against the tourists. However, the North American teams would be made up of 22 players so those selected for the international match could reasonably expect to play against the tourists.

The press stated that the Canadian team was missing several players who would otherwise have been selected. This would have been due to the dispute with Montréal.

With the game in the balance the American batsman Wilby, when only having scored 2, believed he was out LBW and started to leave the field. It transpired that the American umpire Symes had not given him out, but on realising this Phillipps broke the stumps at the strikers end. Wilby then left the field but in the words of the press report "refused to be considered as having lost his wicket."[xv] To avoid bad feeling the Canadians allowed Wilby to continue his innings. The bowler Parsons was furious at the decision: he threw away the ball and refused to finish

---

[9] *New York Times* of 15 September 1858 stated that a challenge was accepted by St George's Club from Mr Rikery of Montréal for a game to be played on 8 October 1858. Mr Rikery objected to the Canadian team being called "all-Canada" due to the exclusion of players from Montréal.

the over. He was replaced by Rogerson who according to the press report did not bowl as well as Parsons. www.cricketarchive.com reports that following this incident the Canadian players gave up on the game, a view supported by the Toronto *Globe*. Wilby made 22, out of a total of 72-6, and the US won by 4 wickets, making this the first match since 1845 to be won by the away team.

A letter appearing in the *New York Times* from an old English player asserted that the umpire should have called dead ball before the stumps were broken to avoid the row. Despite all this the press reported that the players dined together after the match "in the best possible spirit", which I hope was true.

6-7 August 1860 – Eleventh match
This game was the last to be played at the St George's Club in New York, but surprisingly no members from this club played due to a decision taken at their convention not to take part in amalgamated teams. This was also the last match to be played before the outbreak of the American Civil War, which had a detrimental impact on cricket south of the border, as games that required less equipment and preparation such as baseball were favoured.

Three players from Montréal were selected for this match, which helped to ensure that the rival international series was short lived. The Montréal player JG Daly fielded in the crucial position of long stop. He had top scored with 10 in the Montréal 22 first innings against Parr's Englishman. Foudrinier and Hardinge had played in the Series before.

The press reported[xvi] that having a fixed number of runs for certain shots was unsatisfactory and as a 5 was scored I have to assume that although a boundary was used in some matches, it was not used in this one.

Though attendance was free there were only 500 spectators. After scoring 86 in their first innings and 104 in their second, Canada set the Americans 94 to win. Unfortunately the Canadian bowling and fielding were not as good as they had been in the American first innings; 20 extras were conceded, which was double the number in the American first innings of 97, and the United States won by 5 wickets.

Due to the US Civil War the Series was not played for five years, although matches between America and British army officers in Canada were contested.

29 August 1865 – Twelfth match

Astonishingly for a match of such importance the American team only had ten men. The game was played at Toronto but it seems unlikely that there were no eligible players amongst the spectators. It is probable that the names of the team members had been submitted to the umpires and one of the American players failed to turn up. Due to poor management the home team did not consist of Canada's strongest players with nine of them playing in the Series for the first time, a large number after only a five year gap. Once again no players from eastern Canada were chosen. This was due to both the short notice given and poor management[xvii].

Marder cannot trace a club affiliation for the Canadian JM Young[10] and suggests that he was a late addition to the side to make up the numbers, although this seems unlikely as he batted at 5 and made the second highest score in the Canadian second innings.

The pitch was poor and the bowling was superior to the batting, which resulted in a very low scoring game, with Canada's 73 in their first innings being the highest score. Despite this the 10 men of America managed to score the 65 required for victory for the loss of eight wickets. The Canadian captain was criticised for unimaginative field placings, and drops by Parsons and Young were described by the Toronto *Globe* as "the most inexcusable we have seen on the cricket field." Young also failed to run out Rogerson and the narrowness of the defeat suggests that the result would have been reversed had these chances been taken.

There would be a gap of 14 years before the next match, which Marder describes as unaccountable. Possible explanations are discussed in a later chapter. It is possible that resources were directed towards the visits made by touring sides in the mid-to-late nineteenth century at the expense of the International Series. These ground breaking tours are the subject of the next chapter.

---

[10] According to www.cricketarchive.com JM Young opened the batting for the Civilians against the Military of Canada on 28 & 29 August 1863. He played alongside Frank Draper and Ben Parsons in this match, who were also his teammates for the 1865 international game.

Chapter 4: The First Tours

I have from the very outset regarded these tours primarily as imperial enterprises, tending to cement friendship between the Mother Country and her Dominions

Sir Frederick Charles Toone (England Manager) on overseas tours in 1930 Wisden

The twelve 1872 tourists at Montréal, with the great WG Grace at the wicket.

In 1859 the first overseas cricket tour took place when George Parr's team of professionals left Liverpool on 7th September to play in Canada and the United States. The players were a combination of the two strongest teams in the land, the United England Eleven and its rival the United All England Eleven. The amount of cricket played in North America made it the logical choice for such a tour, but in 20 years Australia had taken over this mantle, although this in part was an indirect consequence of this tour.

There is some evidence of previous tours. The Duke of Dorset was due to tour France in 1789, but arrangements had to be cancelled due to the Revolution. An exhaustive study could be carried out of all the rumours and sparse evidence to establish the veracity of the rival claims to be the first overseas cricket tour. However, the findings of this interesting exercise could not detract from the importance of the 1859 tour and its place in history. The first tourists would feature heavily in the second and third tours. Heathfield Stephenson took his own team to Australia in 1861-2 accompanied by William Caffyn who also toured Australia and New Zealand in 1863-4 with George Parr's team, along with five more of his 1859 teammates. Caffyn would stay behind and coach Australian cricketers in both Sydney and Melbourne. It was a combined team from these two clubs that defeated James Lillywhite's touring English professionals in what became known as the first Test match in 1877. Lillywhite toured North America in 1868. The tour of 1859 was the first vital step towards the establishment of cricket as an international sport.

It is unsurprising that the tourists won all their games, even against teams of 22 players. They were selected from the two best teams in England: six players each from the All England Eleven and the United All-England Eleven, who earned a living by touring England and playing against local teams of 22 players. With the exceptions of Edgar Willsher and Richard Daft, it would be difficult to find any other players who were more worthy of selection than the 12 who toured. Daft was named in the original 1859 tour party, but was replaced by Heath Stephenson. Willsher was also included in a list of the tourists published in August[11]. Although neither Willsher nor Daft were part of the 1859 venture they would both lead their own tours to North America.

---

[11] The *Albany Evening Journal* of 9 August 1859 included Willsher and an accurate list of the fixtures. The Toronto *Globe* of 21 September 1859 included the name of R Daft, but not H Stephenson in the touring party. The *New York Herald* of 25 September 1859 stated that Stephenson had replaced Daft.

The tour had first been mooted in 1856, but the players' financial demands could not be met. However, these players eventually settled for half the sum demanded three years earlier. So the reasons for embarking on this adventure were not just financial, although each player eventually received £90, which is just under £4,000 in today's money. This was a good return when in Britain players tended to receive £4-5 each per match[xviii].

Henry Sharpe of New York Cricket Club helped with the financing of this tour[xix] and Robert Waller, also of New York, helped to secure sponsorship. However the man most responsible was William Percival Pickering[12], who had the necessary contacts on both sides of the Atlantic. He had captained Eton, represented Cambridge University and had been involved in the founding of Surrey Cricket Club and I Zingari before emigrating to Canada in 1852. He briefly returned to England and served on the MCC Committee, before resettling in Canada. The Englishmen insisted that some money be paid in advance, which must have required a certain degree of trust. The 1859 tour ended up £100 in the red after expenses had been paid and this shortfall was made up by the Montréal Cricket Club.

The 1859 tour is proof that a history of cricket in Canada is not just a history of cricket in Toronto. Montréal Cricket Club had the finances to ensure that a team of England's best cricketers came to Canada and in WP Pickering they had a President who had the links to make it happen. He played four times for Canada in the International matches of the 1850s and would undoubtedly have represented Canada more times had he not instigated a dispute with Toronto Cricket Club over a perceived bias in selection in favour of players from Ontario. The dispute took the form of a self-defeating boycott and the organisation of games with the Americans with a side of Montréalers, calling themselves Canada. They were heavily defeated and the schism was short-lived. When Pickering first tried to arrange the tour, back in 1856, he was President of Toronto Cricket Club, but as President of Montréal he ensured that no games would be played in Toronto. The wheel would turn full circle and Pickering would become President of Toronto again, where he worked hard to ensure that the 1878 Australian tourists played at the Toronto Cricket Ground. In time he would become the Secretary and Treasurer of the Ontario Cricket Association.[xx] Whatever bitterness was felt in the dispute, clearly there was no long lasting grudge.

---

[12] *Bells Life* published a letter from George Parr and John Wisden on 8 January 1860 stating that Pickering's Montréal Cricket Club were solely responsible for the tour.

When the Montréalers played under the guise of Canada the match was embarrassingly one-sided with "Canada" being bowled out for 42 and America hitting 165 in response and winning the game by an innings and 46 runs. The game in Montréal coincided with the visit of the Prince of Wales and although seats had been provided for the Prince he made his polite excuses and declined to attend.

These tours used cricket to foster a closer relationship between Canada and the old country in the name of Empire. Imperialist motives run as an under-current for all the tours to Canada from 1859 to 1976, although clearly there were other factors that sustained these ventures. The early tours also went to America, where extolling the virtues of the Empire would have fallen on stony ground, although the involvement of New York's St George's Club indicates that it was often anglophiles who the tourists were playing against. The motives for Canadian cricketers were twofold: they hoped that these tours would encourage the growth of the game in the Dominion and encourage more immigrants from the mother country. For their part the Englishmen, both professional and amateur, were seeking financial reward and an adventurous holiday. It is hardly surprising that an excursion to see Niagara Falls became an essential feature of these tours.

*   *   *   *   *   *   *   *   *

After posing for a now famous photograph on a completely different ship, the English players embarked on the *Nova Scotian* on 7 September; they suffered a nightmarish journey, encountering several storms before they finally arrived in Montréal a week later than expected. They would have arrived a day earlier had the crew not made a navigational error in fog and mistaken the Bay of Gaspé for the mouth of the St Lawrence; such were the vagaries of mid-nineteenth century transatlantic travel.

According to the *Toronto Globe* of 27 September, the organisers at Montréal, in particular Mr Balchin the owner of the lease of the property, were criticised by Fred Lillywhite for not advertising the game well enough. This was a little unfair, as the organisers' plans had been disrupted by the unexpected delay to the *Nova Scotian,* causing the game to commence later than originally advertised. Critical press reports originating from Toronto should perhaps be read in the light of the fact that Pickering and the Montréal Cricket Club had snubbed Toronto, by arranging a match at Hamilton[13] but avoiding Toronto, the

---

[13] The Toronto *Globe* of 16 September 1859 reported that although Hamilton wanted to exclude players from Toronto they would be unable to get 22 Hamilton cricketers to play against the English tourists.

capital of cricket in Canada. There were daily adverts in the *Globe* offering special rail tickets to Montréal, but the week's delay would have made it difficult for out of town spectators to attend. The attendance increased in the afternoon as the public became aware that the match was taking place. However, the mood of the crowd was subdued after it was announced that the eldest son of the Governor General Sir Edmund Head had drowned.

The location of Montréal, as well as its attractions as a city, made it a logical place for touring cricketers to play. The ground sounded idyllic; it was on St Catharine Street, with the centre of Montréal visible about half a mile in the distance and the maple trees adorning Mount Royal could also be seen in the background. However, whilst the setting was picturesque the condition of the ground was not conducive to cricket. The 1872 tourists were even more critical of the venue than the pioneers of 1859, which suggests that cricket in Montréal was in decline in the mid-late nineteenth century. Richard Daft's 1879 team avoided Montréal completely, whilst PF Warner's 1898 tourists described the ground as "appalling"[xxi]. The low number of spectators at the start of the game indicates that cricket did not have a wide appeal in Montréal. The elitism of the sport guaranteed the support of those in power and the match on 24 September was attended by the Commander of the Armed Forces, General Sir William Fenwick Williams, the hero of the siege of Kars during the Crimean War. However, the organisers of cricket in Montréal could not get the support of thousands of ordinary members of the public to ensure the upkeep of the facilities and the necessary spectator numbers to make international cricket viable. Toronto and its surrounding area was the centre of Canadian cricket, in terms of players, spectators and facilities.

The first organised overseas tour showed the need for warm-up games as the tourists bowled poorly and allowed Montréal to make 85 in their first innings. They then lost Grundy in the second over and were lucky not to lose more wickets before time was called. Fortunately the next day was Sunday and after a day of rest the Englishman played better on Monday and won the game by 8 wickets.

After an early finish to the game against Montréal the tourists played a game against each other, selecting 10 of the most promising local players to make up the numbers. The estimates of crowd sizes made in nineteenth century press reports should not be relied upon, but according to the *New York Herald* only 2,000 spectators watched this game, whilst at its peak the crowd had numbered 5-6,000 people during the match against Montréal. The crowd wanted to see a meaningful contest and not an exhibition match.

The after match dinner was hosted following the first day's play by Montréal Cricket Club and their arrangements for this were more agreeable to the tourists that those made for the game. The first reference to cricket in what was to become Manitoba can be found in a speech given by the Chairman of the Montréal Cricket Club at this dinner. According to Fred Lillywhite's account Francis Godschall Johnson stated that whilst Governor of the Red River settlement, he had witnessed the formation of a cricket club which had commissioned a carpenter and a shoemaker to construct bats and balls.

The practice of a shoemaker producing cricket equipment has a long history. John Small, a cobbler by trade, started producing some of the first straight bats in Britain in the mid-to-late 1700s, thus replacing bats that had been shaped like a hockey stick. Small is also renowned as being the first batsman to master the use of the straight bat, a technique made necessary by bowlers learning to pitch the ball so that it bounced once, instead of simply "bowling" the ball along the ground.

The accuracy of Lillywhite's account can be questioned, however, and he is unlikely to have brought a notepad with him to record the many speeches and toasts. He has Johnson explaining that it had been "some time since" that he had been the Governor of the Red River settlement. In fact he was Governor of Assiniboia from 26 November 1855 until 1858, hardly "some time since". At the same dinner he hoped that in ten years time an England Team would play in Red River, informing his guests that he had been ridiculed for announcing that a steamboat would arrive in the settlement in a year's time, but his prediction had been fulfilled. The first steamboat, the *Anson Northup*, arrived in the Red River settlement in June 1859, a few months before the Englishmen arrived. It was a notable event, ending the isolation of the Red River Settlement[xxii], but Lillywhite's account made it appear to have occurred longer ago. In August 1937 Johnson's dream was finally realised when an MCC team played against Winnipeg at Assiniboine Park.

Following the game against Montréal, the tourists undertook a journey of 450 miles, which involved travelling by train and then hauling their luggage over a mile to a river boat, which brought them to New York where they played a United States 22. Lillywhite estimates 25,000 spectators at the St George's Club ground at Hoboken. Even when taking into account that this must have been over the three days and may of course be an exaggeration, it still compares favourably to the maximum of 6,000 souls present at any one time at Montréal. The after match dinner was held at the St George's Club, where the Star Spangled Banner was played and toasts drunk to President James Buchanan, suggesting that the members of the Club were being absorbed into the American melting pot. Nevertheless, following the defeat of the Americans by an innings and 64 runs, the American press were keen to point out that only three of the local team were born in the United States. The *New York Herald* challenged the tourists to a game of baseball.

The Englishman proceeded to Philadelphia where they beat the 22 there by 7 wickets. *Bell's Life* stated that the Philadelphians were the strongest team yet faced by the tourists, a point that Lillywhite concurred with. He accurately predicted the rise of cricket in that area.

Following the official game a benefit match was played: a contest between North and South with six English players a side and 10 local players making up the numbers. The expenses of the matches were paid for, but only 2,000 spectators attended and an opportunity for the tourists to make a large profit was lost. In his after tour speech at Godalming, Surrey in December, Julius Caesar was critical of American hospitality but did not elaborate. Lillywhite attributed Caesar's comments to the poor organisation of this benefit match, which the majority of tourists blamed on their hosts. However, Lillywhite asserts that the Englishmen should have taken responsibility for organising a match that was being held purely for their financial benefit. In any case it is always more difficult to entice a crowd to an exhibition match, than to a contest against local opposition.

The English professionals now travelled to Hamilton via Buffalo and the Niagara Falls. The Englishmen were guaranteed a visit to the Falls under the terms of their contract and they ended up viewing it twice, once from the American side before the game against Hamilton and then from the Canadian side a week later after their final match against New York. Jean François Gravelet had made the first ever tightrope crossing of the gorge four months before, under his stage name of *Blondin*.

The early cricket tourists had to overcome the considerable challenge of transporting their baggage, as well as themselves, to and from the cricket pitches of North America. This task was compounded for those on the 1859 tour by having to transport Fred Lillywhite's printing press, which issued scorecards at every ground. According to Caffyn's account a number of players took pleasure in the fact that the printing press went astray between Buffalo and Hamilton, which made the baggage train lighter, but deprived the Hamilton spectators of the scorecards and Lillywhite of an income and a permanent record of the scores.

The weather at Hamilton was too cold for cricket, but the game was played and the tourists won their final scheduled match by 10 wickets. The planned benefit game was cancelled due to the weather. The failure of these benefit matches was a source of embarrassment and contention. It probably explains why an extra match was arranged against a combined 22 of Canadians and Americans at Rochester, New York. Permission was required from the tour organisers to play this extra game and it would have been better all-round if this had been refused. It was now mid-October and the season had turned. The organisers spent a reported $1,200 on fencing[xxiii] and had subscribed generously to the fund required to entice the tourists to play, but it was too cold to play or watch cricket and the pitiful attendance of only 400 souls on the first day ensured that the venture was a costly failure. Lillywhite asserted that the umpires should have called the game off, a claim supported by the fact that there was no play on the second day due to heavy snow. After winning the match by an innings and 68 runs the Englishmen played an impromptu game of baseball to entertain the sparse crowd and attempt to minimise the loss suffered by the game's sponsors.

New York's baseball clubs sent a delegate named Dr Jones to the game at Rochester to arrange a baseball match against the tourists for a sum of $5,000, but logistically it proved impossible to organise. The Englishmen required the permission of the tour organisers for this venture to go ahead and this was not forthcoming. The *New York Herald*[xxiv] stated that this created bad feeling within the touring group as the majority of them wanted to play. The *Herald* blamed the decision on the malign influence of a "Montréal insurance clerk" who was hostile to both New York's press and its cricketers. Presumably this was WP Pickering. Lillywhite dismissed baseball as being similar to the children's game of rounders, but the fact that it could be played at short notice in conditions where cricket could not at least partly explains why baseball would replace cricket as the major bat and ball sport in North America. Parr's criticism of being able to catch a batsman on the bounce was more prescient.

The tourists now returned home on the *North Briton* and when they passed the *Nova Scotian* in the calm waters of the St Lawrence, the Captain of the *North Briton* arranged for the message "Won All Matches" to be written on a board to inform the crew of the *Nova Scotian* of the success of their former passengers. This ensured that those on board the *North Briton* were fortified by the cheers of their fellow Englishmen on the *Nova Scotian* for the crossing that they now faced.

The journey back was even worse than the journey out and the crew suffered a fatality when the jib-boom broke and threatened to become entangled in the screw. A 63 year-old sailor called John Evans had both his legs broken by one of the ship's anchors, which was lifted by the storm. Fred Lillywhite organised a benefit, which began in the name of the sailor, but ended up in the name of his widow. There would have been no way of conveying the news of the accident to her before she emerged on the quay to greet her husband. The £30 16s raised was just over a third of the amount received by each player for the trip.

At the dinner thrown in honour of the cricketers Caesar, though critical of the Americans, praised the Canadians for their hospitality and stated that some of the players wanted to stay there. The history of international cricket could have been very different if Caffyn had decided to stay and coach in Canada instead of Australia.

By Lillywhite's reckoning the first cricket tourists had travelled a total distance of 7,364 miles, although it is unclear if he had differentiated between nautical and statute miles. Lillywhite concluded that many of the players would refuse to go on future tours, due to the hardships just suffered on the many journeys of this tour. This may have been true, but fortunately many cricketers would accept the challenge of touring and so make cricket an international sport.

*   *   *   *   *   *   *   *   *

Edgar Willsher led a team over to North America in 1868, nine years after the first tour. A group of North American patrons arranged the tour with VE Walker[xxv], who was the captain of Middlesex Cricket Club, which at that time was dominated by the Walker family. Separate committees from Montréal, New York, Boston and Philadelphia agreed the pay demands of the 12 professional players for the trip, which included all travelling expenses and a separate allowance for match day expenses. It was calculated that US$1,000 would need to be raised through gate receipts.[14]

Willsher was the captain and the most well known cricketer in the group of touring professionals. On 26 August 1862 Willsher's over-arm deliveries had been no-balled repeatedly by the umpire, the 1859

---

[14] The *New Orleans Times* of 19 September stated that the 12 professionals were to be paid £600 each, which is doubtful as it would represent a massive increase on the £90 paid nine years before. It seems more likely that £600 was the total figure divided 12 ways and supplemented with the US$180 for match day expenses. The *Times*' claim of $1,000 required from gate receipts to break even would equate to a daily crowd of 2,000, with each spectator playing 50 cents each. The crowd size was usually reported to be far larger than 2,000.

tourist John Lillywhite, thus highlighting the reality gap between the rules which prohibited balls delivered from above the shoulder and the fact that this had become common practice. In a scene that would be repeated by Sri Lanka in Adelaide in 1998, Willsher's teammates, with the exception of the two amateurs, stormed off the pitch in protest. Play was abandoned for the day and only recommenced following the substitution of Lillywhite as umpire.

These tensions had also existed in Canadian cricket, prompting George Barber to write a letter published in the Toronto *Globe* of 30 August 1862, which argued that in Canada the bowling already dominated the batting and the pitches were poorer than those in Britain and so the rule restricting deliveries to those below the shoulder should be more rigidly applied. The presence of Willsher in the touring party proved that in both nations over-arm bowling was now accepted and the game could now enter the modern era.

The 1868 touring party also included a number of players who would go on future tours of Australia, linking these early North American ventures with the birth of international cricket. James Lillywhite was a member of the influential Lillywhite family who dominated Sussex cricket in the nineteenth century and was the younger cousin of the aforementioned John Lillywhite. James would tour Australia five times and was England's captain in the first ever Test match. Henry Charlwood accompanied Lillywhite on the 1876-7 tour and played in the inaugural Test match, as did Alfred Shaw, who bowled the first delivery in Test cricket and went on a total of five tours of Australia. Shaw would tour North America again with Richard Daft in 1879. The opening batsman Henry Jupp would accompany Lillywhite on the 1873-4 tour, which included WG Grace, and the 1876-7 tour. Ted Pooley was also on that tour and would have played in the first Test as England's wicket-keeper had he not been arrested in New Zealand after a dispute with a bookmaker who had refused to pay Pooley his winnings[15]. The court in Dunedin found him not guilty, but by then the Test had already been played and he had little option but to return to England, arriving home a month after his colleagues.

The 1868 tourists played five games in America and only one in Canada. Their first game was against the St George's Club of New

---

[15] The bookmaker was offering odds of 20 to 1 for those correctly guessing a batsman's score and the enterprising Pooley had placed 22 bets of a shilling each on the score of 0. He needed only two ducks to make a profit and there were 11. He was fined £5 for assaulting the bookmaker when he refused to pay, but was arrested later on what was then a far more serious charge of destroying property. Information taken from: http://www.cricinfo.com/magazine/content/story/142484.html

York at their ground at Hoboken, which would also be the venue for their last game against a team called America Cricket Club. The Englishmen won their first game by an innings and 26 runs; the victory margin would have been larger had Willsher not refrained from bowling himself in the second innings. They then played a game of baseball, also against the St George's Club, for the entertainment of the crowd who were greatly amused by the mistakes made by the English novices. The fact that George Griffith played for the St George's Club indicates that this was not a serious sporting encounter and the tourists' victory margin of 39 to 14 also indicates that this was an exhibition match. Nevertheless the *New York Herald* reported that the Englishmen were showing a great improvement by the third innings and the Cambridge-born John Smith was cheered for hitting several home runs. The tourists then made the obligatory trip to Niagara Falls before heading north.

For their second game the tourists travelled down the St Lawrence and played a ridiculously one-sided draw in Montréal. The Montréal 22 included a number of cricketers from the military as well as players who had represented Canada in the international match, including JN Kirchhoffer, George Brunel and his brother John. Press reports indicate that the Canadians were confident of putting in a good performance, but what followed was a humiliation. The match commenced a day later than scheduled due to rain. When they finally did get on the pitch the tourists bowled out Canada for 28, although the innings lasted for 64 overs with Willsher and Freeman bowling unchanged and taking 8 wickets and 13 wickets respectively. Apparently the outfield was uneven which the Englishmen benefited from whilst compiling 310 for 9 in response before the weather caused the game to be abandoned. This was an example of how, in an age before declarations, a team could draw a game by failing to bowl out the opposition. George Griffith top scored with 69 and was awarded a bat for this feat by the ubiquitous George Barber.

The tourists then travelled overnight by rail to Boston, to play a team made up of players from New York, Philadelphia and Massachusetts, who played under the auspices of Boston Cricket Club. Unfortunately rain had saturated the pitch, leading Willsher to pronounce it as being the worst he had ever seen. The weather delayed the start of the game, which meant that the games scheduled for the Philadelphia and New York had to be rearranged. Willsher's team scored 109 and then dismissed the 22 men of Boston for 39, meaning that the home team narrowly avoided the follow-on by 10 runs. The tourists made 71 in their second innings and then dismissed their opponents for 37 runs to win the match by the large margin of 104 runs. The Englishmen lost a baseball match by 21 to 9 against a team made up of players from

Harvard, Trimountain and Lowell clubs. They left for Philadelphia on the same day, travelling by train via New York.

Willsher's team played two games of cricket and a baseball game on the grounds of the Germantown Cricket Club. The press gave the baseball game, which was played against the Athletic Club, the same level of publicity as the two cricket games and the entrance fee of 50 cents was the same for all three events. Unlike the other 22s, the Philadelphian team was made up of American-born players and they provided the tourists with their closest game of the tour, which the Englishmen narrowly won by 2 wickets. The *New York Herald* called the game "the best contested match in the annals of cricket in America."[xxvi] The second game was against an American 22 and the press were quick to praise the performance of the native born American cricketers, in contrast to the play of their English born teammates. Willsher's team scored 117 and 64 and dismissed the American 22 for 47 and 62 to win the game by 98 runs.

If the results of the cricket matches dealt a blow to American pride, the baseball matches appear to have been organised to redress the balance. The Athletic Club allowed the tourists 11 players instead of 9, and four outs an innings, which equated to three additional innings. Additionally, the Englishmen were given Harrup, the Olympic pitcher, as one of their players. The Philadelphia Inquirer reported the humiliation of Willsher's men in their 31 to 11 defeat by stating that a "great deal of amusement was afforded the spectators by their queer mistakes in playing the game." A similar ordeal awaited the tourists during their baseball game in New York and it must have been a sobering experience for a professional cricketer to try and learn how to play a foreign game in front of a baying crowd, which was larger than one which had turned up to watch them play cricket. The games only took approximately 2 and a half hours in contrast to their final game against an America Cricket Club 22 in New York, where a sparse crowd saw the Englishmen take 4 days to amass 143 and dismiss their opponents for 76 and 65 to win by an innings and 2 runs. The tourists' departure home had been delayed by the postponement of the cricket matches and this made a rougher Atlantic crossing more likely. It is to the tourists' credit then, that they agreed to play one final match for the Testimonial of the old New York professional Sam Wright. The English 12 provided 6 players for both teams and the remainder of both teams were made up with talented local players. The tourists had won five out of their six cricket games, and the one-sided draw at Montréal a victory in all but name. However, they would also have realised that in America at least the future was baseball not cricket. This point would also be reaffirmed by the next English tourists, who arrived in North America 4 years later.

In 1872 the MCC secretary RA Fitzgerald led a team to Canada and America which included WG Grace and many other leading cricketers of the age. Mr TC Patteson of Toronto and Captain Wallace of the 60th rifles garrisoned at Halifax, visited the MCC secretary, Mr RA Fitzgerald, in the summer of 1871 and managed to arrange the subsequent tour[xxvii]. Apparently the clubs in Québec and Ontario paid for the cost of the tour, with Mr Patteson contributing $1,500 to the tourists' expenses. Wallace's contribution is unrecorded, but the tourists did not play in Halifax. The inclusion of Grace with the touring party was one of the conditions.

Again the results were one-sided, although it is likely that the Canadians extended the invitation to the MCC to encourage more immigrants from the homeland, as well as to develop the game domestically. In places the book of the tour, *Wickets in the West* by Fitzgerald, reads more like a travelogue designed for future tourists, than an account of a cricket tour; complete chapters are dedicated to their excursions to Lake Simcoe and to Niagara Falls, where the opportunities offered to British emigrants are discussed at length; at Hamilton, Fitzgerald details a meeting with an old acquaintance from Buckinghamshire who has become a successful farmer.[xxviii] This suggests that the book and the tour had an ulterior motive unrelated to cricket[16]. It is clear that all involved in the tour wanted to strengthen links between Canada and the Mother Country. Fitzgerald emphasised this by dedicating his book to Lord Dufferin, the Canadian Governor General, who had held a dinner for the 12 at the Citadel, his official residence in Québec City.

It was common practice for captains of eighteenth century sailing ships to announce the destination to the crew after they had set sail, to prevent desertion if the undertaking proved to be a bigger commitment than expected. Fitzgerald must have wished that he had been able to do this as he was forced to find a number of replacements at very short notice. Fitzgerald took his revenge by naming and shaming those who had let him down, in his book *Wickets in the West.* Here he informed the reader that the original squad had taken a solemn oath that they would tour. CI Thornton went back on his word due to a fear of seasickness induced by seeing a picture of a ship in distress and reading an article on the subject. Charles Thornton would live to play against Canadian opposition. He represented the MCC against both the 1880 and 1887 Canadian touring teams and he ensured that the

---

[16] For more on this theory see pp 60-61 *"Wickets in the West:* Cricket, Culture and Constructed Images of Nineteenth Century Canada" by Greg Gillespie in Journal of Sport History Vol. 27 No.1 Spring 2000

latter team played against his side the CI Thornton XI. In the 1872 squad he was replaced by WH Hadow.

RD Balfour was said to have "disappeared" and was replaced by CJ Ottaway, who was a great all-round sportsman, being the first captain of the England football team as well as an Oxford Blue at rackets, real tennis and athletics. His last minute call-up was not his only association with Canada. In August 1876 he scored 102 for Hamilton against Montréal and in August 1877 he had the good fortune to marry a Canadian, called Marion Stinson.[17] It was good fortune too for Fitzgerald, to secure such a talented cricketer and replacement wicket-keeper for his squad at such short notice.

According to Fitzgerald JW Dale "jacked up". I'm not sure what that means but he didn't make the tour; VE and RD Wallace both fell ill as did CK Francis. This left the touring party short of bowlers. The three vacancies were filled by Francis Pickering (who was WP Pickering's nephew), Edgar Lubbock and WM Rose. RAH Mitchell is included in the original list of the touring party, but then never mentioned again. Fitzgerald declared his disappointment that nobody joined the tour at Ireland and so Mitchell could have been one of the players he was expecting. Frustratingly Fitzgerald refers to many players by their nickname, which is confusing as some of the tourists clearly had more than one. After so many players had let him down Fitzgerald was a relieved man when the rest of the squad arrived to disembark with him on the SS Sarmation on 8 August 1872. The crossing took just over 9 days.

The tourists appeared to be a little accident prone, which may have been alcohol related. Alfred Shrewsbury dislocated a toe whilst attempting to hurdle chairs on board ship and Appleby slipped into deep water when off it. Ottaway was lucky to escape serious harm whilst being driven down a rough track outside Québec City during a hunting trip. A bough from a tree, unnoticed by the driver, narrowly missed the cricketer's head and struck the carriage, bringing both horse and trap to an abrupt halt. Hadow injured himself playing an impromptu cricket match at the Stadacona Club, which was a forerunner of the Québec Garrison Club. Hadow was well enough to beat the Stadacona racquets champions in a game of doubles with Harris soon after. Moving 12 cricketers, their baggage and entourage from cricket ground to cricket ground was a big logistical challenge in nineteenth century North America and Hadow's misfortune continued

---

[17] Sadly Ottaway died in 1878 in London, aged 28, leaving behind a pregnant widow. Marion returned to Canada and remarried, leaving her young daughter in England, who would emigrate to Canada at the age of 19.

when he lost his cricket bag in the St Lawrence river when stepping onto a train, which I suppose would have to be seen to be believed[xxix]. He played no part in the next two games.

The tourists' first match was at Montréal, where the playing facilities were poor and the crowd numbers disappointing. The state of the ground at Montréal is criticised with carefully worded praise by Fitzgerald who expresses his admiration for "the spirit that can reconcile cricket to such natural disadvantage."[xxx] It is doubtful whether Charles Francis would have shared this sentiment as the "natural disadvantage" caused him to suffer a blow to the head during practise, thus adding his name to the list of the injured. Tellingly the *Herald* and *Gazette* reported that more might have watched if they had been playing lacrosse[xxxi]. Fitzgerald suggests that the low crowd turn out was due to the popularity of swimming in the St Lawrence at Lacoona. Reading between the lines of Fitzgerald's jocular prose it is clear that cricket was dying in Montréal and it is unsurprising that Daft's 1879 team decided to avoid playing there altogether.

Fitzgerald praised the bowling of Sam Hardinge, who had a lengthy career that included playing against Parr's tourists of 1859, Fitzgerald's of 1872 and Daft's of 1879. He also played in three matches in the International Series, with great success. Fitzgerald was critical of both the batting performance of the locals which he described as "feeble" and the President's speech, which he stated was political and badly received. Unlike the first of WG Grace's speeches which have gone down in folklore. Wherever he went Grace gave the exact speech, with one word difference:

"Gentlemen, I beg to thank you for the honour you have done me. I never saw better **** than I have seen today, and I hope to see as good wherever I go."[xxxii]

Here it was "bowling". In later life Grace, who disliked speaking in public, would sometimes revert to what he called one of his Canadian speeches. After compiling 255, Fitzgerald's team dismissed the Canadian team for 48 and 67 to win the match by an innings and 140 runs

The 12 Englishmen then travelled to Ottawa to their next game at Rideau Hall. Showing his amateur colours Fitzgerald criticised the Ottawa 22 for practising beforehand, which he saw as a "waste of breath"[xxxiii]. Fitzgerald praised the Canadian bowlers but not the batting, describing the first innings as a "slaughter of the innocents", which led him to under bowl Appleby in the second innings for "reasons of humanity". Despite this generosity of spirit the Canadians could only make 49 to go with their 43 in the first innings and Fitzgerald's team won by an innings and 110 runs. After praising John Brunel's innings of 10, Fitzgerald departed from his usual restraint and gave a damning account of the Canadian batting; he exclaimed that it was "past comprehension ... that young and stalwart cricketers should positively refuse long hops and half volleys."[xxxiv] He concluded that the Canadians were playing the reputation and not the bowling.

The haphazard nature of the tour was revealed after the team left Ottawa. Due to a misunderstanding between Fitzgerald and Patteson the Englishmen travelled to Brockville when they were expected at Belleville and as a result a fixture was not honoured, leaving hundreds of spectators disappointed. The Toronto *Globe* makes no reference to this game, it only states that the tourists were hoping to take on some sightseeing and fishing before playing in Toronto.

It was then on to Toronto where Fitzgerald praised the bowlers, who managed to avoid any wides in the English innings of 319. However, he also praised the fielding which seems a little generous considering Grace was dropped twice in his innings of 142, which included five sixes. He was probably caught at Point when in his 40s but according to the Toronto *Globe*[xxxv] the umpire ruled that it was a bump ball, apparently much to the surprise of the fielders and batsman, but to the delight of the crowd. This incident deserves more focus as Grace's score was not only the highest of the tour, it was also the highest score by a touring Englishman on Canadian soil until it was eclipsed by David Gower's 157 against Manitoba at Assiniboine Park, Winnipeg on 22 September 1976. Fitzgerald reported that Grace was clearly not out and he was merely teasing the crowd by pretending to walk on a first bound catch to Point[xxxvi]. It would be more difficult for an umpire to give the great man out if he visibly demonstrated that he considered that the catch had not been fairly made and if he was merely teasing the crowd he succeeded in fooling the reporter of the *Globe* into believing that the umpire was mistaken.

Grace's by now well practised speech praised the batting and the fielding, which seems a little harsh on the bowlers. In a theme that Fitzgerald would repeat later in the book he singled out seven of the Toronto 22 for praise and asserted that these players could form the basis of a good XI. The *Globe* praised the fielding of Whelan at point, Sproull at long stop, Dr Spragge at mid off, Hope at long leg and Gamble at long off.

After lunch on the second day the tourists took the field with only 8 men, much to the fury of Fitzgerald. His humour would not have improved after Ottaway was forced to surrender the gloves to Hornby after injuring a finger. The fielding was not faultless in the second innings with two overthrows allowing Hemstead to register a 7 in his top score of 28.

The *Globe* was critical of the accommodation, both for the tourists who had no chairs in their tent and for the press, who had no accommodation at all. The scorer was not protected and was bothered by spectators resulting in an error. Play was also held up on occasion because there was no effort made to keep spectators away from the area behind the bowler's arm. The pitch was not as good as the one at Ottawa.

The Lieutenant Governor and his wife were in attendance for this match, with over 5,000 other supporters. Lady McDonald, the Prime Minister's[18] wife, attended the pick-up game on 6 September. This was more than just a cricket match, it was a social event. To make up for the early finish, two teams of 12 played against each other, with six tourists on both teams, which were captained by Grace and Fitzgerald. Undoubtedly Grace was the finer captain and he led his team to a 59 run victory. The scores further emphasised the difference in skill between the English and Canadian players, although three natives made scores of note. The Brunel brothers both made double figures in the first innings, with John hitting 15 and George 13. John backed this up with 12 in the second innings, which Fitzgerald said was made "in very good style".[xxxvii] Lieutenant Henley made 22 and 14, although I can find no other record of him playing in Canadian domestic cricket, suggesting that he was as British as the tourists. The withdrawal of British soldiers from Canada had a detrimental impact on cricket in Canada and was lamented by the population. Fitzgerald diplomatically reports this attitude amongst "every class", concluding that "we do not pretend to analyse the policy, we only record the facts."[xxxviii] He confusingly refers to the British soldier as the Red Man.

Following the match the tourists were reminded of their status as honoured guests when, at the Lyceum Theatre in Toronto, the performance was stopped as the Englishmen arrived late and the band struck up Rule Britannia. In the words of Fitzgerald "the prompter had some difficulty in recalling them to their suspended avocation."[xxxix] The views of the paying audience went unrecorded.

---

[18] Derek Birley (page 122 of *A Social History of English Cricket*), the Encyclopaedia of North American Sports History and Donald King (as editor of the Canadian Cricket magazine) all state that Sir John A McDonald declared cricket to be Canada's national sport. I have found no evidence that he said this. If he did I expect it would have been to curry favour with the Anglo-elite and not an insightful comment on cricket's standing in Canada.

Before leaving Toronto, Fitzgerald expressed his gratitude to the public bodies of the city which had been so hospitable to them; he singled out the Royal Canadian Yacht Club and the Toronto Cricket Club. The tourists dinned with the Royal Canadian Yacht Club, with their commodore Dr Hodder in the chair. Many members of this club also played cricket, unsurprising for a pillar of the Anglo-elite.

Those that lament the morals of the youth of today would do well to note that their Victorian ancestors were no angels. Appleby, Ottaway and Francis were late arriving for the match against London because they had been in the company of three young women of Toronto. The official line was that the cricketers had accompanied the young ladies to church; I leave readers to make up their own minds on the veracity of this statement. Suffice it to say that this was the story given to the Captain who gave them leave of absence on the condition that they arrived at the game in time. Fortunately Fitzgerald won the toss and decided to bat first and thus avoided having to take the field with a reduced team, although in the absence of Ottaway, Hornby had to open the batting with Grace. Ottaway turned up in time to bat at 7. Once again Grace was apparently caught, only for it be ruled an unfair catch by the umpire. "Bump balls" are notoriously hard to rule on, although a legendary reputation can help the umpire to rule in favour of the batsman.

Fitzgerald estimated that 7,000 people viewed the first day's play, enough to ensure a profit to the organisers. A ball was held in the tourists' honour at the City Hall in London after the first day's play, but the Englishmen were still able to commence play at the allotted time of 11 a.m. the next morning. Unsurprisingly Grace declined the invitation to the ball, but his fellow opener Ottaway was "languid after his exercise at the ball of the previous evening"[xi] and was dismissed for 6. It is alleged that Ottaway's early death was due to an infection caught after a night's dancing.

It is worth noting that on most grounds on this tour 4 and 6 runs were awarded for boundaries and I expect that the 1872 tour helped to establish the now accepted scoring system on the grounds of Canada. It would be some time before this practice became universal as the comments of the 1887 tourists from Canada prove, but it helped to address the advantage that Canadian bowlers held over the batsman and it remains a vital part of modern cricket.

Fitzgerald's assessment of London's cricketers was similar to that of the earlier Canadian teams. He described the bowling as "admirable" and singled out Wright and Gillean for special praise. The latter bowled in the International Series in 1880 and 1881, taking a total of 10 wickets. He also played twice against Daft's 1879 tourists and toured Britain in 1880. The fielding was seen as "creditable" but the batting showed "the same preconceived dread of the straight long hop."[xli] Hyman's batting was praised although Fitzgerald pointed out he gave two chances in his first innings top score of 18, which should have been taken. His 9 in the second innings was also the highest score. It was the closest game so far as Fitzgerald's team ran out winners by 130 runs; for the first time they had failed to win by an innings. The *Globe* states that this was the first match where betting was apparent.[xlii]

After a four hour trip by rail Fitzgerald's team arrived in Hamilton for their final match in Canada, before departing for America. The pitch was deadened by heavy rain, which encouraged hard hitting in order to score and Edgar Lubbock hit the 72 year old umpire George Barber in the chest, causing him considerable pain and saving a certain 4. In the Hamilton innings Whelan was praised for his 31, which included 12 runs off one of Rose's overs and was the largest score hit by a Canadian on the tour. Eberts, Spragge and Shaw were praised for their batting, but Fitzgerald stated that no other Canadian batsman was worthy of any praise and Hamilton were obliged to follow on. The game ended in farce as the Canadian batsman sportingly allowed the match to be concluded in twilight to allow the tourists to see Niagara Falls the following day. Rather unfairly Fitzgerald details the problems the failing light caused the fielders, which allowed the batsman to steal runs, whilst the difficulty the batsmen must have had in seeing the ball went unrecorded. Swinyard was presented with a bat in mark of his efforts in promoting the tour and he entertained the tourists at his home where Grace made his usual speech, although unusually his compliment was of non-cricketing nature: he praised Hamilton's ladies.[xliii]

Fitzgerald concluded that "we had expected to find stronger batting, but were not prepared to meet such good bowling."[xliv] To emphasise his point regarding the batting, he stated that only Appleby could be considered a first class bowler. He stated that the batting was too "glued to the crease" and too timid, prompting the advice: "hit with judgement but always hit". Fitzgerald hoped that in future games could be between teams of equal number and with the exception of the position of wicket-keeper, he believed that a decent XI could be made out of the best of the players he had competed against. Incidentally on more than one occasion he praised the fielding of the long-stop, which arguably was then a more important position than wicket-keeper. He also commended the fielding of Spragge, Hope, Hyman and Whelan and the bowling of AB Laing, Maclean, Brodie, Swinyard, Wright, Gillean and Eberts. A cursory glance at the records of domestic cricket in Canada suggests that JB Laing was a better bowler than his brother AB, although the latter had more success against the tourists. John

Burnett Laing's greatest achievement in terms of Canadian cricket was to have a son: John Melville Laing, who would become Canada's greatest all-rounder.

Finally Fitzgerald sheds some light on what the tour had really meant to the Canadians: "the heart of Canada is not so much wrapped up in love for the national game, as prompted by the warmest attachment to English institutions."[xlv] He attributes the wide margins of victory to the presence of WG Grace.

Fitzgerald won all his tosses in Canada but lost all the tosses in America. This did not prevent the tourists from beating the St George's Club 22 at Hoboken, New York by an innings and 139 runs. It was estimated that there were only 2,000 spectators present to see the Englishmen's victory, leading Fitzgerald to conclude that cricket was not a popular sport in New York and was "indebted for life to a few determined Englishmen."[xlvi]

Following this game the tourists travelled to Philadelphia where they had their most competitive match of the tour on the ground of the Germantown Cricket Club. There were an estimated 7,000 spectators on the second day, indicating that cricket was far more popular in Philadelphia than in New York. Two Englishmen were run out in their first innings, suggesting that the Philadelphians were competitive fielders. Rose had been the least successful bowler in the Philadelphian's first innings and due to the closeness of the game Fitzgerald decided to rely solely on Grace and Appleby in the second innings. Comparisons were made between the victory target of 33 and the 1868 tourists' target of 32, which they made with only 2 wickets to spare. The wicket was worn, making runs hard to get in the second innings. Grace edged to the wicket-keeper but was given not out by Farrands the English umpire.[xlvii] He made three more runs before being dismissed for an innings of 7, which had taken him nearly an hour. Fitzgerald's XII lost three wickets on 29, but made no more mistakes, to reach 34 for 7 and so win by 4 wickets in this 12 a side contest. There was some bad feeling amongst the crowd when the tourists felt obliged to leave shortly after the conclusion of the match to start their journey for their final game in Boston. Unfortunately they still missed their train and could not travel until the following day. To make matters worse heavy rain rendered the ground at Boston unplayable. Nevertheless the match did start and in the words of Fitzgerald "the Twelve did their best to lose, and nearly lost."[xlviii] After matching Boston's score of 51 in the first innings the tourists reached 22 for 6 in their second innings, chasing 44 for victory, when time was called. Fitzgerald concluded that the Americans did not have the time for cricket and that baseball would remain the major bat and ball sport, although he retained more hope for the future of Canadian cricket. The tourists returned home on the *SS Prussian*.

*   *   *   *   *   *   *   *   *

In 1878 an Australian team toured North America for the first time, on their way home from their successful inaugural tour of England. Their manager was John Conway and he arranged games in Canada against Ontario and Montréal, sandwiched between matches at New York and Philadelphia and later games at Detroit and San Francisco. Originally the Australians were only going to visit Toronto, but they added Montréal to their fixtures list. Following negotiations with the Toronto Cricket Club President WP Pickering and groundsman RB Blake, Conway declared himself impressed with the Toronto Cricket Club's facilities, although he added that nothing could compare to the Melbourne Cricket Ground.[xlix]

The drawn game against Philadelphia had been a controversial one. Chasing 100 to win the Australians had reached 56 for 4 in reply when time was called. However, the Philadelphian umpire had allowed the home bowlers to overstep the crease with impunity. According to the tourists the umpire continued to make partisan decisions but their request to have him changed was refused and the Australians finished the game under protest.

The first match played by an n team on Canadian soil created considerable interest; the *Globe* dedicated more than a complete column to its pre-match report of Friday 4 October, which stated that 6 runs would be awarded for shots hit out of the ground (a distance of over 100 yards), whilst 4 would be scored for shots hit over the boundary. The evergreen Rev TD Phillipps was included in the original 22, but he was unable to play. His replacement CRW Postlethwaite bagged a pair. The captain of the Ontario 22 was going to be ER Ogden, but he hurt his wrist whilst practising and was replaced by JN Kirchhoffer, who like Ogden would captain Canada in the International Series. Kirchhoffer became a Senator in 1892, a post he would hold until his death in 1914.

The Ontario 22 included seven players who would represent Canada in the International Series, including R Adams, who top scored with 17 and was run out trying to steal a single to the long-stop, and S Ray who opened the innings and made 16. The only other man to make double figures in the first innings was GF Hall, who scored 12 and would play for Canada in the 1879 International. No batsman made double figures in the second innings and after conceding a lead of only 23 runs in the first innings, Ontario were defeated by 10 wickets.

Only 5 of the Canadian team attended the after match dinner, which heard Colonel Cumberland praise the Australians for showing what colonists could do in competition with the Old Country on land, adding that he fully expected the rower Ned Hanlan would show them what colonists could do on water. The message was clear. Cricket might be Australia's national sport, but it was not Canada's: she led the world in rowing. In reply Conway studiously avoided comment on the cricket and played it safe by praising the impartiality of Canadian crowds, contrasting them to those in Philadelphia and New York.

In Montréal a combined 22 of players from Montréal and Québec were comprehensively outplayed and would have lost by an innings had the weather not intervened. The home team made 91 and Australia amassed 319 for 9 in reply with Charles Bannerman hitting 125. The Australians diplomatically attributed this to a good wicket although the under-arm bowlers were treated with disdain.

To be defeated so comfortably by a touring English team was one thing, but a thrashing by a fellow colony demanded some form of post-mortem. A *Globe* article of Thursday 10 October 1878 demanded 5 points of action:
1. Cricket should be made Canada's national sport
2. The setting up of a national association, which serves to assist clubs in their communication and to keep good records of performance, so that players could be assessed at the end of each season.
3. Select the best players, no matter in which part of the province they reside.
4. Allow time for the selected players to practise together.
5. Encourage diligent practise amongst Canadian players.

The article also noted that the best players were often not available, either due to a lack of adequate warning or the absence of "a small pecuniary outlay." The simplest of these five points, to form a national association, was not realised until 1892, although the Ontario Cricket Association was set up in 1880. Two days later the editor published a letter arguing that Canadian cricket had improved in the six years since Fitzgerald's tour, as the Ontario 22 had reached 100 and the Australian bowling was superior to that of the English tourists. All these points were true, but a Philadelphian team had played the Australians on level terms and given them a far closer game that the Canadian 22. Canadian cricket may have improved, but at a lesser rate then their rivals in Pennsylvania.

The Australians finished their tour by thrashing both the 19 members of the Peninsular Club of Detroit, by an innings and 66 runs, and then a Californian 22, by an innings and 134 runs in San Francisco. The Peninsular Club included a Thomas Dale, who opened the bowling. The Yorkshire born Dale was a colourful character and his story will be told in the next chapter.

*   *   *   *   *   *   *   *   *

In 1879 Richard Daft led a team of Englishmen to Canada and the United States. Daft's team set sail from Liverpool on 28 August and arrived in Québec on Sunday 7 September after enjoying a calmer crossing of the Atlantic than some of their predecessors. They played five one-sided games in Ontario and a number of Canadians played more than once. As already detailed, they decided not to play in Montréal. The press had stated during Fitzgerald's tour of seven years before that lacrosse was more popular in Montréal than cricket and this was the justification given by the 1879 tourists to continue on to Toronto without playing in Montréal, where they considered cricket was poorly supported in a population which was mostly French.[i]

On 10 September 1879 the tourists took the field against a Canadian born 22. The match commenced in dramatic fashion when Alfred Shaw bowled H Totten with the first delivery of the game. The rest of the Canadian batsmen fared little better and the team were bowled out for 31. The superiority of the English bowling over the home team's batting was commented on by the tourists[ii]; an assessment that mirrored the comments of Fitzgerald seven years earlier. Like Fitzgerald, Daft's tourists felt able to praise the Canadian fielding if not the batting. The Canadians did manage to score 72 at their second attempt and thus avoided an innings defeat. They lost the game by 10 wickets and, as was the custom, an exhibition game was then played to entertain the crowd.

The adverts publicising the match against the 22 stated that the Governor General, the Marquis of Lorne, and his wife HRH Princess Louise would be in attendance, which they duly complied with, although they did not arrive until 5:15pm. In a reverse of how the English amateurs had been honoured at the Lyceum Theatre in 1872, the game of cricket was suspended to allow the professional Daft to be summoned from the field to meet the Canadian Governor General and his royal wife.

There was no break for the tourists. After finishing their match against the 22 Canadian born players on 11 September, they started their next game against 22 Anglo-Canadians the following day. Canadian born cricketers played an annual game against a team made up of "Old Country" cricketers who had been born in Britain, hence the decision to select two teams of 22 players based on their birthplace. However, it meant that the 22 players were not the best cricketers that Canada could have selected and by spreading their talent too thinly the organisers ensured that the matches were too one-sided. It appears that selection was based on social standing as well as cricketing ability. At one of the three games played at Toronto on this tour a Member of the Provincial Parliament was dismissed by Shaw and "knocked down the stumps with his bat and ran off the field as fast as his legs could carry him."[lii] The MPP could have been one of two people: Cook and Baker played in two of the three matches in Toronto are the only cricketers who could have been MPPs at this time, although Kirchhoffer did become a Senator. Herman Henry Cook had been the Member for Simcoe North and was 42 years old at the time and he is the most likely suspect. The only other candidate is Adam Jacob Baker, but he would have been 58 years old and it is unlikely that he would have played in two important matches at this age, without any prior notable record as a cricketer.

When it became apparent that a short match would mean a loss of revenue the tourists started to deliberately field badly to try and ensure a more competitive, longer match.[liii] Daft set the example as captain, by deliberately dropping Kirchhoffer, who went on to top score with 21, out of a total of 76. Daft's men made 209 in reply and the game was drawn with the home team 64 runs in arrears with 7 wickets remaining. The gamesmanship by the Englishmen failed in its purpose and the low crowd attendance for the first two matches threatened the financial viability of the venture.[liv]

Naturally no cricket was played on a Sunday, but on Monday 15 September the tourists' third game began. Daft did not play in this match against an Ontario 22 due to an injured finger, one hopes from deliberately dropping a catch. In any case the tourists did fine without him and won the game convincingly by an innings and 3 runs in front of a small crowd. GB Behan was the only Canadian to reach double figures, a feat he managed in both innings with scores of 23 out of 65 and 13 out of 54. He would represent Canada in the International matches of 1880 and 1881.

The fourth match was against Hamilton, who put 17 players into the field. The team was to have 16 players, but an extra man was added to the team at the 11th hour according to the *Globe* of Friday 19 September. Hamilton had just completed a successful tour of the United States where they had beaten Detroit, St George's Club of New York, Staten Island and Young America of Philadelphia. It is unsurprising that they were considered stronger than the composite teams and so fielded five fewer players. The result was an even more comprehensive thrashing: by an innings and 103 runs, where they made disappointingly small scores of 48 and 35 with only one player making double figures. The pitch was of such a poor standard that it prompted George Ulyett to declare after compiling the match's top score of 44 that he had more bruises than runs. To allow a result the game was extended into a third day, although play started late, as the tourists did some sightseeing in the morning.[IV]

They then defeated a Western Ontario 22 by 135 runs at London before embarking on a tour of the US. They were back in Liverpool on 3 November 1879.

Daft's tour of 1879 was a disappointment. The general lack of interest of the wider population was reflected in the low crowd numbers. Whilst those that supported cricket were keen to invite touring teams of high calibre, there can be little doubt that those who held influence over Canadian cricket preferred the touring teams to be made up of amateur players. TC Patteson declared at the annual dinner of the Toronto Cricket Club in December 1871 that the professional tour of 1859 had done more harm than good to Canadian cricket, even going as far as belittling the efforts of Caffyn and other professionals who had coached in Australia in the 1860s. History has shown Patteson to be incorrect in his estimation of the value of professional coaches, but the first Canadian cricket tour of Britain emphasised the weakness of professional cricket. The second would highlight the strength of amateur cricket. This was a long-term weakness of Canadian cricket. Professional cricket was sustainable; amateur cricket was not.

Chapter 5: The First Canadian Cricket Tour

"With a Persistence Worthy of a Better Cause": *Toronto Herald's* view of the tour

The first team to call itself Canada outside the International Series was not the 1880 side. The 1874 team that contested the Halifax Tournament included two players of the 1880 Tour: Rev. TD Phillipps(sitting furthest left) and E Kearney

"Heroic failure" is the kindest description that can be given to the first Canadian cricket tour of Britain that took place in 1880: it was ridiculed in the Canadian press, which criticised the right of the players to represent Canada on grounds of skill, geographical representation and nationality.

A report in the *Toronto Herald* asserted that the tourists would be unable to compete with an English village team, let alone the sides they would encounter and to avoid humiliation the whole venture should be cancelled. This article was reprinted in the *Sportsman*, which no doubt contributed both to the lack of interest shown by the British public, and to the great interest shown by the authorities in the presence of the Canadian captain, Thomas Dale. The report stated he was previously a member of the Royal Horse Guards, but, as Trooper Dale had deserted this regiment in November 1872, it must have taken an injudicious mixture of courage and stupidity for him to return to the country of his birth following this publicity. The published squad also included a T Jordan, which was nothing more than an alias for Dale, proving his awareness of the threat of arrest before the tour started.

The views of the press have coloured history's view of the tour and their concerns were not without reason. A glance at the tour averages suggests that the majority of the players were selected on availability, not ability.

Batting

Player's Name	Innings	Runs	Highest Score	Average	50s
Thomas Dale	7	126	52	18.00	1
RW Hibbard	23	327	61	15.57	1
W Wright (Notts professional)	16	199	81	13.27	1
AH Lemmon	28	281	44	11.71	
W Pinkney	28	274	67*	11.42	1
JS Howard	28	291	29	10.78	
TD Phillipps	20	191	50	9.55	1
GF Hall	29	236	47	8.43	
J Dewhurst	26	185	33	7.71	
John Smith	20	131	23*	7.28	
JL Hardman	27	172	38	6.88	
AS Treloar	26	117	25*	5.32	
H Miller	19	37	13	2.64	
JS Gillean	26	44	10	2.44	
Edmund Kearney	16	32	9	2.29	

Dunn, Dutton, F Henry and W Gilbert were local cricketers who played in only one match

I have not managed to locate complete bowling figures for this tour. Nevertheless, a simple examination of the number of wickets taken indicates who was in the side as a bowler. Gillean, for example, was clearly in the team as a bowler. However, Kearney's position at the bottom of the batting averages is misleading, as he was an all-rounder who had batted in the top six in both the 1874 Halifax Tournament and in the following year's contest in Philadelphia. He hit 45 for Halifax against all comers in the 1874 tournament and 47 against the British Garrison the following year. His poor performance on the 1880 tour was due to an injury, of which more later.

Bowling

Player's Name	Matches Played (Total: 17)	Matches Bowled	Innings Bowled	Total Wickets	Wickets per Innings
JS Gillean	15	14	18	68	3.78
W Wright (Notts)	9	8	12	59	4.92
T Dale	5	5	7	33	4.72
E Kearney	10	7	9	15	1.67
H Miller	11	5	5	10	2
JL Hardman	16	4	5	7	1.4
RW Hibbard	13	3	3	6	2
GF Hall	17	4	5	6	1.2
AS Treloar	16	1	1	6	6

W Gilbert and F Henry also bowled, both taking 4 wickets in a single innings.

H Miller was the tour manager and probably would have played fewer games had the tour not been so eventful. Miller's first challenge had been to select the squad; a task that was made more difficult when players who had originally agreed to tour changed their minds. CJ Logan and FW Armstrong were both of international calibre and were both named in the squad, but neither toured.

Thomas Dale was their best player, but as a Yorkshireman living in Detroit, his selection was based on ability and availability more than nationality. Whilst living in Britain Dale developed into a fine cricketer, whose exploits were reported in *Bells Life* and it is possible that he played for United North of England Eleven against WJ Page's 22 at Tufnell Park in August 1872.[19]

---

[19] The T Dale in that game was absent in the second innings, which fits Dale's description, although the Dale who played for the United North did not bowl, which does not.

Dale joined the army and served in the Royal Horse Guards, now known as the Household Cavalry. However, in November 1872 he deserted from the Royal Horse Guards and emigrated to the New World, leaving his wife behind. She would have her revenge.

Dale did not keep a low profile. He immediately started making a name for himself on both sides of the North American border as a talented cricketer. Incredibly, he coached the Garrison team of Halifax for the important tournament of 1874 and then umpired in the following year's tournament in Philadelphia. He seemed oblivious to the risk of being identified as a deserter by any of the British soldiers he coached or rubbed shoulders with in the two tournaments.

It is probable that some of the Canadian players were British-born emigrants who saw the tour as a chance to visit family and friends from the old country. The tourists' ship took them past Canada Hill on the Isle of Bute, where families of nineteenth century emigrants would gather to watch the boats sailing off to the New World with their loved ones on board. Many hearts were broken on that hill, as the watchers knew that this would be the last that they saw of their kinsmen; in many cases they would never hear from them again.

The Canadians' arrival in Glasgow on 14 May allowed them a week to practise and this helped them to win their first game, defeating West of Scotland by five wickets. Dale was undoubtedly the man of the match, taking more wickets (12) and scoring more runs (60) than any other player. The victory came at a price, as Kearney broke his finger. He had represented Canada in the 1874 tournament in Halifax and the following year's contest in Philadelphia. This injury denied the tourists the services of one of their best batsmen for the next three games and a glance at the averages shows that although he played ten more matches, his form never recovered.

In the first example of an unhelpful itinerary, the Canadians headed west to Greenock before then travelling over 70 miles back the way they had come, playing in Edinburgh the day after the game in Greenock had finished. This was no way to prepare for a match and the Canadians lost by 10 wickets. However, it was clear that, provided their skipper continued to score runs and take wickets, the team could defy the pessimistic pre-tour reports.

The team's luck ran out during the fifth match against Leicestershire when Dale's thin disguise of playing under the name of Jordan was exposed by arresting officer Detective Crisp, who had the decency to wait until the end of Leicestershire's innings before depriving the

Canadians of their captain and star player. It is difficult to piece together Dale's colourful story from the existing records. He was living at the barracks of the Royal Horse Guards at the time of the 1871 Census and by all reports he deserted this regiment in November the following year. In September 1873 he turned up playing for St Louis in a 43 run victory against Toronto. After his spell as a coach in Halifax, already referred to, he became a professional for the Peninsular Cricket Club of Detroit, where in July 1877 he impressed the visiting Toronto Cricket Club with both his batting and bowling. Daft's 1879 tourists considered Dale of Detroit to be the finest bowler on the continent. He appeared to settle down here and married a woman from Natchez, Mississippi. However, this union was declared void when his first wife tracked him down and had him arrested for bigamy. A report from the Toronto *Globe* of 19 June 1880 stated that the divorce settlement included a promise that Sir Garnet Wolsely, Britain's then Quartermaster-General to the Forces, would ensure an amnesty from arrest for desertion. If true, this could explain why Dale felt confident enough to tour, although not why he saw it necessary to play under a false name.

When a Sergeant of his old regiment identified him, Dale fully admitted the charges and travelled from Leicester to the Knightsbridge Barracks in London for his court martial. Perhaps he was confident that the amnesty promised to him in his divorce settlement would protect him from a custodial sentence. Some form of extenuating circumstances would explain Dale's lenient sentence of thirty-six days and also his reaction to it. A trooper could expect a week's detention and a fine for swearing, so a punishment of just over a month would perhaps equate to a charge of insubordination, certainly not desertion. Dale's captors were completely unprepared for his reaction: he broke free and managed to make it far enough away from the military complex to be apprehended by a civilian. The court martial reconvened and increased the sentence by three hundred days. The 1881 Census, taken on the night of 3-4 April, finds Dale languishing in Millbank Prison.

Cricket has a habit of closing ranks on players subject to a public scandal but somehow Dale was immune to this. By May 1881 Detroit Peninsular Cricket Club had re-employed him as their professional. He repaid this loyalty by joining the Windsor Cricket Club, just before their important Ontario Cricket Association semi final match in August 1881. Windsor were defeated by Hamilton and by July 1882 Dale was back playing for Detroit.

To be fair to Dale player loyalty was flexible in late nineteenth century Canadian cricket and many players competed for more than one team to maximise the amount of cricket that they played, but it is surprising that there was not more media comment[20] when a professional player, who was contracted to Detroit and had a shady past, swapped allegiances just in time to play in Windsor's most important match of the season. The short-lived periodical the *Canadian Cricket Field* reported the controversy when fellow tourist JS Gillean elected to play for Pickwick Cricket Club against the Asylum Club. He was a member of both teams and arguably it was the Asylum Club that had the stronger claim to him. The fact that Dale's actions resulted in no more than a footnote in the *Globe*, and a comment in the *Canadian Cricket Field* that he strengthened the Windsor team, suggests that like many rogues he led a charmed life.

Press reports continued to be favourable on Dale's play and he was selected to tour with the Western Cricket Association team and for other important matches, such as East versus West and United States versus Philadelphians. The media reported purely on the cricket and made no mention of Dale's tumultuous past. He continued to play for Detroit up to 1885, but there was no mention of him in their averages for the 1886 season. In 1893 he played for a Detroit 18 against the touring Australians, making two scores of 6 and not taking any wickets as the fourth bowler used. Dale died on 2 August 1921 in the United States.

The tour did not end with the arrest of Dale. Even the game against Leicestershire continued with the opposition generously allowing the Canadian substitute, J Dewhurst, to bat, albeit at number 10. The Reverend Thomas Phillipps took over the captaincy. This was his first game of the tour and, as there is no evidence that he fielded during Leicestershire's first innings, it is possible that Phillipps was also a substitute[21]. Considering the ability of some of the Canadian players and the fact that Phillipps had played for Canada against the United States the previous year, it is surprising that he had not played in the earlier games. At the age of 47 he was probably accompanying the tour principally to assist the overworked Miller in an administrative / diplomatic capacity. Certainly the presence of such a well-known Canadian cricketer gave credence to the tour.

The presence of a W Gilbert in the Canadian team is a mystery. There was no Gilbert in the touring party and he played only once for the Canadians. It is tempting to conclude that this was WR Gilbert, the

---

[20] The Toronto *Globe* of Monday 8 August 1881 merely stated that Tom Dale has joined the Windsor cricket club and will play for them in future.

[21] In page 5 of his article "North America in International Cricket", Rowland Bowen states that Phillipps travelled from Canada to save the tour following the arrest of Dale, but the fact that he played in the Leicestershire game disproves this. He was also included in the list of the original touring party in the *Sportsman* of 6 April 1880.

cousin of WG Grace, who emigrated to Canada in 1886 after being caught stealing from his teammates' dressing room. However, the absence of the middle initial and a suggestion of an "s" at the end of his name in Haygarth's *Scores and Biographies* make this unlikely. It is true that the Canadians included local players to make up the numbers, but Gilbert's performance seems too good for that. There was a W Gilbert who played for Sussex, but it is unlikely that he would have scored the runs made in the Leicestershire match, or been entrusted with the task of opening the batting. WR Gilbert was an amateur at the time and so would have been prohibited from taking any payment other than expenses for representing Canada. The tourists were not particularly popular either side of the Atlantic, so I suppose it is possible that the scorers fudged the issue by omitting the middle initial of one of the country's most well-known players, knowing that the powers-that-be would turn a blind eye.

Most summary accounts of the tour imply that it fell apart following Dale's arrest and sentencing and although it is true that matches against Swansea and Cardiff were cancelled, twelve more games were arranged in addition to the five already played. Miller, the tour's manager, contacted Swansea Cricket Club and asked for £15 to be forwarded to them, as the games against Leeds and Leicester had been financial failures. The money was not forthcoming and so the two games were cancelled. Apparently the telegram was not read in time.

Miller also tried to secure the services of CJ Logan, whose name had been included in the original tour party. He had enjoyed great success against Daft's 1879 tourists, taking 7 for 35 for Canada and 6 for 39 for Hamilton against the Englishmen. In 1880 he played for Canada against the United States, where he opened the innings and took match figures of 6 for 70 in the drawn game. According to the *Sportsman,* Miller hoped that Logan would be able to receive the desperate plea, drop everything and cross the Atlantic all within the timescale of three weeks. In an age when all trans-Atlantic communication had to be carried by boat this was hopelessly optimistic and Logan remained in Canada.

Unfortunately the next match was against the MCC, the most important game of the tour. The Canadians were thrashed by an innings and 123 runs in a single day in front of a small crowd: another financial failure as well as a humiliation. Despite having 15 players Canada could only score 33 in their first innings, which included a hat-trick by Fred Morley, and 36 in their second innings, which included a hat-trick by Alfred Shaw, who had toured Canada in 1879. Both bowlers played Test cricket for England. George Ulyett, another Test cricketer and tourist of Canada in 1879, scored 30 in MCC's innings of 192.

The tourists had been hopelessly outclassed and, in order to ensure that they were competitive in their remaining fixtures, they needed to replace Dale. The services of Nottinghamshire's Walter Wright were secured, thus substituting a Yorkshire-born American resident with an English professional. Wright was an immediate success making 81, the highest score of the tour, in the next game, a drawn match against Crystal Palace. The home team were fortunate to get away with a draw, finishing on 47 for 5, still needing 194 more to win the game. Wright took 10 wickets to go with his runs and it was clear that the touring team relied on him the same way they had relied on Dale.

Despite his performances with both bat and ball, there were two drawbacks to employing Wright. Firstly the team's right to be called Canada, which was questionable from the outset, was lost. Haygarth's *Scores and Biographies* quite rightly calls the team "Canada with W. Wright of Nottinghamshire." The second drawback was the cost of employing a talented professional. Wright ensured that the team could continue to play competitive cricket against the English club sides, but his wages were paid from the tour's meagre budget. Without an increase in gate receipts the tour was destined for an untimely finish.

The team now had to travel from Crystal Palace in London up to Stockport, a journey of over 200-miles which had to be travelled in two days. Overall the schedule was gruelling and hinted of desperation. The team had three separate stays in London between lengthy journeys north to Stockport, Halifax and Longsight (near Manchester). A team that was in demand would have agreed a more sensible schedule, although it is possible that Miller was merely trying to save accommodation expenses by arranging overnight travel.

Distance travelled by the Canadians in 1880

Date	Venue	Distance from previous venue (on modern roads)
21 & 23 May 1880	Hamilton Crescent Glasgow	-
26-27 May 1880	Glenpark, Greenock	37 miles
28-29 May 1880 (drawn 1 day game on 29 May)	Holyrood, Edinburgh	73 miles
31 May -1 June 1880	Woodhouse Hill Ground, Hunslet	222 miles
2-3 June 1880	Grace Road, Leicester	98 miles
10 June 1880	St John's Wood, London	108 miles
14-15 June 1880	Crystal Palace Park	7 miles
18-19 June 1880	Higher Hilgate,	212 miles

	Stockport	
22-23 June 1880	Hales Road Cricket Ground, Cheltenham	130 miles
24-25 June 1880	Kennington Oval	99 miles
26 June 1880	Scott Street, Walsden	237 miles
28-29 June 1880	Thrum Hall, Halifax	14 miles
30 June- 1 July 1880	Orleans Club Ground, Twickenham	209 miles
2-3 July 1880	East Road, Longsight*	207 miles
5-6 July 1880	County Ground, Derby	71 miles
9-10 July 1880	Wavertree Road Ground, Liverpool	92 miles
12-13 July 1880	Amblecote, Stourbridge	100 miles

*Longsight to Halifax 33 miles

Wright had a rare failure with the bat against Stockport, scoring 1 and 0, and although he took five wickets for 68, the touring team lost by an innings. RW Hibbard top scored with 41 in the second innings and he had plenty of time to wonder whether the Canadians were getting value for money from Wright as the team began its long journey south to Cheltenham.

Cheltenham appeared to have been a weak team, with only three of their number having played first-class cricket. Rather unusually, the home team were permitted to field 12 players against the touring side's 11, who had the better of a drawn game. Wright again failed to make much of an impact with the bat, but he took 9 of the 13 wickets to fall.

The tourists now travelled east to face the Surrey Club and Ground. The standard of the opposition meant that the Canadians were allowed to field 15 players against the 11 home players for the second time in the tour. The Surrey team were not as strong as the MCC side and had three players who never played any first-class cricket. None of the Surrey men had played Test cricket, compared to six of the MCC team who had thrashed the 15 man Canadian team earlier in the tour. This time the Canadians, with the services of Wright, did themselves justice. After being dismissed for only 41 in the first innings, the Canadians rallied and amassed 171 in their second innings, with Rev. TD Phillipps top scoring with 50. Wright took 10 wickets in the match and the tourists won the game by a handsome margin of 110 runs.

The tourists now had to travel more than 200 miles to play a one-day match against Walsden in Lancashire the next day! Walsden were clearly a weak team and even though they were allowed to field 15 players the 12 Canadians had the better of a drawn game, scoring 120 in their first innings compared to Walsden's 62. The tourists then played a two-day game against Halifax on level terms two days later, suggesting that the match against Walsden was a late addition to their itinerary: it was not included in the fixtures list published in the pre-tour press reports.

The drawn game against Halifax finished on 29 June and the Canadian team now travelled 209 miles to play the Orleans Club at Twickenham the next day. The following match was at Longsight the following day, necessitating yet another journey of over 200 miles, which must have seemed ridiculous to all involved as Longsight is only 33 miles from Halifax. These lengthy journeys would have been taken at night and so support my theory that Miller arranged for the squad to travel during the night to save on accommodation costs.

The game against the Orleans Club was supposed to have been 13 a side, but for some reason the tourists were only able to field 12 men. The Orleans team was a strong side, as the majority of the team played regular first-class cricket. They defeated the Canadian team by an innings and 24 runs. This result should have convinced the tourists that they could not take on first-class players on level terms, but after a rain-ruined draw against Longsight the Canadians were humiliated by Derbyshire. The home team amassed a huge total of 473, which allowed them to thrash the tourists by an innings and 229 runs.

The Canadians then took on two far weaker teams called Wavertree and Stourbridge, beating them both in what were the final two matches of the tour. The provisional fixture list had included four matches after the final game against Stourbridge on July 12, so it is fair to assume that the tour ended prematurely, presumably due to a lack of funds as by all accounts the gate receipts were disappointing.

Miller deserves praise for successfully arranging 17 fixtures and along with Phillipps he was quite rightly spared the more scathing press attacks. In the words of the *Toronto Herald* he had dedicated himself to the tour "with a persistence worthy of a better cause". The players also deserve credit for achieving five wins, seven draws and five defeats. It would have taken considerable effort to play with any heart knowing that, as the money ran out, they could expect indifference to any success and ridicule for their failures. They earned their place in cricketing history.

The 1880 tourists were the first Canadian cricketers to cross the Atlantic, paving the way for the more successful 1887 tour, who as shown in the following chapter, learned lessons from these pioneers.

Chapter 6: The Second Canadian Cricket Tour

And he that will not play or pay to help the manly game,
May lie forgotten in the grave – an unremembered name
Last lines of the poem in the book on the 1887 tour: *Cricket Across the Sea*

One of the highlights of the 1887 tour was the game against WG Grace's Gloucestershire, where the Canadians proved how much their cricket had improved since 1872. Dyce Willcocks Saunders is in the back row, sixth from the left, wearing a striped blazer and cap. The Canadian captain ER Ogden sits two places to Grace's right (our left).

George Lindsey first mooted the idea of a tour to Britain during a committee meeting of the Toronto Cricket Club in the winter of 1886-87. The venture was supported in principle but practical objections were raised. Clearly no repeat of the 1880 tour would be tolerated. The players needed to be representative of Canada, both nationally and geographically, and of the highest standard if they were to compete with British teams composed of first-class players. Furthermore, it was also clear that gate receipts alone could not finance the tour.

Lindsey ruled that each player should pay half his own expenses. Only a small percentage of society would have been able to meet these costs whilst taking what was essentially a three-month unpaid holiday. The fact that Canada's top cricketers were part of this elite group indicates both the strength of, and the long-term weakness of, cricket in Canada. The sport could rely on this group from the late nineteenth to the early twentieth century, but certainly not much beyond the First World War. By relying on the rich amateur, whilst shunning the vital role of the professional, those who ran Canadian cricket made its decline inevitable.

The other half of the tour costs was made up of gate receipts and of public subscriptions of the great and the good, including the Governor General of Canada and the Lieutenant Governors of Ontario, Nova Scotia and Québec. The support of such notables assisted the tour both financially and in terms of public relations. The manager Lindsey and the wicket-keeper Saunders astutely dedicated their book of the tour, *Cricket Across the Sea,* to Governor General Lansdowne. His support, and that of the Toronto Cricket Club and the press, ensured the official status of this Tour, in contrast to the unofficial nature of the 1880 venture.

Had the gate receipts been plentiful the subscribers would have been entitled to some return but this does not appear to have been the case. *Cricket Across the Sea* asserted that, although there was little or no financial return for the subscribers, the value in terms of Canadian cricket meant that "we are still confident that the subscribers, to whom no sordid motives of gain can be attributed, will yet feel that they have made a good investment."[lvi] After reading this, any of the numerous subscribers would have found it difficult to object without suggesting that they had a motive of gain. The subscribers' role was more like that of patrons, although whether they felt their money had been well spent is unrecorded. One hopes that they found solace in the last lines of the poem replicated above. With half the expenses being paid by the tourists and an impressive list of subscribers / patrons one might speculate on how little was raised in gate receipts and, in turn, how many people turned out to watch these games.

Lindsey argued that the three consecutive victories against the United States in the International match showed that Canada ought to be able to put a team together that could emulate the success of the 1884 Philadelphian tourists and avoid some of the humiliations of the 1880 Canadians. The press, although highly critical of the 1880 venture, were supportive of the 1887 tour from the outset. The Toronto *Globe* ran an article on 3 February 1887, reporting that the annual meeting of the Toronto Cricket Club had voted unanimously to support the tour and included the names of the players who were expected to be in the squad. It was important to secure the best players to be able to compete in Britain, but the following leading cricketers were unable to go: CJ Logan (for the second time, making it no further than the provisional squad list), BTA Bell, F Harley and M Boyd. *Cricket Across the Sea* does not give reasons for their refusal,[22] but it meant that all those who toured were born in Canada - another contrast to the 1880 tour. Those who were selected were cricketers of note and included representatives from Halifax and Montréal, although the squad membership was heavily drawn from Toronto and Hamilton.

The tour meant that there was no International match in 1887, although the tourists defeated New York at Seabright by five wickets, before sailing on the *Furnessia* on 2 July 1887. ER Ogden did not play in this game as he decided to travel separately from the team, preferring the company of his wife, who was also the tour's official scorer. He met his teammates in Ireland, whilst the tour manager Lindsey was forced to make up the numbers, as, in contrast to modern tours, the twelve-player squad was small enough to ensure that all the players could expect to play in most of the games. This provided little cover for injuries, which explains why so many of the batsmen would also bowl and why, from a modern perspective, nineteenth century touring teams often appear unbalanced.

It was clear that WJ Fleury was regarded as the twelfth man, playing only due to injury to others. When Saunders was unable to play against Northumberland due to a sprained foot, Fleury was drafted into the side where he batted at 10 and did not bowl. That he was unfairly underrated is proven by the fact that he would play in a total of nine matches and come sixth in the batting averages. George Lindsey was pressed into service seven times, only two fewer times than Fleury, but when Lindsey was selected he proved that his playing ability did not match his administrative skills.

---

[22] The *Globe* of 26 April 1887 stated that Bell had decided to retire.

Good relations had been established with the Irish cricketers following their 1879 tour of North America and so it is unsurprising that the 1887 tourists sought to include Ireland in their itinerary, albeit for only one game. The cricketers and their entourage had to land in Londonderry, then travel overland to play in Dublin, a journey that took an entire day. The main party met up with their captain Ogden in Dublin; where they played cricket for three days before crossing the Irish Sea to play the rest of their tour on the British mainland. The original intention had been to return to Ireland at the end of the tour, but this proved impossible as the tourists had their own individual plans. As the tourists had paid half their tour costs, it was not unreasonable for them to expect time off for sightseeing. Some of the cricketers would tour Europe following the end of the tour and so it is reasonable to conclude that the decision to include Ireland in the itinerary was influenced by those who wanted to sightsee as well as play cricket.

The Irish team was a strong side mostly made up of the Leinster[23] and Phoenix Clubs but it also included J Dunn, an Australian studying at Trinity College, who top scored with 67. Two of the Irish players, the opening batsman David Trotter and captain Jack Nunn, had played against Toronto, Hamilton, Whitby and Cobourg in their North American tour eight years earlier. Before the game the Canadians were entertained by a Mr Barrington who had been the 1879 tour manager and, at the after-match dinner, the Canadians met two of the Hone brothers who had also been part of that venture. There were five members of the Hone family on the 1879 tour and it is impossible to identify which of them were there to welcome the Canadians eight years later. Sadly the '79 tourists William Hone junior and Jeffery Hone both died in 1888.

The 1880 pioneers, whether by design or by accident, found themselves with several days to prepare for their first game. In contrast, the 1887 tourists had only one day, which did more harm than good, resulting in Ogden damaging his finger and some minor injuries to other players, suggesting that the squad were still feeling the effects of the ten-day voyage and overland journey. They were not helped by the social obligation of attending a dinner arranged in their honour following their arrival in Dublin. This led to a baptism of fire on a fast pitch where the tourists' fielding was poor (in contrast with the rest of the tour) and Ferrie strained his side bowling his fifth over, an injury which would affect his bowling for the first half of the tour. The result was a defeat by an innings and 102 runs to the Irish Gentlemen. The Canadians never recovered from allowing Ireland to reach 319 at the

23 Leinster CC was formed in 1852 (source: The Cricketer 31 May 1952, p.187) The Canadians were made honorary members of both clubs.

start of the match, which included a ninth wicket stand of 94. Ferrie opened the second innings after being the not out batsman in the first innings. As stated previously, opening with the not out batsman was not unusual in Canadian cricket, but it had no tactical value as Ferrie batted at 11, and can only be explained as the sporting thing to do, in effect, allowing the one unbeaten player from the 1st innings to complete his innings.

After being defeated early in the second day the teams decided to begin another match, presumably for the entertainment of the crowd. Ogden won the toss but although batting first would have been tactically the correct move, he demurred from doing so as it would have been ungentlemanly to keep his opponents in the field for the third innings in a row. Nevertheless the Canadians gave a far better impression of themselves in the second match, dismissing a weakened Ireland for 166 and scoring 202 in reply, thus giving themselves a moral victory by leading on the first innings.

Whenever a group of young men are brought together on a cricket tour, roguish behaviour inevitably follows. Before they left Dublin one of the Canadian players decided to finish the evening by arranging a horse cab race down Stephen's Green by eight drivers for half a sovereign. The driver who finished last boasted that he could outpace the other seven on foot, a feat that he then achieved in a second race back up the Green. The noise attracted the attention of the local constabulary and the Canadians were obliged to return to bed.

The Canadians had time to tour the Guinness factory in Dublin, before departing for Edinburgh via Holyhead. Twice the main party left their teammates behind to make their own way to a game, presumably at their own expense. The first instance occurred in Dublin when Saunders and Britten, the general dogsbody, missed the train after having one too many pints of the famous Irish stout. They had to make their own way across sea and land to Edinburgh, where they claimed to have been delayed by attending church on the Sunday morning. The second instance occurred in Scotland, when WC Little was left stranded sightseeing at Rob Roy's cave after missing the tour boat. It says something for Scottish hospitality that, although he had no money with him, he managed to rejoin the touring party the next day.

When the team arrived in Holyhead they boarded their own private railway carriage, which would transport the whole squad, its entourage and 78 pieces of luggage throughout mainland Britain. The carriage had the numbers 147 painted on it and was much beloved by the players.

The Gentlemen of Scotland were a strong side and included RJ Pope who had played for Australia in their last tour of England. Once again Ogden lost the toss and Scotland were allowed to compile a match winning total in their first innings. Saunders was added to the injured list when he was struck on the foot by a throw-in to the stumps from the outfield. He continued in the field, but was unable to bat the next day. The Canadians were further handicapped by having to bat until 7pm. The sun does not set in Edinburgh in mid-July until after 9:30pm, but the Canadian batsmen would have been unused to staying out that long and the captain was criticised for agreeing to such a late hour for the close of play.

The school boys at Merchiston College were given a half-day holiday to allow them to watch two former students, George Jones and William Henry, play against the Gentlemen of Scotland. Jones and Henry were born in St John, New Brunswick and Nova Scotia respectively and were sent to Britain to complete their education. The College students saw Henry hit 76, the highest score of the match for either team. Despite this the Canadians could only make 146, forcing them to follow-on. They went on to lose the match by 10 wickets, only avoiding an innings defeat by forcing the injured Saunders to come in at 11.

The Canadians travelled south to Newcastle to play the Gentlemen of Northumberland, who were a strong team and included the Oxford Blue Hylton Phillipson in their team, who kept wicket and opened the batting. Unfortunately Saunders needed a walking stick to move about and his place was taken by Fleury, who batted at 10 and did not bowl. Ogden lost the toss again and saw the opposition pass the 200 mark in their first innings. Ferrie's side strain finally got the better of him and he retired from the game after bowling 16 overs. Northumberland sportingly allowed the manager Lindsey to take his place and bat in both innings. It is probable that they knew of Lindsey's standard as a cricketer before agreeing to the request. Canada managed to avoid the follow-on for the first time in the tour and were left three hours to bat to secure a draw. They slumped to 18 for 5 and although Henry's 57 allowed Canada to recover to 118, they were heavily defeated by 212 runs.

The Canadians now proceeded to Sunderland where they played against Durham. The names of all their previous opponents had the prefix "Gentlemen of" and the reason that this team does not was due to the selection of five professionals in their team. This contravened a prior agreement that the tourists would play only against amateur cricketers. However, on accepting that this was an honest oversight, which was too late to reverse without huge inconvenience, the Canadians allowed Durham to play unchanged. In turn Durham allowed

Saunders to bat with a runner, despite the fact the injury had occurred in a different game. Ogden lost another toss and again their opponents ran up an impressive first innings score. Durham's top scorer AA Mewburn was dropped twice, once before he scored and once on 50 in an unbeaten innings of 87 out of a total of 281.

For the third time out of four matches the Canadians were obliged to follow-on, this time with a deficit of 97 runs. In their second innings Canada slumped to 35 for 4 before Ogden and Henry made a partnership of 115 in less than an hour to save the game. Ogden made 98 and Henry made 77. Batting at 11 Fleury made an unbeaten 27, which was the third highest score and made up for being *adjudged* LBW in the first innings by Shanly, the Canadian umpire. With Canada 196 ahead, Durham were obliged to bat and the tourists ended the game with satisfaction, reducing the home team to 12 for 1 before time was called.

The tourists were obliged to stay overnight in Manchester before travelling on to Buxton to play the Gentlemen of Derbyshire. Unfortunately there was an exhibition on at Manchester and, in the first example of poor organisation, the cricketers were forced to try six hotels before finally managing to book themselves into The Brunswick at 1 am, knowing that they would have to be up in six hours to travel to the Park Road cricket ground at Buxton.

Against the Gentlemen of Derbyshire Ogden finally won his first toss - and the tourists finally won their first game by the handsome margin of an innings and 40 runs. The wicket was wet and difficult to bat on, with the bowlers assisted by a crosswind. In these conditions Saunders played an anchor role, taking two hours to make the top score of 46 in a total of 150. Ogden and Gillespie then bowled unchanged to dismiss Derbyshire for a paltry 42. Following on they fared little better and could only make 68, with the captain giving the manager Lindsey a bowl. Victory was completed shortly after noon on the second day.

In the first example of an unhelpful itinerary, the tourists were now obliged to travel from Buxton to Brighton, too far to travel in a single day, necessitating a stay in London. They arrived at their hotel in Euston at around midnight and, whether through chance or design, found that a young actress, whom they had met on the boat out, was staying at the same hotel.

At Sussex's County Ground at Hove the tourists continued to struggle without Ferrie and again Lindsey was pressed into service. The manager of the 1872 tour, RA Fitzgerald, had observed that he had not seen a single Canadian wicket-keeper worthy of the name. In this match Saunders showed that Canadian cricket had made advances in this field as his performance, which included a smart stumping and involvement in three other wickets to fall, drew favourable comparisons with domestic amateur wicket-keepers. Sussex made 206 and in failing light Canada were reduced to 27 for 3 in reply. It was clear that Aubrey Smith was too good a bowler for the Canadians and he took 8 for 19, forcing the tourists to follow-on 133 runs behind. That winter he toured Australasia with Arthur Shrewsbury's team and the following year Smith would play in his only Test match, against South Africa at Port Elizabeth, where he would take 5 wickets for 19 in the first innings. According to the *Toronto Star* of 20 July 1910 Smith would tour Toronto as a successful comedian. Following his retirement from cricket he became an actor, moving from theatre, to silent films and then playing stiff upper lip Englishmen in the talkies. He formed the Hollywood Cricket Club in 1932 and was knighted in 1944. He died four years later at Beverly Hills, California aged 85.

When it became clear that the Canadians would lose the match, the contest changed into whether an innings defeat could be avoided. Lindsey came to the crease as the last man, with Canada needing 2 to make Sussex bat again. This was achieved by an all run six, which included two separate overthrows, the first of which allowed an extra four to be run suggesting that all runs had to be run out. A Major Edwards lost half a sovereign, by making separate bets that Lindsey's dismissal was imminent.[24] Edwards was clearly a man who liked a bet and he induced Aubrey Smith and WA Henry to have a sprinting race. The first race was a dead heat, but Smith won the second and bets were honoured in the pavilion after the race.

In a further boost to Canadian pride, they managed to remove one of the Sussex batsmen before the home team won the game by nine wickets. To entertain the crowd Sussex batted on, but could only reach 100 for 8 by stumps[25], which was a fielding performance from which the tourists could take strength. The tourists now returned to London to play against the MCC at Lord's, in their centenary year.

This was the most important game of the tour and the Canadians faced a strong MCC team, which included ten cricketers who had represented the Gentlemen in their annual match against the Players. Ferrie was back in the team, but his lack of match practise showed and he took only two wickets in the match. Ogden lost the toss and a heavy

---

[24] Page 113 of *Cricket Across the Sea* states that the bets were a shilling each, but this would mean 10 separate bets, which seems unlikely. Either the loss was exaggerated or made with more than one person.

[25] Score as stated on p.116 of *Cricket Across the Sea*. Cricketarchive records the Sussex score as 123 for 9 by stumps.

defeat for the Canadians looked likely as the MCC amassed 306. Welman was badly dropped by Gillespie and he went on to make an unbeaten 50, which allowed the MCC to add 76 for the final wicket. The Canadians finished the day on 161 for 7, still needing 69 more to avoid the follow-on.

The dinners thrown in honour of the Canadians were usually held on the evening of the first day's play and here the tourists were entertained in the pavilion, which was unfortunate as their dinner suits were at their hotel. It is possible that these dinners helped the Canadians, as they were young men whose performances were less likely to be impaired by the indulgences of the night before than those of some of their older opponents. Canada fought back on the second day, with the last three wickets adding nearly 100 to reach 254, only 54 behind the MCC innings. Allan's 78 was the highest score for either side.

In their second innings the MCC started strongly with Cl Thornton, who had played in the corresponding fixture in 1880, scoring 58 while batting at the top of the order. However, after putting on 112 for the first wicket the home side collapsed to 191 all out, with the skipper Ogden taking 9 wickets for 83. The Canadian wicket-keeping and fielding was praised, with Henry's catch to remove Farmer, just by the pavilion, described as the best of the tour.

Unfortunately a lack of time robbed the spectators of a tight finish. Chasing 248 to win the Canadians reached 139 for 6, with Allan unbeaten on 35 not out. The Canadian tail had shown in the first innings that they would have been capable of making the 109 more runs to win. Many notable Canadians watched this impressive display by their fellow countrymen, including: Rev Dean Jones, Head Master of Trinity College School, and George Brunel, a noted Canadian cricketer who played for Toronto Cricket Club and represented Canada twice in the International Series against the United States.[26]

The official nature of the 1887 tour and the social standing of its players ensured that they were well treated. In contrast to the hectic nature of the 1880 tour the 1887 players had time to visit various tourist attractions often with a prestigious guide who could access sites that would have been out of bounds to the public. After the important match against the MCC, the Canadians had two days in London where they

---

[26] Mr and Mrs Reynold Gamble, Mr and Mrs Harcourt Vernon and D'Arcy Boulton were also reported as present, but I have been unable to discover why p.129 of *Cricket Across the Sea* considers these spectators to be worthy of note. I presume that D'Arcy Boulton was related to William Boulton, who had been Mayor of Toronto and was mentioned earlier.

shown round the Houses of Parliament (where the Irish Land Bill was being discussed) by Lord Oxenbridge the President of the Surrey Club and were given a tour of Windsor Castle by Sir Henry Ponsonby Fane who ensured that they saw the private and State apartments of the Queen's residence. Following the game against Combined Services at Portsmouth, Colonel NW Wallace, formerly of Halifax, and a Major Lambart showed the Canadians round the Spithead Fort. They were invited on board a torpedo boat and shown how a torpedo worked, and, during the Hampshire game, shown round the Ordnance Survey where "all the strategical points of the realm are exposed to view on paper."[lvii] From a modern perspective it appears extraordinary that non-essential personnel were allowed to view the latest navy technology and maps which the nation's enemies would have been keen to see. The Canadians also saw the battleship *Trafalgar* which was under construction. It was the third ship of that name and would become the largest battleship afloat. Following the Surrey game they were taken round the Bank of England: all evidence of the esteem in which the cricketers were held.

The tourists now returned to the south coast to play against a Combined Services XII at the United Service Recreation ground at Portsmouth. The weather was hot and the pitch in good condition, so Ogden had no hesitation in opting to bat first. Considering the conditions, the Canadians were disappointed with their total of 159, especially when the Combined Services made 351 in reply, with Major Bethune scoring 105. The tourists were now facing a deficit of nearly 200 and the prospect of a heavy defeat. However, the team rallied; with scores of 66 from Henry and 86 from Allan they reached 267 for 10 and drew the game 75 runs ahead, with one wicket remaining in this 12 a-side contest.

The Canadians now went back to the capital to play against Surrey at the Oval. A more sensible itinerary surely would have been to play this game directly after the match against the MCC and to have played the game at Portsmouth after playing Sussex at Hove. Instead the tourists were forced back to the south coast after the game against Surrey, to play Hampshire at Southampton. The Canadians were required "to bundle out of London on Tuesday night without any dinner"[lviii] to travel down to Southampton to play Hampshire, reaching Southampton at 11pm. That said, the schedule was not as hectic as that of the pioneers of 1880 and the later tourists at least had their own carriage.

The Canadians won the toss against the Gentlemen of Surrey and opted to bat. Unfortunately the pitch played very badly and the Canadians had done well to reach 33 without loss when Trollope, the Surrey Captain, after consulting with his teammates, offered the batsmen the option of playing on an alternative pitch. This offer was gratefully received, but rather perversely, on a far easier pitch for batting: both openers were promptly dismissed. The Canadians made a disappointing total of 141 and, in reply, the Surrey team amassed a huge total of 432. The tourists' fielding was uncharacteristically poor, with several chances missed. To make matters worse Saunders had to stand down as wicket-keeper due to a bruised hand. Despair appears to have set in and the Canadians were reduced to "offering up fervent prayers that the batsmen might inadvertently knock over their wickets, or handle the ball, or do anything else contrary to the rules of the game which would procure their dismissal"[lix]. LA Shuter made 102 and Ogden was the best bowler, taking 6 for 129.

By allowing their opponents to bat for so long the Canadians had to bat for only two hours to save the game. To their credit they saved it in style reaching 149 for 2, with the injured Saunders making a match-saving 71 not out. There were two curiosities of note: the Surrey wicket-keeper bowled four overs, taking one of the two wickets to fall; and the not out batsman from the first innings, WC Little, opened the second innings.

When the Canadians reached the ground at Southampton, where they played the Gentlemen of Hampshire, they found that the dry weather had made a hard ground where batsmen got full reward for their shots. Canada won the toss and unsurprisingly chose to bat first. Ogden was dropped on 42 and went on to make a captain's innings of 133, which was the highest score of the tour and the only century. The next highest score was 22 by GW Jones out of a total of 219. Jones also kept wicket, as presumably Saunders' hand injury had not healed sufficiently. Two players, Cave and Wynyard, who had played for United Services, kept wicket for Hampshire. The Canadians fought back to reduce Hampshire from 114 for 3 to 225 all out. Saunders made 55 in Canada's second innings of 211, where the tourists lost their last five wickets for 33 runs, either in pursuit of quick runs, or possibly through a tactical decision to give themselves as much time as possible to dismiss Hampshire for a second time and win the game. Only one hour forty-five minutes were left for Hampshire to bat before the scheduled end of the game at 6:30. Fleury took a memorable catch on the boundary on the off-side to dismiss Lacey, but it was to no avail as Currie and Wood managed to hold out for a draw, with Hampshire finishing 61 runs behind with two wickets in hand. The result then could be described as a "winning draw" for Canada.

After the Hampshire game the team had a quick meal before reaching Salisbury at 11pm, checking in to the Cathedral Hotel, where a number of players were attracted to the pretty barmaid, or, in the prose of

Cricket Across the Sea, the "female custodian of the pewters and the 'opped hale', like Potiphar's wife, was fair to look upon."[ix] Unfortunately for the amorous cricketers, they had to be up in time to catch the 6:05 to Bristol the next morning.

The captain had arranged to cross the Atlantic with his wife, instead of with the main touring party, and it no doubt gave his subordinates much harmless pleasure when he almost missed the train to Bristol, arriving in a dishevelled state with his wife a minute after it was due to leave. On this train journey the tourists had a heated debate on whether the White Horse near the village of Uffington was made by cutting into the hillside or by piling stones on the ridge. *Cricket Across the Sea* asserts that the matter was still undecided, probably because it is a pile of stones in a cutting. The authors also state that the feature was half a mile or 2640 feet long, when it is actually less than 400 feet in length, suggesting that the argument was more important than the facts.

Due to a refusal by Bristol rail to transfer their 78 pieces of luggage, the players had to carry their own cricket bags to the private ground of Mr Tankerville Chamberlayne at Yatton, to play Gloucestershire, who usually played at Clifton. The ground was impressive with beer and dancing tents, as well as an elegant little pavilion, which the Canadian team was photographed in front of. Mr Chamberlayne was not there in person due to a family illness. Through his representative Mr Radcliffe, he apologised for this and for not assisting the Canadians with their luggage, as he had not know when the Canadians were to arrive. Whether this was through poor organisation of the hosts or the visitors remains unclear.

Many of the tourists had seen the great WG Grace play at the old Toronto Cricket Ground in 1872 and they were no doubt delighted to be able to play against him and his Gloucestershire team. Grace made a point of shaking hands with all of the Canadians and made favourable mentions of his Canadian tour. Gloucestershire usually played amateurs, so were capable of fielding a strong team including both EM and WG Grace.

The Canadians batted first but could manage only 140, with Little, whose batting had improved throughout the tour, left stranded on 31 not out. Doctors EM and WG Grace opened the Gloucestershire innings and kept up a continuous conversation during their stand of 49. Herbert Page was reportedly stung on the tongue by a wasp during the lunch break, but was well enough to top score with 79 in the Gloucestershire first innings of 239, so this may have been some obscure metaphor or an in-joke. Ferrie took four wickets, all bowled, including the prize of WG Grace for 59.

The Canadians started their second innings 99 runs behind, with defeat looking the most likely outcome. However, the tourists rallied and made a brisk 283 to force their opponents to bat out a draw. The highlight of the Canadian innings was Henry's 88, which was made in 46 minutes and included 13 fours and one six; he bludgeoned 27 off two consecutive overs. This prompted WG Grace to call him the "Canadian Bonner" after the Australian George Bonner, who had toured America in 1882. Gloucestershire had time to make 113 for 3 before stumps, still 81 runs from victory. Ferrie bowled EM Grace in the second innings, giving him the rare achievement of bowling both Graces in the same match. He was given the match ball as a memento of this feat; he attached a silver band to the ball, which he had engraved[lxi].

It was with good reason that WG Grace commented on the great improvement in Canadian cricket since 1872, when the Canadian teams on that tour had been soundly beaten despite putting 22 players into the field. The 1872 tour manager, Fitzgerald, had concluded that cricket in Canada would improve if games were played on level terms: the 1887 tourists proved him correct.

During this match the Canadians stayed with Mr Cox, RB Ferrie's brother-in-law. At the end of the tour Ferrie would stay with his sister and her husband for a month before sailing home. *Cricket Across the Sea* suggests that Ferrie's experience on this tour and the time spent with his family in particular convinced him to abandon his planned career in the church and get married instead.

The tourists now had a journey of well over a hundred miles to Stoke-on-Trent to play the Gentlemen of Staffordshire. Again the itinerary can be questioned as the next two games would take them back south to play in Birmingham and then in Leicester, before heading up north to Liverpool. It would have made more sense to play in Stoke after the Leicester game, as Stoke lies almost equidistant between Liverpool and Leicester. The journey from Bristol was too far for one day and the tourists stayed at the Queen's Hotel two hours from Stoke.

The County Ground pitch at Stoke was prone to deteriorate and so the Gentlemen of Staffordshire were at a considerable advantage after winning the toss and electing to bat first. Their innings of 229 appeared to be above par, but the Canadians responded with 313, their highest innings of the tour. The runs were not made effortlessly: Ogden had to retire hurt on the first day after receiving a blow on the head. He was able to bat the next day adding 17 to his 20 already scored. Fleury, who had begun the tour batting at 10, made an unbeaten 56 and shared a 100-run stand with Little. Lindsey, who was also playing in this game, had bet that Fleury would not make a 50 and so presented him with a cricket bag for his endeavours.

Staffordshire reached 111 for 3 before collapsing to 145 all out, although this was in part due to the state of the pitch which was becoming unplayable. The Canadians required 62 for victory in 55 minutes, which in normal circumstances would have been a perfectly feasible task. However, the wicket was now badly worn with "gravel and refuse from the furnaces which formed the sub-soil"[lxii] coming through the pitch. At one end the batsman was forced to stand in a hole three or four inches deep. Despite this the batsmen went all out for the win; though understandable, it soon became clear that this tactic was not the right one. The Staffordshire wicket-keeper, GB Capes, disgracefully stumped Fleury after he went to pat down the pitch following a delivery that had nearly hit him on the head. One wonders who was umpiring at square leg. Saunders was also stumped by his counterpart and it was left to Ferrie to bat with WW Jones to hold out for a draw. When stumps were drawn the tourists had struggled to 37 for 8. Despite his poor sportsmanship the Canadians praised Capes for his agility and Allcock for his seven wickets, although the pitch, bad light, and the Canadians' desperate attempt for a rare victory, were all contributory factors.

The close finish was watched in front of 2,000 spectators.[lxiii] This was a comparatively large audience compared to others during the tour. A report from the Toronto *Globe* of 13 August 1887 stated that there was a good attendance for the game against Derbyshire but not as many as for the Sunderland game where there was a daily tally of 500 spectators. Clearly gate receipts alone could never fund a venture of this nature.

After a tour of the potteries, arranged by the Mayor of Stoke, the touring party travelled to Birmingham to play against the Gentlemen of Warwickshire. At their hotel they encountered a lady from New Jersey they had met on the *Furnessia*, who they had called the "Skylark". During the game with Warwickshire they also met Whitby, who toured Canada in 1885, but could not play for Warwickshire due to a hand injury. At the train station the Canadians met Stewart, who had toured Canada with the West Indies and who they had met before at the Oval. Clearly the young cricketers were gaining admirers who, for different reasons, were prepared to travel many miles to see them.

The Edgbaston wicket was wet due to overnight rain and Warwickshire were perhaps unwise to elect to bat first as Gillespie exploited the conditions excellently, reducing the home team to 86 for 9, before a thunderstorm followed by gentle rain prevented any more play that day.

The innings was brought to a close swiftly the following morning for 106. George Jones took three good catches in the outfield.

The amount of time lost to the weather made the draw the most likely option. After compiling a swift 204, which included an innings of 56 from Ogden, the Canadians now pressed for an unlikely victory. Cox bowled underarm for Warwickshire, a fact remarked upon, presumably because by the late nineteenth century this was rare.

Warwickshire reached 64 for 9 at 6pm, the allotted hour for the end of the game; however, the skipper Herbert Bainbridge sportingly offered to play an extra hour, which allowed Canada to dismiss Warwickshire for 73 runs and complete a victory by an innings and 25 runs. Ogden completed a good game, taking 8 wickets (all bowled) for 27 runs, to go with his 2 wickets in the first innings. The President of the MCC, Hon E Chandos Leigh was present to shake hands with all the Canadian players and congratulate them on their victory.

The tourists travelled that evening to Leicester, where they stayed at the Bell hotel, so sparse that one of the team members was forced to sleep on a bed made up of a table and four chairs. Leicestershire won the toss and unusually elected to bowl first. It allowed Canada to make 228 and to reduce Leicestershire to 67 for 4 in fading light. The following day the Leicestershire opener AE Wright made a match-saving innings, carrying his bat for an unbeaten 63, which was made in three hours and 20 minutes. The Canadians lost their chance of victory partly through poor fielding, which was blamed on too much cricket without a proper break. The Canadians could manage only 141 in their second innings, leaving Leicestershire with the impossible task of scoring 158 to win in less than an hour. They reached 40 for 3 before the close, suggesting a close finish had the match been allowed to run into a third day. Following the Leicester game a number of the team stayed with friends, possibly a reason for their touring in the first place.

After arriving in Liverpool the team decided to rest instead of tour the city, evidence perhaps that the tour was grinding to a halt. The following day they arrived at Aigburth, then considered to be outside Liverpool and now a suburb of the city. The cricket ground there was described as the prettiest the Canadians saw on the tour, although the trees provided a difficult background for the fielders. Lancashire still play County games at this ground, although it has not become one of the leading grounds in England as the tourists had predicted.

The Canadians lost the toss and were made to toil in the field, as the Gentlemen of Liverpool compiled a first innings of 233. Ogden had the satisfaction of dismissing his opposite number caught and bowled for a duck. The tail failed to wag, but by quickly bringing the Liverpool innings to a close the Canadians found themselves having to commence their first innings in poor light, which they blamed for their collapse to 61 for 7.

The Canadians were all out for 78 and although they hit 229 after following-on the Canadians were defeated by 6 wickets as the Gentlemen of Liverpool and District hit off the runs required for victory a mere eight minutes before the scheduled end of the match. The fielding was not good, although there were some memorable catches. Henry top scored in both Canadian innings with 48 and 69, the latter being the highest score of the match for either side. Liverpool owed their victory to Thomas Evans, who took 11 wickets[27] for 94 runs in the match and had played first-class cricket for Derbyshire.

The Canadians had two more fixtures to honour, but for three of their best players the match against Liverpool was their last of the tour. Saunders now started on his journey home, whilst Gillespie went to Scotland to trace his family roots and Ferrie to Weston to spend time with his sister. A farewell dinner was held at which each player spoke of his experiences. Apparently George Jones spoke for an hour and a quarter, wandering onto such topics as his Acadian home[28] and the fact that his uncle had been defeated at the last election. The manager George Lindsey was presented with a locket by the other players, in gratitude for his efforts in arranging the tour.

The remaining cricketers now travelled a short distance to Oxton to play against the Gentlemen of West Cheshire. Bearing in mind the depleted nature of the squad it is surprising that the tourists agreed that the game should be 12 a-side. This forced them to include the Assistant Manager Coote Shanly in the team. Shanly had played for the Toronto Cricket Club, but he was not a regular in the first team. As a cricketer he played in the shadow of his more talented elder brother Cuthbert, who died of a terminal illness in 1882, aged just 23. Coote moved into cricket administration and received a silver pencil for his efforts as the official scorer at the 1887 AGM of the Toronto Cricket Club. He had umpired in a number of the tour matches but had not been selected for any of the earlier games and he probably thought his days of playing, at least at a high level, were behind him. He batted at 12, but was allowed to bowl, taking 1 wicket for 21 off 6 overs. Harris Hodgson, a former President of Montréal, was also drafted into the

---

[27] p.192 of *Cricket Across the Sea* incorrectly states 13 wickets
[28] The Acadians were forced from their homes in the mid eighteenth century for refusing to swear allegiance to the crown. Whilst this was a despicable act akin to ethnic cleansing it at least benefited Canadian cricket as their lands were given to those of British descent who brought their sports with them.

side. He had also played one match for the 1880 tourists, where he had opened the batting in their debacle against the MCC. He was clearly a Canadian living in Britain who was happy to answer his nation's call in time of dire need. Lindsey was also called upon to play and these three gentlemen batted at numbers 10, 11 and 12.

The ground of Oxton Cricket Club was picturesque, with the Cheshire Hills and Mount Snowdon in the background. A number of the West Cheshire players had also represented Liverpool and they provided the backbone of their score of 210. In reply Canada made 134 for 5, collapsing to 162 all out the next morning. The Canadians bowled out Cheshire for 138, with Little taking four catches, as the wicket started playing up. Perversely by dismissing their opponents so promptly, the Canadians greatly increased their chance of defeat. They slumped to 90 for 9 chasing an impossible 187 to win in two hours, but managed to hold out for a draw, with 2 wickets remaining.

Charles Thornton had played for the MCC against both Canadian touring teams of 1880 and 1887 and at Lord's he had invited the tourists to play one final match at JW Hobbs' ground (no relation to Jack Hobbs) at Norbury Park. Presumably this invitation was accepted before it was realised that the team would be missing five of its players, as the Canadian skipper Ogden and Vickers had now also left the squad. This meant that the touring team needed to field four players who would not normally have expected to play. One of these was Lindsey, who also decided to step into the role of captain. Shanly was again elevated from his normal position as umpire and Ogden's brother Lyndhurst brought the number up to 10. Finally the brother of Aston, one of the entourage, made up the 11.

Surprisingly there were over a thousand spectators to watch this makeshift team, including the owner of the ground James Hobbs, who presided over the lunch. The ground was described as having an outfield like a billiard table and an excellent wicket. Lindsey won the toss and decided to bat. He played a captain's innings at number 10, hitting a crucial unbeaten 26. Despite the fact that the tourists were deprived of their regular bowlers they managed to dismiss Cl Thornton's XI for 178 to complete an unlikely victory by 13 runs in this single innings contest. For the entertainment of the crowd the Canadians batted for the final half hour as if the game had been a two innings contest, ending the tour in style by hitting 78 off 12 overs, without loss.

The tour officially ended at this point and it appears that the players and their entourage essentially became free agents. Henry, Ogden and Vickers managed to play some additional cricket for a local team at

Hawarden. Shanly went to Jersey, whilst Lindsey, the Jones brothers and Aston toured mainland Europe. Gillespie, Vickers, Shanly and Little all boarded the *Ethiopia* on 15 September, which brought them back to North America, whilst Ferrie, Henry, Dickson, Ogden and his wife began their journey home on the *City of Rome* on 28 September.

Legacy

The 1887 tour was a success. By touring Britain in a year when no other teams did so, and by proving that a Canadian team was capable of taking on first class cricketers on even terms, the Canadians encouraged reciprocal tours.

For their part the Canadians would have learned from their experiences in Britain and would have brought these ideas back to Canada. The fact that boundaries were used in almost all grounds in Britain would have been noted and no doubt contributed to that practice being adopted in Canada.

At first glance the records of the 1880 and 1887 tours appear very similar, with five wins and five defeats for both teams and the 1887 tourists drawing nine games, which was two more than on the 1880 tour. However, this does not tell the whole story. All the 1887 games were played between teams of equal size, whilst the 1880 tourists were permitted 15 players against the MCC and Surrey. A glance at the team names indicates that the 1887 Canadians faced stronger opponents and that they managed to avoid the number of one-sided contests suffered by their predecessors. It should be noted, however, that the 1887 tourists arranged to play against amateur opponents, in most cases denying the British teams from fielding their strongest sides. The opponents of the 1880 tourists had no such restrictions, which explains why their games on level terms were against club and not County teams.

A report of the tour in the Toronto *Globe*[lxiv] stated that in cricket the result was not important, a sentiment that sounds ridiculous by today's standards. However, in an era before declarations it was possible to avoid defeat by bowling badly thus giving your opponents less time to bowl you out. Naturally this would have been seen as "not cricket" by the Canadians, who would have preferred a defeat in which they had competed well against their opponents to a one-sided draw where they had been hopelessly outclassed. This fact should be borne in mind when comparing the draws of the 1880 and 1887 tours. Many of the 1880 drawn games were one-sided affairs, where the tourists were spared from defeat only by bowling too poorly to give their opponents time to dismiss them twice.

The 1887 tour marks the zenith of Canadian cricket. There would be no dramatic collapse, just a decline leading up to the First World War.

Chapter 7: Canada vs America: the Series from 1879 to 1912

*"The US is our trading partner, our neighbour, our ally and our friend...
and sometimes we'd like to give them such a smack!"*
Rick Mercer, Canadian Comedian, on "This Hour Has 22 Minutes"

The great Philadelphian all-rounder Bart King, who regularly tormented
Canada in the Series and would have graced any team.

The gap of 14 years between the 12th match in 1865 and the next game in 1879 is hard to explain. Perhaps the excitement generated from touring sides in 1868 and 1872 made the International Series superfluous. They inspired a Philadelphia and Boston combined team to tour England in 1874, playing baseball and cricket. However, touring teams from Britain and Australia continued to visit Canada in the 1880s and 1890s, when the International Series was at its peak, suggesting that there was no correlation between the two.

The Toronto *Globe*[lxv] suggested that the withdrawal of British troops from Canada was a reason for the cessation of the International, but matches between American clubs and British Officers based in Canada continued, for example in 1868 the Knickerbocker Club toured the US, with the press[lxvi] calling their games international matches. Major Hoagge played for the Knickerbocker Club in addition to representing Canada in the 1865 International.

The preference to play games between clubs instead of between nations was one of the reasons for the cessation of the Series in 1912 and so may well also be an explanation for the 14 year gap. There was a tournament played in Halifax in August 1874 between Philadelphia, Canada and British Officers. This was won by Philadelphia who hosted a return tournament the following year, which they also won. These two tournaments indicated that there was an appetite for international cricket on both sides of the border, but the wheels turned slowly.

In 1877 the Hamilton Club from Ontario contacted a Mr JT Soutter from New York to suggest a resumption of the Series. Toronto Cricket Club's secretary, Mr Herbert J. Furlong, offered to pay the team's hotel expenses. There was a dispute about the venue before Ottawa was decided as a compromise choice, suggested by John P. Green, the secretary of the newly formed Cricketers' Association of the United States. In August 1879, 14 years after the previous match, the Series restarted.

The Canadians George Brunel and the renowned Reverend Thomas Phillipps were the only players to take part in international matches before and after the interval. They would have found that much had changed in 14 years: overarm bowling had been legalised and the majority of international matches were now played with boundaries.

It could be argued that by making it permissible for the bowler to raise his hand above the shoulder in delivery the MCC were merely legalising a practice that had being going on for years. Before the rule change the bowlers would attempt to push the boundaries of what was acceptable; but after it they were at liberty to raise the arm as far over the shoulders as they liked. Far from being insignificant, the revision of the laws brought about an evolution in the game which forced batsmen and groundsmen to adapt to faster, more accurate bowling.

The Series came of age during 1879 to 1912 and with only three exceptions it was an annual contest. The games played during this time became what all international matches should be: a contest between the best players from both countries. This is proven by the cancellation of games scheduled for 1887 and 1889 because the best players of Canada and America respectively were touring Britain. The International game became the match of the season for players and supporters on both sides of the border.

13th Match: Ottawa on 19-20 August 1879

Rowland Bowen asserted that had the Civil War not intervened cricket would have become a major sport in America[lxvii]. Before the conflict, cricket in New York was declining and Philadelphia was becoming the new centre for American cricket. New York was relatively unaffected by the Civil War, whilst Pennsylvania was ravaged by the conflict, hosting arguably the most important battle at Gettysburg. If the War had been a bane to cricket then it would be reasonable to assume that the game would have declined in Philadelphia, but not in New York. All evidence is to the contrary. Philadelphia became the unquestioned centre of American cricket, whilst the sport declined in New York and elsewhere in the States. Baseball did increase in popularity during the war, as, unlike cricket, it requires no pitch preparation, but claims regarding the long-term impact of a four-year conflict on the popularity of cricket are highly questionable. As we shall see, similar unfounded claims with regard to baseball and cricket were made after the First World War. Philadelphia was now the dominant force in American cricket, providing seven of the players for the 1879 match.

The Cricketers' Association of the United States had been instrumental in arranging the restart of the Series, but its role in selecting the national team would be usurped by the Association of Cricket Clubs of Philadelphia by the mid 1890s. Selection for the Canadian team for this game was determined by the secretaries of Hamilton, Ottawa, Toronto and Montréal cricket clubs[lxviii], although clearly selection did not necessarily mean participation. Both Hamilton and Montréal declined to release players for this match, claiming that their club games were more important, which given the gap of 14 years was hardly a surprising reaction. In addition, the compromise choice of Ottawa as the venue instead of Hamilton or Toronto had not placated those in Hamilton. The Canadian team was significantly weakened as the vacancies were filled by players from the Ottawa Cricket Club, purely on grounds of expediency.

In 1880 the Ontario Cricket Association was set up by the principal clubs of that province. They were responsible for the selection of the national side until the Canadian Cricket Association came into being in 1892. The vast majority of players would continue to be from Ontario, with a few from Montréal, Halifax and Winnipeg. Charges of bias made by cricketers from outside Ontario were regularly met with exhortations in the Toronto press to select the best team to face the Americans. The influence of the Canadian Cricket Association over provincial cricket would ebb and flow, but the aim of selecting a geographically representative Canadian team was never lost.

The famous Newhall brothers, Dan and Charley, dominated this match in 1879 by taking 19 Canadian wickets between them (Dan 8, Charley 11); the only other dismissal being a run out.[29] The Canadian wicket-keeper FW Armstrong appeared to be the only batsman to cope with these two bowlers. He hit 29 in the second innings, more than double the next highest score. It was not enough and America scored the 60 runs required for victory for the loss of 5 wickets.

The hospitality which had typified the earlier matches continued. A moonlit trip on the Ottawa River was arranged and a number of Ottawans accompanied the Americans to the station to see them off.

14th Match: Nicetown, Philadelphia on 13-14 September 1880
For the first time in the Series the Americans hosted a match outside the New York area, reflecting the rise of Philadelphian cricket and the comparative decline of the New York clubs. Fifteen games would be played in America between 1879 and the outbreak of the First World War and all but one would be played in Pennsylvania. The 1886 match was played at Seabright, New Jersey because this was a popular summer resort for affluent Philadelphians, many of whom owned second homes on this coastline.

The 1880 game was twelve a side, a practice which was repeated in 1881, 1884, 1885 and 1886. Both teams had nine new players, as the selection for the previous year's contest had been done more on availability than merit.

There were about 3,000 people present on both days' play, whilst the wider public were updated by carrier pigeons sent from the ground at

---

[29] In the second innings the records show that the Newhalls bowled unchanged with Charley bowling 77 deliveries (15.2 overs) and Dan bowling 74 deliveries (14.4 overs) thus illustrating the fallibility of record keeping of that era. The two extras in the innings were both recorded as byes and so the extra deliveries were not wides.

the fall of each wicket.[30] Those at the ground saw Canada score 83 in their first innings, to secure a lead of 13 runs. However, after their opponents made 168 in their second innings there was insufficient time for a result. In poor light, with the surrounding trees casting lengthening shadows on the ground, the Canadians collapsed to a potentially disastrous 7 for the loss of 6 wickets, before time ran out[31]. Canada had unintentionally avoided defeat by failing to bowl out the Americans promptly in their second innings, but the Canadians had been as keen as the Americans to finish the game, an attitude that would be repeated later in the Series. This kind of sporting behaviour was more common in an age before declarations.

Unusually the Canadian tourists played an additional tour match, two days after the Series game, which would have allowed them only a day to recover from the contest and the evening entertainment provided by their hosts on the night of the 15th. This possibly explains why Merion managed to complete a victory against the Canadians by eight wickets in a game that was poorly attended.

15th Match: Hamilton on 29-30 August 1881
Hamilton was probably chosen as the venue to smooth over any bad feeling caused by the non-appearance of Hamilton players for the 1879 match. This was the only time that Hamilton hosted an International and the pitch was poorly prepared, which explains the comparatively low scores.

The start was delayed to allow Charles Newhall of America and George Hall of Canada to arrive. Neither managed to turn-up on time and George Hall's place was taken by Edward Ogden, who would captain the 1887 touring team to Britain. He did not bowl and made 11 not out batting far too low at 10, although by finishing unbeaten he was allowed to open the second innings.

The twenty year old debutant Alec Gillespie was the only Canadian batsman to reach double figures in both innings and his 27 runs for the match was the highest of either team. Gillespie played in 14 Internationals, which was more than any other player of either side. He took a total of 48 wickets at an average of 11.04, with his accurate medium pace bowling, and he scored 302 runs, which was more than

---

[30] Referred to in *New York Herald* of 14 September 1880. One imagines that they may have run out of pigeons during Canada's second innings.
[31] There is confusion surrounding the end of the match. Marder states that the game was abandoned due to a storm (see p.87 of The International Series), whilst the Toronto *Globe* does not mention the storm or poor light, only that the game concluded at 5:55pm. The *New York Herald* of 15 September refers to poor light, but not the storm, and states that the match ended at the scheduled time of 5:45pm.

any other Canadian. He made two centuries for Hamilton, both against Toronto: 117 on 2 July 1881 and 101 not out on 29 August 1892, which shows his longevity as well as his ability. Like his father, George H Gillespie, Alec was a keen curler and played for Toronto Curling Club.

The United States finished the first day on 43 for 5 in reply to 76 all out. They were assisted when the Hamilton groundsman rolled the pitch at the end of the day's play[lxix], in contravention of accepted practice. The United States made 107, a lead of 31 runs, and Canada's second innings total of only 50 was never going to be enough. The Americans knocked off the 20 runs required without loss to complete a victory by 11 wickets in this 12 a side contest.

The Toronto *Globe* states that although the Canadian bowling was better than the Americans', this was outweighed by the difference in batting and fielding between the two sides. The article added that the Canadian fielding was shockingly bad at the end of both American innings. The *Globe* criticises the umpiring, with the proviso that it did not make a difference to the result. The complaints included the stumping decision against Adams in the second innings and the giving out of Morrison even though the ball had clearly hit the pad. To make matters worse the umpire then asked the batsmen where it hit him and there was also an instance where the two umpires disagreed on a decision. This must have been painfully embarrassing for all concerned, but indicates incompetence rather than biased decision making.

The Toronto *Globe* criticises the selection policy which was governed by personal feelings and not merit, resulting in the erroneous selection of at least four players. The paper predicts that the discontent with the Selection Committee will either result in a "regime change" or the early death of the Ontario Cricket Association, which was established in 1880. Waud was commended for his wicket-keeping and captaincy, whilst Ferrie, Ogden, Guerrier, Behan, Gillespie and Ray were also singled out for praise. Gillean took four wickets, more than any other bowler, so presumably the four deemed unworthy of selection were Morrison, Saunders, Adams and Logan. None of these players would be successful in the Series, but only Adams was not selected again suggesting that despite the paper's predictions there was little change in the selection policy.

16th Match Nicetown, Philadelphia on 18-19 September 1882

The choice of the home ground of Germantown Cricket Club in Philadelphia as the venue for this match was fitting as the home team was made up entirely of Philadelphians. The Canadians would have preferred an earlier date for the match, which was late in the season for the cricketers from north of the border. The fact that the Americans gave the Canadians a generous gratuity for their expenses[32] made it more difficult for the away team to protest, especially as a later date ensured a larger crowd as the Philadelphians came home from their summer retreats.

The Ontario Cricket Association were unable to put their first choice XI into the field and for this reason the team was not geographically representative of Canada. Kirchhoffer, a Toronto lawyer who had business interests in Manitoba, had been selected as captain and his refusal to play was blamed on the Association's Secretary. Apparently the notification of selection came too late for Kirchhoffer to rearrange his commitments in the North-West. Edward Ogden's residency in Chicago counted against him[33] two-fold: as a cricketer living in America his selection could have been challenged and the logistical difficulties in travelling to the ground made any last-minute call up impossible. AH Stratford, of the touring Winnipeg team, was unable to obtain his captain's permission to play, which was a pity as the usual stumbling block for western cricketers, the distance required to travel, would not have applied. According to the *Canadian Cricket Field* CJ Logan, who took 7 for 39 against Daft's tourists in 1879, had too far to travel. He appears to have been a player for Cobourg, Whiby and Port Hope, so this excuse requires more explanation.

Whilst the Ontario Cricket Association were striving to make the team representative of Canada they were thwarted by the refusal of cricketers from outside of Ontario to play. The selectors also found it difficult to assess the abilities of players from other provinces, who never played against the cricketers of Ontario[34]. Four players withdrew at short notice and unsurprisingly their places were filled by cricketers from the Toronto area. The wicket-keeper EH Hamilton, who was from Montréal[35], was the only player selected from outside Ontario. It is worth noting that supposedly only players who were members of a team that belonged to the Association were considered for selection.

---

[32] According to the 23 August 1882 edition of *The Canadian Cricket Field* the Canadians were unable to pay the Americans a gratuity when hosting the matches of the International Series. Presumably they simply paid subsistence expenses.

[33] According to the *Globe* of 2 August 1886 Ogden's Chicago residency was the reason for his non-selection for the 1886 International.

[34] According to *The Canadian Cricket Field* of 13 September 1892 those cricketers residing in Ottawa were not considered due to their distance from the Toronto area, so strictly speaking it was not just players from outside Ontario who were unlikely to play in the Series due to their location.

[35] The *New York Herald* of 19 September stated that Hamilton was a Montréal player, which appears to be supported by cricketarchive.com, but Marder claims that he played for Peterborough Cricket Club (see page 104 of The International Series).

This rule was not rigidly applied, as Montréal only became a member in 1883, although it does show that membership was not restricted to Ontario clubs. Before 1892 the Ontario Cricket Association were doing the job of a national organisation that would later be carried out by the Canadian Cricket Association.

There were over a thousand spectators to see Canada bat first and be dismissed for 108. That this was considered to be a low score indicates how the game had changed compared to matches played before the legalisation of overarm bowling. In the American first innings Alec Gillespie was the pick of the bowlers, as he removed the top four batsman helping to reduce the Americans to 30-6. However thirties from batsmen 8 and 9 allowed the Americans to secure a first innings lead of 18. Gillespie took no more wickets in the innings and only one more in the match suggesting that the Americans had learned to cope with his bowling. At the end of the first day's play the Canadians had to bat in poor light, not helped by the shadows cast by nearby trees onto the wicket. HB Morphy hit 39, but was given not out by the Canadian umpire, G Elmslie of Hamilton, after clearly edging behind. His was the joint highest score, matched only by EW Clark in the American second innings, but despite this Canada could only manage 106. The Americans required 89 to win, which they managed for the loss of just two wickets, only losing their second wicket when the scores were level. The Americans continued to bat for the entertainment of the crowd[36] and finished on an impressive 175 for 8. The *New York Herald* of 20 September 1882 stated: "The United States has had its own way for too many years to make these meetings of startling interest". Canada had not won since 1857.

17th Match: University of Toronto grounds on 15-16 August 1883

The Ontario Cricket Association once again selected the Canadian team and inevitably they failed to satisfy everybody. A letter from an Uxbridge member, which was printed in the *Globe* of 26 July, accused the Association of an urban bias for not including their star player called Crossthwaite, who had averaged 23 that season after 13 innings. This player would not have been unknown to the selectors as he had played against the touring Irishmen in 1879. In a self-defeating move the letter concluded that Uxbridge would have no dealings with the Association, a decision which was hardly likely to build bridges. Efforts would be made to encourage rural cricket, with the Association agreeing at the following year's AGM to divide the province into districts, with the best clubs in each district competing with each other for the Association Cup. By placing the Toronto teams in the same district, matches

---

[36] The *New York Times* of 20 September 1882 stated that the spectators showed no interest in the play after the result had been determined, but stayed to watch it anyway.

between urban and rural clubs were ensured. In September 1912 the Association held a knock-out tournament for 16 rural teams. The contest was held in Canadian National Exhibition week, when train fares were cheaper.

The Canadian team played a warm-up game against an Ontario 16, beating a team which included Ferrie and Behan. Both played in the 1881 match and although Behan's international career was over, Ferrie's was just beginning. The warm-up game was an important development, which ensured that Canadian team had a chance to develop as a team. Unfortunately this innovation would not reap immediate dividends.

Approximately 1,000 spectators witnessed the match in which Canada were totally outplayed and had to endure reports in the press which included the words "lamentable" and "disastrous", whilst the Americans were praised for their batting, bowling and fielding. Canada won the toss and batted first and were dismissed for 43. In response the Americans compiled a match winning 148, forcing the Canadians to try seven different bowlers. Gillespie was the best of a bad bunch, taking 2 for 32 off 27 overs, but he took some of the blame for a last wicket stand of 50, which he could have ended had he managed to gather a wild throw from Brock with the American batsman Lowry stranded half-way down the pitch. Brock and Harley both dropped Lowry before Gillespie finally ended the innings by completing a catch off his own bowling. The Canadians could only manage 56 in their second innings and they lost the match by an innings and 49 runs.

In Britain, the amateur club I Zingari was formed in 1845. Translated from the Italian it means "The Gypsies" as the team had no ground. In 1888 an I Zingari club was formed in Australia and three years later it was recognised by the famous British club and allowed to wear their black, red and gold colours. This was not the second Zingari club however. In September 1883 a team called Canadian Zingari toured Philadelphia and won every game, beating Belmont, Merion and Germantown.[lxx] The tour allowed the best Canadian cricketers to play together and the two Hamilton bowlers, Ferrie and Gillespie, had particular success on this tour, taking 19 of the 20 wickets to fall against Merion. It is no coincidence that this bowling partnership would dominate the next three International matches and be instrumental in reversing Canada's fortunes.

The Americans had won the last three matches by 10 wickets, 8 wickets and an innings and 49 runs. Only rain had prevented another one-sided result four years previously. There had been little evidence since the re-start of the Series in 1879 that the Canadians could compete with their American opponents. Fortunately this was about to change.

18th Match: Nicetown, Philadelphia on 15-16 September 1884

For the third time in a row the Americans chose to host the game at the Germantown Cricket Club's ground at Nicetown. Spectators were charged $5 for entry into the club house, 50 cents for a reserved seat and 25 cents for admission. The game was sportingly delayed by 15 minutes to allow for the late arrival of the Canadian captain Dr ER Ogden. He then won the toss for Canada, elected to bat and top scored with 39 in a total of 179.

The Americans started badly in reply and at one stage were 22 for 5, but they recovered to 109, just managing to avoid the follow-on[37] courtesy of a last wicket stand of 20. RB Ferrie and Gillespie opened the bowling, as they usually did for Hamilton, and took nine wickets between them. The Canadians scored 151 in their second innings, with Ogden again top scoring, this time with 49. Canada suffered a middle order collapse going from 109 for 3 to 109 for 7, although in an age before declarations this had tactical value, even if it was not deliberate, as the lead was 179 at this point and the Canadians would have been going for quick runs in a two day match. Chasing 222 to win, the Americans were reduced to 29 for 4, effectively leaving them with just pride to play for. This they achieved thanks to Brewster and Morgan who joint top scored with 27, although Morgan was dropped twice in consecutive deliveries and Brewster once later in his innings. They ensured that the Americans reached a respectable total of 121, losing the game by 100 runs. This was the first Canadian victory since 1857 and was mainly down to the bowling of Ferrie and Gillespie who finished with a match total of 9 wickets and 11 wickets respectively in this 12 a side contest. Their partnership during this and the next two games prevented the Series from becoming a one-sided contest. Unfortunately the crowd size for this game was very small, only 400 souls present on both days[lxxi].

19th Match: Rosedale Athletic Ground, Toronto on 4-5 August 1885

The Toronto players were unhappy that the game was being played at Rosedale[38] instead of on their ground. The facilities and outfield were

---

[37] The MCC brought in the follow on law in 1857, which stated that a team was obliged to bat again if they were 80 runs behind in the first innings. In 1894 this was increased to 120 runs and in 1900 it was increased again 150 for a three day match (100 for a two day match) and perhaps more importantly the fielding captain could decide whether to enforce it. (See http://acscricket.com/Articles/2/2352.html)

[38] Toronto and Rosedale amalgamated into one club in 1898, because Toronto had no ground. The Toronto-Rosedale club was in existence for three seasons, reverting back to two clubs in 1901 when Toronto secured a ground on the University campus.

ideal for the occasion, but the wicket was inferior, which explains the low scores. The great patron of Canadian cricket, Governor General Lord Lansdowne, was in attendance, accompanied by heroes (or oppressors, depending on your view)[39] of the North West Rebellion which had been suppressed that spring. Lansdowne unexpectedly conversed with players from both sides during the lunch break on the second day. He was then formally introduced to the American players at the end of the match. Cricket in Canada still had a good relationship with the social elite.

GW Jones of St John, New Brunswick was selected on the strength of what sounds like a phenomenal season. The *New York Times* of 24 July 1885 stated that he was averaging 113 before the match between the Eastern Association and Longwood of Boston. He was the only Canadian player from outside the Toronto area to be selected by the Ontario Cricket Association for this International match.

The match was played on a bad wicket made worse by heavy rain just before the game started which waterlogged the ground. The pitch deteriorated as the match progressed, suggesting that the American captain Law made a mistake when he won the toss and put Canada into bat. Gillespie top scored and was run out for 21 in an innings of 87. America were routed for 43 in their reply. Only three Canadian bowlers were used: Ferrie who took 7 wickets and Ogden and Gillespie who took two apiece. On this occasion Ogden rated his bowling more highly than Gillespie's and bowled 16 overs, taking 14 for 2 compared to Gillespie's 4.1 overs, where he conceded 1 run for 2 wickets. The American score could have been even lower had Gillespie bowled more.

In Canada's second innings Gillespie top scored again, this time with an unbeaten 18 which allowed Canada to recover from 20 for 7 and total 57. Thus the Americans were set an unlikely target of 102. It is always difficult for a team batting last to score the highest total in the match to win the game and so it proved. At 48-5 a close finish looked likely, but the run out of Morgan ended a 23 run partnership and precipitated a collapse: America lost their last six wickets for 14 runs, closing their innings for 62, leaving the Canadians as victors by 39 runs. It was a reasonable effort on a treacherous wicket against accurate bowling. Ogden had realised Gillespie's worth and ensured that he bowled nearly half the overs to return with 5 for 24 off 19.2. He had top scored in both innings and taken 7 wickets, including the last two in successive deliveries to win the game for Canada; a fine all-

---

[39] It is possible that one of these was the Canadian hero Sam Steele, who had commanded a small force of Mounties which defeated the insurgents at the Battle of Loon Lake.

round display. His performance, accompanied by double figure scores in both innings from WW Vickers, and 10 wickets in the match for RB Ferrie ensured that Canada won their second International in a row. The *New York Times* stated that Canada had only won the previous year's contest because the best American players had been unavailable, but they had been beaten again by a Canadian national team which was approaching its zenith.

20th Match: Seabright, New Jersey on 13-14 August 1886

For non-cricketing reasons the venue was switched from Nicetown to Seabright, New Jersey, where many Philadelphians spent their summer vacations. Despite a great deal of effort being expended, the pitch was uneven at both ends and this was reflected in the comparatively low scores. The wicket was sited east-west, making batting hazardous from one end in late afternoon, as the sun began to set behind the bowler's arm. Half-way through the match the American skipper suggested moving to a new pitch, a proposal that was properly rejected by the Canadians. Playing on a pitch unfamiliar to both teams negated home advantage. This venue was clearly unsuitable and this was the only time it was used for a match in this Series.

Dyce Saunders won the toss for Canada and opted to bat. They recovered from 29 for 5 due to the efforts of WA Henry, A Gillespie and F Harley. Batting at 6, 7 and 8 respectively, their scores of 19, 19 and 39 ensured that Canada reached a competitive 123. "Slogger" Harley. lived up to his name as his top score of 39 was made whilst batting with the tail, none of whom made double figures.

Once again Ferrie and Gillespie combined to torment the Americans by reducing them to 11 for 6, with Ferrie taking two wickets with his first two deliveries. There were 8 ducks in the American innings and only three of their batsmen reached double figures in this 12 a side contest. The three batsmen were the wicket-keeper WC Morgan, who carried his bat for an unbeaten 17, MacNutt who scored 15 and Lowry who made 14. The latter two had taken 10 wickets between them earlier in the day. A last wicket stand of 21 between Morgan and Lowry ensured that America avoided the follow-on, but Canada had a lead of 68.

In their second innings Canada reached 106, due in no small part to Harley.'s 27, which was the top score. Gillespie batted one place above him and finished unbeaten on 11 indicating that he had been considerably outscored. In desperation the Americans used seven different bowlers.

The Americans needed to score 175 to win and although they batted better than in the first innings the task was clearly beyond them and they were all out for 77. Canada only needed to use three bowlers to complete the win: Ferrie, Gillespie and Wilson who took all 22 wickets to fall in the match. Little took seven catches in the game, fielding at point, which indicates poor batting technique as well as good fielding. When Canada won the game by 97 runs their players' celebrations were described as follows in the press[lxxii]:

> the Canadians went wild with happiness. They cheered, shouted, sang and gesticulated for an hour before they relieved their feelings.

How the Americans felt about such behaviour on one of their grounds is unrecorded, but there was no dinner or entertainment after the game and the Canadians started their journey home that evening. The victory was watched by TC Patteson, who had helped to organise the 1872 MCC tour which had included WG Grace and is referred to in a previous chapter.

There was no match in 1887 due to the Canadian tour of Britain. The match could have been played in September but this idea was not met favourably south of the border. Canada's last tour game was on 24 August in Cheshire and the 1884 match was played on 15 and 16 September so theoretically it would have been possible to schedule a game on a date when the touring Canadians could have played, providing the tourists had returned home promptly. However, this would have required better planning than the organisers of the fixture had hitherto shown. It would have been easier to schedule a game before the Canadians sailed for Britain and they did play a New York team at Seabright on 30 June and 1 July, but a game against a club side was not an international, although the New York Times of 2 July carried the wonderfully oxymoronic headline "New York loses the International match by four wickets"[40]. The International match was not formally called off until early September with the Canadians stating that the Americans could not raise a team, a claim that an editorial of the New York Times on 8 September 1887 called "incomprehensible". Poor organisation and/or communication led to bad feeling on both sides.

21st Match: Toronto on 4-5 July 1888

Canada only had one player, JH Senkler, who had not played in one of the last three victories against the Americans. The Canadians were playing at home and had a well experienced team which had reason to expect success, but it was not to be.

The American captain Dan Newhall won the toss and decided to bat first on a wearing pitch. Canada had relied heavily on the bowling of

---

[40] The match was a 12 a side game and so by overhauling the New York total with 6 wickets down, Canada actually won by 5 wickets.

Ferrie and Gillespie in their run of three consecutive victories. The two Hamilton players had taken a staggering 51 wickets in these matches, but in this game they were innocuous and failed to take a single wicket. Ferrie was suffering from a side strain, a recurrence of the injury he suffered on the 1887 tour of Britain, and Gillespie was under-bowled. The Toronto *Globe* blamed the lack of a quality spinner and overreliance on pace bowling, which could not cope with superior batting. ER Ogden opened the bowling and ended up sending down 43.2 four ball overs out of the 103.3 overs bowled. He took 5 wickets for 94 runs but bowled nearly three times as many overs as anyone else. In contrast Gillespie only delivered 15 overs for a miserly 11 runs and no other bowler came close to his economy rate. Given recent history it is surprising that Gillespie did not open with Ferrie and that Gillespie was so under-bowled. Canada's captain, WA Henry, was from Halifax and the only Canadian from outside Ontario. He did not know the strengths of his team and had a poor game as captain.

The Americans amassed 205, which was the first time either team had made over 200. Canada needed a good start but all of the top five batsmen were out for single figures. The only partnership of note was between F Harley and GW Jones who made 35 for the sixth wicket. This was a good effort from Harley, who was suffering from rheumatic fever. Unfortunately nobody else made double figures and Canada finished on 79 all out. Having been largely overlooked as a bowler, Gillespie hit 7 not out after being made to bat at 9, which was far too low for a player of his ability. In the previous three games he had batted at 4, 4, 8, 7, 7 and 7 and these were all 12 a side contests. He would be promoted up to 4 in the next match.

Canada followed-on a massive 126 behind. The second innings was a disaster, with AC Allan top scoring with 11. Brown and Brewster bowled unchanged and Henry Brown was irresistible taking 6 wickets for 13 with his left arm slows and Canada were dismissed for 39 to lose the game by the huge margin of an innings and 87 runs. At the time this was the largest victory in the Series and only the second time that a team had won by an innings.

For the entertainment of the crowd a game between smokers and non-smokers was played, with Canadians and US players making up the teams. Extra Canadians made up the numbers as not all those who had played in the International game were available for the extra match, or perhaps there were too many smokers in both teams.

The Philadelphians toured Britain in 1889 and the match was cancelled that year, following the precedent that had been set in 1887.

22nd Match: Wissahickon Heights, Philadelphia on 14-15 July 1890

Canada had no fewer than six players who had not played in an International before, but only two of these (Lieutenant Hamilton and KH Cameron) would not play in another International. GS Lyon and HB McGiverin were both debutants and would become stalwarts of the Canadian team.

The American captain W Brockie won the toss and decided to bat and when two quick wickets from KH Cameron reduced America to 73 for 5 this looked like the wrong decision. However, GS Patterson and FE Brewster then put on 91 for the sixth wicket and Patterson, who could have been stumped early in his innings, went on to score the first century of the Series. He hit 126 out of a daunting American total of 269, beating their own record score of two years before. The Canadian captain M Boyd used seven bowlers, but not GS Lyon who was a useful change bowler and would take five wickets in the Series. Cameron was evidently the best bowler, taking 3 for 18 but Boyd only gave him 15 of the 126 overs delivered in the American innings. This was a poor decision given that he took more wickets and had a far better economy rate than the other bowers.

Canada was bowled out for 141 in reply and had to follow-on 128 runs behind. The debutant TSC Saunders had top scored with 39 and so was promoted to open, but he could only make 2. GS Lyon top scored with 34, to go with the 26 he had made in the first innings to round off an impressive debut. Baily and Henry Brown took 5 wickets each and Canada was bowled out for 97, leaving the Americans as the victors by an innings and 31 runs. Canada had been competitive at times but for the second match in a row the Americans had won by an innings, and once again the Series was threatening to become a one-sided affair.

23rd Match: Toronto on 13-15 July 1891 (no play on 14 July due to rain)

The Americans protested about the state of the pitch that was rough and bumpy at both ends, which explains the low scores. When their captain GS Patterson won the toss he reasoned that the wicket would not get any better and so opted to bat. They made a terrible start with four out of the first five batsmen making ducks. America lurched from 0-2 to 5-4 to 31-7, before an eighth wicket partnership of 32 between the two top scorers, the opener JH Patterson (22) and the number 9 batsmen S Welsh (13), ensured that the Americans reached a competitive 82 all out. WR Wilson and the debutant E Hall took 4 wickets each, whilst amazingly Gillespie did not bowl at all. This was a clear mistake by the Canadian captain Dyce Saunders, who was also keeping wicket and opening the batting. This was too much responsibility and he was forced to relinquish the gloves to FW Terry in the American second innings. This did not assist his batting as he bagged a pair. Terry completed a swift stumping as stand in wicket-keeper, suggesting that he should have kept wicket for both innings.

GS Lyon, who had batted so well the previous year, came in at 9. He joint top scored with 13 in a disappointing total of 77. Gillespie took six wickets in America's second innings; his victims included the first five opposition batsmen. He was the fourth and final bowler to be used and showed everyone how different the match could have been had he bowled earlier.

Canada were set 110 to win, but were dismissed for 73, with the Reverend FW Terry top scoring with 20. Canada lost the match by 36 runs and the low scoring hides the fact that the victory margin was a relatively comfortable one. The Toronto *Globe* suggested that the Canadian batting was at fault and more practise and coaching were required. The Canadian team had practised against 16 players selected by the Ontario Cricket Association on 10-11 July before the International match commenced on the 13th. The playing of games between sides of an unequal number was becoming increasingly outdated.

24th Match: Manheim, Pennsylvania on 16-17 September 1892

This was the first match for the two great all-rounders: Bart King of Philadelphia and Jack Laing of Toronto. The *New York Times* called the team Philadelphia in its headline[lxxiii], but labelled the team All America above the scorecard. All the American players were Philadelphians. Nine of the Canadian players had battled out a draw against the touring Irishmen less than a week before. This gave the Canadians hope for this match and incentive for the Philadelphians, who were due to meet the Irishmen the following week.

The Canadian captain WA Henry won the toss and decided to bat. That was about the only thing that went right for the Canada team, as they collapsed from 42 for 3 to 65 all out, Gillespie top scoring with 21. It was King who helped trigger the collapse taking 3 wickets for 6 runs off 4 overs. All his victims were bowled without scoring. King was the fourth bowler used and one wonders how many Canada would have made had King opened the bowling, as he would in the future.

In reply the Americans compiled a mammoth 352, eclipsing their own 269 made in 1890 as the Series' highest score. AM Wood scored 129, which was only the second century of the Series. The lower middle order did not perform, but it scarcely mattered. HP Baily batting at number 11 made 24 not out, in a last wicket stand of 54 with FH Bohlen who was the last man out for 90. Laing was the pick of the bowlers, taking 5 for 72.

Canada batted like a broken side, knowing that the 287 deficit would be too much for them. Gillespie was the only player to make double figures, scoring 23 out of a total of 65, as Canada repeated their score of the first innings and lost the game by the huge margin of an innings and 222 runs. This thrashing was the nadir for the Canadian team in the International Series. It also gave the Philadelphians false hope for their match against the Gentlemen of Ireland who defeated them later in the month by the comfortable margin of 127 runs.

The early finish to the International gave time for a meaningless exhibition match for the entertainment of the crowed. The Philadelphians Downes and Brockie took the places of Gillespie and Fleury for the Canadians, who made 136 all out. There was insufficient time for any further play.

25th Match: Rosedale Cricket Club, Toronto on 11-13 September 1893

The *New York Times* referred to the contest as being part of the "annual match between Canada and Philadelphia, the latter representing the United States."[lxxiv]

The Canadians played their usual practise match against a side selected by the Ontario Cricket Association, but this time on level terms. Walter Cooper, who would play in the 1896, 1897, 1899 and 1901 Internationals, bowled for the Association XI and gave the international team a scare when he removed their first five batsmen cheaply, all bowled. They rallied to win the match by an innings and 14 runs. Cooper was then a corporal, but as we shall see in the next chapter, he died a private.

WA Henry won his second toss in a row as Canadian captain and again decided to bat. Canada were reduced to a disastrous 20 for 8 with none of the top seven batsmen reaching double figures. The team were rescued by two batsmen who had a history of being made to bat too low. A Gillespie at 8 and GS Lyon at 10 added 47 for the ninth wicket and GS Lyon then added 20 with the last man F Grew to ensure that Canada reached 87 and avoided humiliation. GS Lyon was left stranded on 30 not out. He was elevated to number 5 in the second innings, but the proverbial horse had bolted.

Calvert the American umpire from Detroit was criticised for miscounting the number of deliveries in Patterson's overs, once allowing six deliveries and twice seven deliveries in the five ball overs.

In response the Americans reached 116 for 8 and according to the Toronto *Globe* of 12 September bets were made that the Americans would not make 130. These bets were lost as the American number 9, AG Thompson, batted superbly with the tail, and ensured that the last two wickets added 61 runs. Thompson finished on 52 not out while LA Biddle and CT Cowperthwaite contributed only 2 and 4 respectively. Jack Laing continued his excellent form with the ball and took 7 for 54.

The Canadian second innings was a reverse of the first as the top order scored 183 for the first three wickets, the second wicket contributing 153, a Canadian record. The Reverend FW Terry became the first Canadian[41] to score a century in the Series, by hitting 111, an innings which lasted 165 minutes and included 18 fours. Terry survived a confident appeal for a catch, which was given not out by the American umpire. His innings was ended when he was run out going for a fifth run, the decision was described by Marder as a close call. The Canadian innings then subsided to 236 all out. It had been an impressive fight back, but America only needed 147 to win the match. Laing was the main threat in the American second innings and he took 4 for 69, all his victims being bowled. Laing's total of 11 wickets in the match was not enough to prevent an American victory by 4 wickets. The American Captain GS Patterson denied reports that he considered Laing to have thrown the delivery that had dismissed him on the last ball of the second day[lxxv]. A denied report is hardly proof of a suspect action, but clearly there was some speculation at the time. In 1895 TC Patteson suggested that Laing's action was questionable in his reminiscences, published in *Sixty Years of Canadian Cricket*. In an attempt to smooth over any bad feeling GS Patterson used his after match speech to praise the Canadian crowd for its impartiality and its appreciation of good cricket.

A glance at the International records suggests that Jack Laing was a great bowler who batted too high in the International matches, when he was actually a great all-rounder. He scored eleven centuries in domestic cricket, at a time when hundreds were uncommon. On 16 October 1893 he hit 43 not out against the touring Australians, proving that he could bat against the best and his abysmal form with the bat in the Series remains a mystery. He averaged 6.56 over eight innings, with a top score of 23, which he made twice.

---

41 Terry was actually born in Wells, Somerset in 1860, and played for Somerset from 1882-85. The *New York Times* of 17 September 1893 argues that unlike the Canadians, the Americans were all native born, overlooking the fact that AM Wood was born in Derbyshire. For the record three of the Canadian players in the 1893 game were born in England and one in Sri Lanka.

Interestingly JE Hall, who was the Secretary of the Canadian Cricket Association and often fulfilled the role of scorer in the International Series, and GS Patterson agreed that annual matches between teams from Ontario and Philadelphia should be played every July at Ontario when the International match was played in Philadelphia and vice versa. I can find no evidence of this actually happening; I imagine that the issue of spreading the talent too thinly was considered to be a terminal problem.

The Americans were entertained at the Albany Club at the end of the second day's play. Major Cosby, the President of the newly formed Canadian Cricket Association, was in the chair.

26th Match: Manheim, Pennsylvania on 17-18 September 1894

The practise match for the Canadian team was held on 11 and 12 September against a touring team from the Maritime Provinces. There was controversy when four of the touring cricketers were not invited to the dinner organised by the hosts, allegedly due to their social status. The finger of blame was pointed at the Maritimes captain WA Henry, as the Torontonians would not have had the knowledge to discriminate. Henry accompanied the Canadian team to Philadelphia, with his teammate George Jones. Alec Gillespie was also there as a spectator, unable to play due to injury.

Lord Hawke's tourists were in New York at the same time and to prevent a clash the International match was rearranged for 10 and 11 September, but due to either poor organisation or communication it reverted to its original date.

The previous month the Canadian captain GS Lyon had scored an unbeaten 238 for Rosedale against Peterborough, a Canadian record. He won the toss and decided to bat, a decision that may have been influenced by the fact he was a man short. WW Jones had missed a connection and his late arrival explains why he batted at 9 after opening in the previous match. Canada amassed a respectable 155, but a glance at the scorecard suggests that it should have been more. Three players joint top-scored with 23 (Laing, AFR Martin and Lyon) and eight players made double figures. The Americans' reply was frequently interrupted by rain. They lost their third wicket on the final ball of the first day, when Wood, who top scored with 36, was adjudged LBW in a controversial decision by the Canadian umpire. America reached 177 for 9 before the weather intervened. No play was possible on the third day and the match was abandoned. Laing gave a rare all-round performance by taking 6 for 69 in the American innings.

The weather may have had the final say in this match, but the Canadians had fought on level terms for the best part of two days. This gave them reason for optimism at the following year's contest when poor organisation south of the border robbed the Americans of their best players.

27th Match: Rosedale Cricket Club Ground, Toronto on 2-4 September 1895

This match was rescheduled at the request of the Philadelphia Committee, who selected the American team. However, the rescheduling failed to convince GS Patterson, EW Clark, WW Noble, C Coates, AM Wood, JB King and HC Thayer to play in a game that they were chosen for. Canada selected one player[42] from outside Ontario, Herbert G Wilson, who had scored the first century recorded in Winnipeg cricket in 1888 and would finish the 1894 club tournament held by Winnipeg Cricket Club with an average of 95 and by all accounts was having a good season in 1895 where his scores of 0, 63, 62, 67 and 72 resulted in the *Globe* calling for his selection for the International match[lxxvi]. Wilson was an adventurer who was a member of the 1884 expedition to relieve General Gordon in Khartoum and in 1897 he took part in the Klondike gold rush. Like many adventurers he did not die in his sleep. He committed suicide in December 1925 after being suspended as Winnipeg's Commissioner of the Workmen's Compensation Board earlier that year.

The game was scheduled to commence at 11, but the Americans arrived late and then indulged in practise, delaying the start until just before noon. FW Terry won the toss for Canada and decided to bat. Dyce Saunders opened the innings and made 26, but when he was out the Canadians collapsed to 69 for 7 and a low total looked probable. WR Wadsworth then hit a brisk 70, batting at number 9 and shared an 87 run stand with ES Jacques at 8 who only made 14. No other batsman reached double figures, in a total of 156, giving the score card a very uneven look.

The inexperienced American team, with seven debutants, were in trouble straight away when Jack Laing bowled Cole with the first ball of the innings. Laing and PC Goldingham bowled unchanged, taking 7 for 21 and 3 for 36 respectively as the Americans were dismissed for 65. Laing ended the innings in spectacular fashion by taking the last three wickets, JW Sharp, S Goodman and LK Mallinkrodt in an all bowled hat-trick. A law change the previous year had recognised that higher

---

42 There is some doubt surrounding the residency of ES Jacques. Marder states that he was from Toronto on page 173 of The International Series, whilst the *Globe* of 2 September 1895 calls Jacques a Winnipeg player.

scores were being made and increased the margin required to follow-on from 80 to 120 runs. Thus the Americans were not obliged to follow-on.

With a lead of 91 the Canadians were now in the ascendancy. They rearranged their batting order, promoting M Boyd from number 11 to open the batting at number 2, presumably because he had been not out 0 in the first innings and the long suffering Gillespie was dropped down to number 10. Boyd could only manage 2 runs, whilst Gillespie was left stranded on 15 not out. FW Terry, who as skipper was responsible for this re-ordering, redeemed himself with a captain's innings of 70. Apparently Terry had a reputation for running out his partners and this was how the opener Martin's innings was ended. The next highest score was 26 by ES Jacques, one of four batsmen who was out in his 20s. This consistency of batting ensured that Canada made 255, leaving the Americans a victory target of 347. This was always going to be beyond them although 80 from FH Bohlen and 48 from EM Cregar ensured that the Americans reached a respectable 205 all out, thus losing the game by the large margin of 141 runs. On the last day, the former International Bristowe substituted for the injured Gillespie; he took two catches including an impressive one-handed effort to dismiss Cregar for 48. Laing's 3 for 71 ensured that he took 10 wickets in the match for the second time in the Series. He bowled 30 five ball overs out of a total of 70 overs, delivering nearly three times as many as anyone else.

Canada had won for the first time since 1886 and although it was against a weakened American team this was still an important result. It would have been truly disheartening if the Canadians had lost against effectively a reserve team. This result made the Philadelphian Committee realise that they required their best players to beat the Canadians. One of the spectators was John Beverley Robinson, who was the last surviving Canadian player from the first match played in 1844. Robinson had been the Lieutenant Governor of Ontario and was the Chairman of the Toronto Athletic Club.

28th Match: Manheim, Pennsylvania on 4-7 September 1896
The Canadian team was described by the press[lxxvii] as being "fairly" representative in comparison to the American team which was exclusively Philadelphian. Five out of the seven players who opted out of the previous game (GS Patterson, WW Noble, AM Wood, Barton King and EW Clark) were playing in this encounter. Seven of the Philadelphians selected would tour England in 1897 where they played first class cricket. The Americans were back up to full strength and were playing at home.

WA Henry won the toss for Canada and decided to bat. Canada were bowled out for a meagre 87, GS Lyon top scoring with 23. King took 4 for 37 and GS Patterson returned figures of 6 for 22. There was controversy in Laing's brief innings when the fielding side believed him to have been bowled, but one of the umpires was unsighted and for whatever reason the other umpire felt unable to give him out. He was out two deliveries later, so even with luck on his side Laing was unable to make an impression with the bat.

Intermittent rain had made batting difficult and the Canadian bowlers Laing and HB McGiverin, who opened the bowling together for the first time, fully exploited the conditions. They bowled unchanged throughout the American innings and at one stage had reduced them to 26 for 9. The number 11 batsman FW Ralston top scored with 14 not out and was the only man to reach double figures. America were all out for 52.

Canada now carefully built on their 35 run lead, making only 17 runs in the first hour of the second day on route to a total of 117, with Laing top scoring with 23, equalling his highest score of the Series. King and Patterson took 6 for 41[43] and 3 for 38 respectively. These two bowlers took 19 wickets between them, with the only other dismissal being a run out.

America required 153 to win. As stated before, making the highest score to win a match is always a difficult task and with Laing in top form it was never likely to happen. He took the first five wickets to fall and finished with 8 for 37 off his 27 overs, which included 11 maidens. Like America, Canada relied heavily on just two bowlers, with McGiverin and Laing taking 19 wickets between them. Laing was unquestionably the man of the match with 24 runs and 14 wickets for only 54 runs. This was a terrific result for Canadian cricket and the players returned to Toronto to a heroes' welcome and a civic reception.

29th Match: Rosedale, Toronto on 6-7 September 1897

It was reported in the press in July[lxxviii] that there would be no International match in 1897, due to the Philadelphian tour to England. In fact the match was played on 6 and 7 September, but none of the touring Philadelphians were selected for the game, which greatly weakened the American team. The last game of the Philadelphian tour of England, against Surrey, ended on 31 July and so it would have been possible for these players to participate in the International. The

---

[43] According to cricket archive, King bowled Goldingham in this innings with a "hellbender". This presumably was an inswinging yorker, as it is unlikely that King would have used an aquatic salamander to dismiss a batsman.

New York Times confirms this by stating that the American team had "left the majority of their crack players at home."[lxxix]

EW Clark won the toss for America and decided to bat. Clark had batted at number 10 in the previous match, but was promoted to 6 for this game and top scored with 34 not out. Unfortunately for the Americans, only one other batsman reached double figures and they were all out for 85. Canada used four bowlers, Laing, Goldingham, McGiverin and the debutant HC Hill. They shared the wickets evenly, but Hill's 3 for 2 off 7.2 overs with six maidens stands out.

The Canadian captain Dyce Saunders opened the batting after keeping wicket for 42.2 overs. Saunders was a talented batsman who underperformed in the Series and he could only make 5 on this occasion. Canada made 179 in their first innings, recovering from 15 for 3. They were indebted to M Boyd who top scored with 51[44] at number 7.

America began their second innings 94 runs behind and was reduced to 39 for 4, with Hill and McGiverin taking two wickets each. Middle order resistance was crushed by Laing who came on first change and took 4 for 30 and only a ninth wicket stand of 44 ensured that the Americans avoided an innings defeat. JH Forrester, who would play in five consecutive matches from 1899-1903, substituted for AFR Martin on the second day, as he was unwell[lxxx]. The US total of 129 all out left Canada requiring only 36 runs for victory. After wicket-keeping for 41.2 overs, Saunders decided to drop himself down to number 3, but chasing 36 to win Canada lost their first wicket with no runs on the board, giving Saunders little time for a rest. He hit 23, whilst only 6 runs were made at the other end, to bring Canada within 3 runs of victory. The Reverend FW Terry then won the game with a boundary. This victory by 8 wickets was Canada's third win in a row, although two of these triumphs had been against weakened American teams.

30th Match: Haverford, Pennsylvania on 29-30 August 1898

Canada organised four tour matches earlier in the month against Staten Island, New Jersey, Manhattan and then New York, under the captaincy of EJ Fawke, who never played in an International. Unfortunately the organisers failed to meet the perennial challenge faced by all amateur cricket teams: to ensure that their best players practise together. GS Lyon, AW McKenzie, AW Philpotts and DW Saunders, who all played in the International, were unable to play in the warm-up matches. New York won the final tour game by 31 runs,

---

[44] Marder credits Boyd with 58 runs but this raises the Canadian total to 186, which if true means that they scored 10 runs more than necessary to win the game.

although Laing top scored in both Canadian innings with 35 and 22. He would make scores of only 11 and 4 in the International match.

The American captain RD Brown won the toss and decided to bat; his choice may have been influenced by the fact that Canada were missing three players, forcing the use of three substitute fielders. These players managed to get to the ground half an hour after the game started; whether their absence restricted Saunders's bowling options is not recorded. Bart King opened the batting as well as the bowling in this game and put on 66 for the first wicket, before being run out for 39. His opening partner was the eighteen year old NZ Graves who scored 128. Apart from the two openers, no other batsman made 20 runs in the impressive score of 250. AW Philpotts of Montréal's McGill University was the only Canadian player from outside Ontario and statistically he was the pick of the bowlers taking 4 for 44. Perhaps he would have played more if geography had not been against him. Inevitably Laing was amongst the wickets again and he took 4 for 76.

Once again Dyce Saunders was keeping wicket, captaining the side and opening the batting. He top scored with a defiant 27, AG Chambers made 22 and McGiverin was one of the few other batsmen to reach double figures with 10 not out, batting at number 11. The quality of the American attack, spearheaded by King, was indicated by the fact that seven of the Canadian batsmen fell to slip catches. Canada scored 113 and followed on 137 runs behind. In two years time the MCC would increase the margin required to enforce the follow on from 120 to 150 runs.

After Dyce Saunders was removed for a duck, Canada were playing for honour alone. King was the fourth bowler to be used through fear of causing injury on the worn pitch. He dismissed the last man Philpotts by having him stumped, so when he did bowl it cannot have been at full speed. AG Chambers top scored with 34 and once again McGiverin was the not out batsman, this time with 13 runs batting at number 10. Canada were bowled out for 136 and lost the game by an innings and a single run. American supremacy had been restored.

31st Match: Toronto on 7-8 August 1899
Monday 7 August was a civic holiday, which ensured that a large crowd was in attendance. America were without Bart King, JH Patterson and AM Wood and this arguably made the teams more evenly matched.

JH Scattergood won the toss for America and opted to bat on a good wicket. In his second match NZ Graves opened the innings and hit 37, although he edged safely between wicket-keeper and slip early in his innings. HC Thayer had last played in an International in 1892 and he justified his selection with a top score of 50. At 156-4 America looked destined for a large score, but their innings subsided rather than collapsed to 206 all out. The Canadian captain McGiverin was the best bowler, taking 5 for 68.

In their reply Canada started well with an opening partnership of 73 between WH Cooper and Saunders, who was still opening the batting despite keeping wicket. Saunders' 45 was the top score of the innings, although Graves dropped him at slip, returning the favour Saunders had done him in the American first innings. The middle order underperformed with the exception of HC Hill who hit 28 batting at 6. At 190-9 it appeared that Canada would concede a small first innings deficit, but McGiverin scored 23 not out batting at 11 in a last wicket stand of 32 in an innings that the press[lxxxi] described as containing some vigorous hitting. Canada scored 222 to achieve a first innings lead of 16. There were 25 extras in the Canadian innings compared to just 13 in the American innings.

The Americans batted steadily in their second innings, with seven of their batsmen making double figures. JH Mason top scored with 51, batting at number 6. Laing and McGiverin took 3 wickets each. HC Hill bowled only 4 overs as first change. He went wicketless but only conceded 9 runs and so it appears that he was underbowled. America scored 219 to leave Canada needing 204 for victory.

Canada's top order failed in their second innings, for although the opener WH Cooper scored 38 the batsmen at 2, 3, 4 and 5 were all out for single figures. At 58 for 6 the situation looked desperate[45]. McGiverin came in to bat with the score at 119 for 8, with Canada still 85 short of victory. According to the press[lxxxii] he "hit everything and scored at a marvelous rate and as the American total was approached the cheering was loud." McGiverin scored 39 not out, helping to add 50 for the last two wickets. Unfortunately nobody could stay with him and America won the game by 34 runs. The game concluded at 6:45pm[lxxxiii]. This late finish was presumably agreed by both teams, to avoid having to return for a third day, but it may have made batting more difficult.

McGiverin scored 62 in this match without being dismissed and had the captain been persuaded to bat higher up the order Canada might have won the game. In the eight matches he played in the Series McGiverin had 16 innings and was not out in 10 of them. This is an extraordinary record given the reports of how quickly he scored. He may have been a

---

[45] Marder states that at around this stage the Canadian batsmen were trying to save the game, rather than to win it, which seems an odd comment, given that according to cricket archive this was a three day match that was completed in two.

tail-end slogger, with a charmed life; or he could have been a genuine all-rounder whose batting talent was wasted by batting too far down the order.

32nd Match: Manheim, Pennsylvania on 21-22 September 1900:

The Americans had originally requested that the game be played on 4-6 July, but this was rejected by the Canadians as too early. The date that was eventually agreed was late in the season, the weather was overcast and the pitch helped the bowlers[46]. Gillespie was back in the team[47], but the Canadians were missing Laing, Saunders, McGiverin and WH Cooper. It is worth mentioning that both Laing and Saunders were on the Canadian Cricket Association selection panel that opted for youth over experience. Why Saunders was representing Vancouver on this panel is a mystery, but with WA Henry of Halifax also present the national character of the CCA was evident. Henry was the only player on the Canadian team from outside Ontario. McGiverin was unable to play due to his business interests, a problem for all amateur players.

The Canadians won the toss and opted to bat first where they struggled against the bowling of Barton King and Percy Clark. King dismissed Major CC van Straubenzie with the first ball of the match and of the first seven batsmen only the opener Captain HS Logan made double figures with 15. HF Lownsborough top scored with an unbeaten 17, not counting extras which totalled 24. The Americans were to concede 44 extras in this match, compared to just 17 for the Canadians. There were more leg byes as well as byes in the Canadian innings suggesting that leg side bowling was to blame for the surfeit of extras. Canada's first innings totalled 108, with King and Clark taking eight wickets between them and bowling 39 of the 44.3 six ball overs to be delivered.

King was dismissed by a stunning catch at point by Straubenzie off the bowling of Chambers who dismissed both openers. The opener CC Morris top scored with 38 and when America reached 100 for 6 they would have been expecting a large first innings lead. However, they were bowled out for 119, gaining a lead of only 11. Thayer was left stranded on 33 not out, batting at number 5. HC Hill was the pick of the bowlers taking 7 for 58.

Lownsborough was promoted to open, a common practice for not out batsmen, but he was dismissed at the end of the first day in fading

---

[46] The *New York Times* of 22 September stated that "a poor wicket handicapped the bowlers", but I don't imagine that it helped the batsmen much either!
[47] Page 1 of the Toronto Star of 13 September 1900 erroneously stated that Gillespie was unable to play and that Somerville of the Upper Canada College would take his place. Perhaps Gillespie had his arm twisted.

light, along with Gillespie. There could be no such excuse for the next two batsmen and Canada were reduced to 35 for 4. The captain JL Counsell then came in and top scored with 30. JH Forrester hit 21 not out batting at 9 and Canada reached 120 all out, to leave the Americans needing 110 for victory. King and Clark did the majority of the bowling and shared seven wickets between them, in an innings that had two run outs.

It was Chambers again who tormented the top order taking three of the first four wickets to fall with one run out. When Chambers' bowling partner Hill took the fifth wicket the Americans were in real trouble at 38 for 5. However CC Morris and Clark then put on 44 for the sixth wicket and turned the game. They both fell in quick succession and when RH Patton was dismissed for 1 America were 96 for 8, still needing 14 to win. The wicket-keeper JH Scattergood and JN Henry saw them home without further loss and America won the game by 2 wickets[48].

After the first day's play the *New York Times* referred to the American team as Philadelphia, but called them the United States in the report on the second day after it was known that the game had been won.

33rd Match: Ottawa, on 9-11 September 1901
The thirty-third game was played at the ground of Ottawa Cricket Club, which had last been used for an International match in 1879. Canada had toured America in the July and August of this year and had beaten Philadelphia by the huge margin of 179 runs. Only three of the Canadians who played in this game were selected for the International match.

The American team was considerably weakened by the fact that Bernard Bosanquet's touring team were due to play the Philadelphians later in the month. Bosanquet invented the googly, an off break bowled with the action of a leg break. He stated[lxxxiv] that he conceived the idea of a googly in 1897 when playing an after dinner game called Twisti-Twosti[49], which involved bouncing a tennis ball on a table with such spin as to prevent your opponent from catching it. Bosanquet maximised the googly's impact by keeping it secret for three years whilst he learned to perfect it, before finally unleashing it on first-class cricket in 1900. However, he also revealed in Wisden that he bowled it "occasionally in unimportant matches" during the development period.

---

[48] Confusingly the Americans continued to bat after winning the game and the score book and the American Cricketer both state that the Americans won the game by 15 runs, obviously an impossible result by a team batting last. The *New York Times* correctly recorded the victory margin as two wickets.

[49] Christopher Martin-Jenkins stated that the game was called twisty grab or billiard fives. See page 20 of "The Complete Who's Who of Test Cricketers".

Bosanquet toured North America twice during this time, firstly in 1898 with PF Warner's XI and again in 1899 with KS Ranjitsinhji's XI. The pitches of Canada and America would have provided Bosanquet with an ideal opportunity to try out his new delivery without revealing it to the wider world. It is possible then that the first ever googly bowled in a competitive match was delivered in either Canada or America.

America won the toss and chose to bat first, which was the correct choice as the wicket deteriorated as the game went on. America were reduced to 89 for 6, but a wagging tail brought the total up to an impressive 168. The bowlers shared the wickets but not the overs, with McGiverin and Bristowe delivering a combined total of 49 overs out of a total of 76.3 for figures of 3 for 59 and 2 for 31 respectively. In contrast Laing, who was playing in his final International at the age of 28, was entrusted with only 6.3 overs for his 2 for 16. It is possible that the strains of being an all-rounder had taken its toll, which would explain why a player who usually opened the bowling, and had taken 10 wickets in an International match on three occasions, was used so sparingly and was the fifth and final bowler to be called on. In the second innings Laing conceded 10 runs in the first over and only bowled three overs for 16. According to the *Globe* he was easily played by both batsmen.

These International games took at least two days to complete, not including travel time and it is possible that Laing decided to focus on his career as a barrister. A decision that more and more amateur cricketers would be forced to take in an increasingly professional world. He continued to play cricket and when living in Chicago he hit a massive 249 for the Wanderers against Douglas Park in 1903. Laing died on 25 October 1947 and was buried in a mausoleum in the cemetery at St Thomas Church, Shanty Bay.

The Canadian innings started badly with Dyce Saunders being dismissed for a single, after having to keep wicket. The Canadians were reduced to 77 for 9 and were looking at a huge first innings deficit. McGiverin batting at number 11 and JH Forrester batting at 9 fashioned together an extraordinary last wicket partnership of 51 to ensure that Canada reached 128 all out. McGiverin was the top scorer with 26 and Forrester finished unbeaten on 25. The Americans conceded 20 extras in this innings, 15 of them byes, compared to just 8 extras in the American first innings. Clark and JA Lester bowled 54.1 overs out of a total of 60.1 and took 5 wickets each.

The Americans built on their 40 run lead with NZ Graves who top scored with 56 and PH Clark who added 28 runs to go with his five wicket haul. At one stage they were 150 for 6 but this time the tail collapsed and the Americans were all out for 156. Canada's attempt to score 197 to win the game started badly when Dyce Saunders was stumped without scoring, an embarrassing dismissal for any wicket-keeper. However, although the scorecard shows that Saunders has the wicket-keeping obelisk it also credits a stumping in the American second innings to Ackland. A hand injury to Saunders had forced him to relinquish the gloves. Henry Ackland missed Clark, but this did not change the course of the match.

The Canadian second innings went the same way as the first but this time Forrester, who had been promoted to 5, and McGiverin who was batting at 9, only managed to score 3 runs each and it was left to AW Mackenzie to ensure that Canada reached three figures by hitting 24 not out, whilst batting at 10. His innings was described as "defensive" by Marder and "dashing" by the New York Times of 12 September, either way it was not enough to prevent an American victory by 94 runs as Canada were bowled out for 102[50].

Canada had the worst of the wicket, which had been deadened by a thunderstorm on the first night, just before America batted for the first time. However, the Canadians were playing at home and had an experienced team with no debutants, in contrast to the American team who introduced five new players and were missing Barton King.

34th Match: Manheim, Pennsylvania on 11-12 September 1902

The Canadian team had travelled all night to get to the ground and their wicket-keeper Ackland was still absent when play commenced. This possibly influenced the decision of the Canadian captain, Hal McGiverin, to bat first, which was made to look like the wrong choice. McGiverin's previous scores with the bat had finally been recognised as he batted at number 5, where he played a captain's innings and was comfortably the top scorer with 23 not out. AW Mackenzie was the only other batsman to reach double figures; his score of 10 was made at number 6, suggesting that his exploits in the previous match had also been noticed. No other batsmen could stay with McGiverin and Canada's innings was closed for the humiliating score of 49, with Ackland still absent. Bart King took 7 for 28.

King then opened the American innings and scored 56 in an opening partnership of 111. His opening partner CC Morris went on to score 73

---

[50] Both the New York Times and Marder state that the Americans won by 94 runs and Canada scored 102, not 100 in their second innings, whilst cricketarchive.com records the victory margin as 96. The discrepancy being Mackenzie's innings which cricketarchive.com records as 22 whilst Marder and the New York Times state 24. I would usually trust the detailed scorecards of cricketarchive, but on this occasion I accept that 102 is the more likely score as the runs in the bowlers' analysis added to the extras totals 102.

before being stumped by Ackland, who arrived part way through the American innings to join a match that was effectively already lost. The Americans did not lose their third wicket until the score was 196 and at this stage a huge total looked likely. Some credit is due to the Canadians for restricting them to 287 all out, with McGiverin delivering 33 overs for figures of 5 for 84. He bowled almost 20 overs more than any other bowler and had the best economy rate, an impressive performance in a losing team. A Lucas deserves a mention for his 3 for 43 off 14 overs.

Canada started their second innings 238 runs behind and were swiftly reduced to 33 for 5. With victory assured King was removed from the attack and perhaps Lucas' top score of 24 should be seen in this light. McGiverin made 18 and the Canadians were bowled out for 134[51]. There were 29 extras in this innings, 8 more than in America's innings of 287. Unfortunately this was the only area which the Canadians could claim superiority and their administrators were rightly criticised for the side's travel arrangements and for selecting a team exclusively from the Toronto area.

35th Match: University of Toronto, on 24-25 August 1903

The date for this match had been suggested by the Canadian Cricket Association in June to allow the Philadelphians touring Britain time to return and participate. The last tour game was played against Scotland on 10 and 11 August and so unsurprisingly none of the touring Philadelphians were able to play in this International match. The game was at home and America were forced to bring in eight new players. With these advantages the Canadians had an opportunity to avenge their recent defeats.

America won the toss and opted to bat, putting on 48 for the first wicket. The opener JL Evans hit the top score of 35 and seven other batsmen made double figures as America scored 167 in their first innings. WC Baber, who had last played in 1899, took 5 for 44. In the Canadian first innings the strength and depth of the American bowling became apparent. In the absence of King and Clark, Canada found two new tormentors in Norris and O'Neill, who bowled unchanged throughout the 27 overs of the torrid Canadian innings of 47, finishing with figures of 7 for 21 and 3 for 19 respectively. Batting in his last International match, McGiverin was unaccountably batting at number 11 again. He finished unbeaten on 0.

---

[51] The batting order is uncertain. Cricketarchive.com states that Ackland batted last, but this is impossible as he scored 6 and the last wicket partnership was only 4. The *New York Times* of 14 September 1902 states that he batted at 5.

With a substantial lead of 120 the Americans batted again and scored 110. H Beatty was arguably the pick of the bowlers. In his only International match he took 4 for 22 off just 7 overs, suggesting that he was underbowled.

Canada needed 231 to win, a task that was always going to be beyond them. The opener Lownsborough completed a pair and Canada were reduced to 14 for 4. WC Baber salvaged some pride by top scoring with 32. The practice of allowing the not out batsman to open the innings was not repeated here and McGiverin was again batting at 11, where he scored 12 and Canada were all out for 83. He finished his International career with a batting average of 29.67, the second highest for any Canadian. This was partly due to the fact that he was not out 10 times, but he scored 188 runs in the Series, with only five other Canadians contributing more. It is glaringly obvious that he batted too low in the order.

Canada had been heavily defeated by 147 runs by a Philadelphian second team, which indicates that Canadian cricket was in decline and Philadelphian cricket was deserving of first class status.

36th Match: Haverford College Ground, Pennsylvania on 11-13 July 1904

The Canadian captain JL Counsell won the toss and decided to bat. TSC Saunders, who was the brother of Dyce Saunders, opened the innings. He had last played in an International match in 1893 and justified his selection with the top score of 61. His fellow opener Captain Symons scored 51 and, had the middle order not failed, Canada could have made an imposing score. JL Counsell continued the practice of the Canadian captain batting lower than he should and made the third highest score of 23 whilst batting at number 10. Canada made 182, with only four batsmen making double figures. For once King had not dominated the Canadian batting and he finished with 2 for 56, conceding more runs that any other bowler. RH Patton was the most successful bowler, taking 4 for 39.

Once again King opened the batting and made 49. The top six all contributed, with PN LeRoy top scoring with 77, and America made a huge 329. Only two of their batsmen failed to reach double figures. The debutant AA Beemer was the most successful bowler, taking 5 for 67. He was under bowled, delivering 14 overs compared to Baber's 24, which resulted in the disappointing figures of 1 for 109.

Canada started their second innings 147 behind and when they were reduced to 17 for 2, with both openers back in the pavilion, an innings defeat looked likely. However a battling 52 not out from H Ackland ensured that Canada reached 162 for 8 at the end of the second day's play. It was mutually agreed to add an extra day to the two-day match, due to the time lost to rain. It was sporting of Canada to agree to this as it robbed them of any chance of drawing the game.

Inevitably American won the game on the third day, Ackland reaching 54 before running out of partners. A Canadian total of 172 left the Americans needing only 26 for victory. They opened their innings with RH Patton and WW Foulkrod, who were the only two batsmen to have failed to reach double figures in their first innings and the Canadians would have taken some satisfaction from dismissing them both for single figures a second time.

America won the game by 7 wickets, but Canada had shown more resolve than in the past and their efforts had ensured that the Series was still a meaningful contest.

37th Match: Rosedale, Toronto on 28-29 August 1905

In 1905 the Americans arranged to play an Ottawan team after the International game, when it would have made more sense to have played the less important match first. The game may have been organised to placate the Ottawans who had expected the International to be played at their ground at Rideau Hall. This venue was supported by the Montréal cricketers who cancelled the inter-provincial game between Québec and Ontario in protest at the game being held at Rosedale's ground. The reason for the switch was that the Ottawa Club announced that they would not pay the pre-agreed sum of money to the Canadian Cricket Association for hosting the fixture[lxxxv]. The new Governor-General Earl Grey, who became the Patron of the Canadian Cricket Association in March 1905[lxxxvi], unsurprisingly supported the game being played at his residence at Rideau Hall.

JH Mason won the toss for the United States, who decided to bat first. Inevitably Bart King opened the innings and made the top score of 29, before he was run out. The Jamaican JJ Cameron was a spin bowler and he opened for Canada taking 6 for 55 to restrict the Americans to 127. Cameron would play for the West Indies in their tour of Britain in 1906 and represent Jamaica against the touring Philadelphians in February 1909. He qualified for Canada on the grounds of residency and only played in the one match.

Canada's innings got off to the worst possible start when Lownsborough, who was playing in his last International, was dismissed for a duck in what turned out to be his last innings in the Series. Fortunately his fellow opener FC Evans top scored with 67, in his first International match. Eight batsmen made double figures, including the 43 year old Dyce Saunders who had decided, or been convinced, that he could not captain, keep wicket and open the batting. He scored 22 batting at number 9 and Canada made 245, assisted by 30 extras. King was the most successful bowler, but his 3 for 61 was a return that Canada would have accepted.

This was Dyce Saunders' 12th and final game for Canada in the International Series, with only Gillespie (14) having played more times. His extensive influence over Canadian domestic cricket is described in other chapters. Saunders would enjoy a swansong in 1922 when he toured Britain with Norman Seagram's team 35 years after the 1887 venture.

The Americans started their second innings 128 runs behind and King once again top scored as opener. His 20 was not enough to save the Americans from an innings defeat as only three other batsmen made double figures. WA Whittaker, JJ Cameron and SW Mossman did all the bowling in both innings and it is fitting that they finished with 3 wickets each in the second innings.

Canada had won for the first time since 1897, by an innings and 29 runs, but their victory owed much to the 9 wickets taken by the Jamaican Cameron, opening the debate about who should be allowed to play in the Series and whether the team selected for 1905 could honestly be said to represent Canada or Canadian cricket. This is an issue that is relevant today and to which there are no easy answers.

It should be mentioned that Dr John Cameron had two sons who both played Test cricket for the West Indies. The younger son, Francis James "Jimmy" Cameron, studied in Canada and played in Canada's 1954 tour of Britain. Whilst the influence of black West Indians[52] on Canadian cricket would have its greatest impact after the Second World War, its history clearly goes further back.

The MCC toured Canada in 1905 and there were strong protests from Cameron's cricket club St Simons[53] when Cameron was not selected to

---

[52] Whilst it is to the credit of Canadian cricket journalists of the early twentieth century that they rarely mention the ethnicity of the cricketers, it does make it very difficult to assess the impact of black cricketers on the game in Canada during this time. Judging from a grainy photograph in 1905 I believe that Cameron and his Jamaican born brother-in-law EG Hull were the first non-whites to play for Canada. Cameron's eldest son John Cameron was clearly black, but this proves nothing. See his player profile on www.cricinfo.com

[53] St Simon's Cricket Club was a church team. I have found further evidence of Canadian church teams defying prejudice and selecting black West Indians. This could be because

meet the tourists. It is possible that ordinarily the Canadian Cricket Association would not have considered choosing a black Jamaican to represent Canada but felt pressurised into doing so after the protest over his non-selection earlier in the summer. The protest from St Simons' captain E McElroy makes no mention of race and merely accuses the selectors of a pro-Toronto Cricket Club bias at the expense of the St Simons Club[lxxxvii].

38th Match: Manheim, Pennsylvania on 9-10 July 1906

JA Lester won the toss for the Americans and decided to bat first. They recovered quickly from losing their first wicket with no runs on the board and would have scored more had their two top scoring batsmen not been run out. King was responsible for running out Bohlen for 52 and then was similarly dismissed himself for 63. Two scores of 44 from Lester and PN LeRoy helped America to an impressive total of 274. Canada used eight different bowlers and none of them took more than two wickets. Mossman and Whittaker being nothing like as effective as they had been the previous year.

Canada made a disastrous start to their first innings, losing their first four wickets for 6 runs, the old firm King and Clark taking two wickets each. The innings was then interrupted by a thunderstorm, which for the Canadians probably came as something of a relief. When the weather abated Canada managed to limp to 31 for 5 before the close of the day's play. On the second day Canada reached a total of 90 and so would have been expecting to follow-on 184 runs behind, however a change in the law made the follow-on optional. The Americans decided to bat again and scored 131 for 3 before declaring, leaving Canada with an unlikely target of 316 to win the game.

Canada's second innings was even more calamitous than their first as King reduced them to 6 for 5. At 34 for 9 another thunderstorm hit the ground, but the two Canadian batsmen insisted on continuing, despite the heavy rain and that the time was 6:20 in the evening. The Canadians could have drawn the match had they decided to come off, but they sportingly decided that playing cricket was more important than the result. JS Hynes and SR Saunders added 28 for the final wicket before Clark bowled Hynes to dismiss Canada for 62 at 6:35 p.m. and win the game for America by 253 runs. King took 8 for 17 in the innings and 10 for 42 in the match.

39th Match: Toronto on 5-6 August 1907

The Americans won a warm-up game against Eastern Canada which included the following former Internationals: H Ackland, WC Baber, MG Bristowe, WC Little and HB McGiverin. None of these players represented Canada in 1907, suggesting that there may have been another dispute between cricketers from Toronto and those from outside. King and Clark were missing from the American team, whilst Canada selected seven players who had not played an International before.

The Americans won the toss and decided to bat. Scores of 36 from the opener RL Pearson and 40 from CJB Dixon helped America to a total of 207. HG Wookey was the most successful bowler, with 4 for 52. The Americans were assisted by 32 extras, compared to just 5 in the Canadian innings and 8 in the American second innings.

Canada's response was greatly reliant on the opener HC Hill's top score of 57. Unfortunately, the middle order imploded rather than collapsed with FC Evans, G Heighington, WA Whittaker and F Hamilton, batting at 4, 5, 6 and 7 respectively, all being dismissed without scoring. Canada put on 40 runs for the last two wickets and finished with a total of 120 and a deficit of 87 runs to avoid the follow-on.

America's second innings was built around FH Bohlen's top score of 57 and WH Sayen's 33, which allowed them to recover from 10 for 5 to post a total of 140[54]. LG Black, who had not bowled at all in the first innings, took 7 for 46. He was the fifth bowler to be used and the game might have gone differently had he been bowled earlier. Black was born in London, UK and played four matches for Hampshire between 1903 and 1919. He died in Yorkshire in 1959, suggesting that he qualified to play for Canada on grounds of temporary residency.

Canada hopes of an unlikely 228 to win all but evaporated when both openers were dismissed without scoring. It is unclear why FC Evans was promoted to open in place of HC Hill who was dropped down to 5, despite top scoring in the first innings. HG Wookey hit 55 batting at 6 to ensure respectability. Canada were all out for 147 and so were defeated by 80 runs. In his last innings for Canada the Reverend Francis William Terry made 20, the second highest score of the innings. Terry suffered from mental illness, which appeared to be related to his duties as a priest. He was ordained by the Bishop of

---

[54] Unless there were multiple cases of batsmen retiring hurt the batting order for the American second innings at www.cricketarchive.com is not possible when compared to the fall of wickets.

Gloucester in 1886, but fell ill in 1889 and was advised then to give up his clerical duties. He immigrated to Canada in poor health, but in September 1893 he went off to Red Deer Alberta to resume his job as a priest. He received a rousing send off at Walker House from fellow members of the Toronto Cricket Club, who presented him with a fur coat and expressed the wish that he would return to Ontario one day. The strain of the priesthood was too much. The Toronto *Globe* simply stated on 1 December 1893 that "Rev. F. W. Terry of Innisfall, Alberta, who was Captain of the Canadian Cricket Team in the last international match, is insane." No further details were given of what appears to have been a relapse. Given the stigma attached to mental illness it must have taken great character for Terry to return to Toronto and resume playing cricket with those who had said goodbye to him so generously only a few months before.

40th Match: Manheim, Pennsylvania on 14-15 September 1908

In early September the Philadelphian Cricket Club toured Canada playing against Ottawa and Toronto. Only two cricketers, JL Evans and AG Scattergood, played in this tour and the International match. Four of their opponents also played in the International: AH Gibson, WS Marshall and GH Southam played for Toronto and HJ Heygate played for Ottawa. Marshall and Southam were both killed in the First World War. Heygate had played five first class games for Sussex at this point. He would play once more after the war, against Somerset on 21 and 22 May 1919. He was due to bat last but, with the scores tied, he was so incapacitated with rheumatism he failed to make it to the wicket before being dismissed timed out.

Canada won the toss and elected to bat first. They effectively lost the game when they were dismissed for 36 in 13.4 overs. The debutant JR Vetterlein took 7 for 17, whilst King took 3 for 19. Even the first-class cricketer Heygate, who was probably in Canada on diplomatic service, could only make 8 and 0 against these two bowlers. WS Marshall top scored with 10.

King opened the American innings and made 35 and his fellow opener JL Evans made 32.[55] JR Vetterlein top scored with 40 to go with his seven wickets and America finished with a match-winning 173. WH Montgomery was the most successful bowler taking 5 for 40.

Canada required 137 just to make America bat again and this appeared unlikely when Vetterlein took the first three wickets, all

---

[55] Marder's scorecard on page 252 states that the first wicket was lost with 5 on the board, whilst cricketarchive states 4, which is impossible unless multiple batsmen were retired hurt.

bowled, to reduce Canada to 13 for 3. WS Marshall, who top scored with 52, at least ensured respectability, but only two other batsmen reached double figures and Canada were dismissed for 116. America thus won the game by an innings and 21 runs.

41st Match: Montréal, on 23-24 August 1909

Canada won the toss and decided to bat. The opener O Wallace hit 24 to joint top score with Heygate. Wallace was making his debut and would surely have played more times for Canada had the Series not ceased in 1912. The wicket-keeper H Ackland hit 18 not out and Canada scored a challenging 156. RH Patton and WM Fellowes did the bulk of the bowling, taking 4 for 63 and 5 for 34 respectively.

The American innings top order struggled to cope with CB Godwin, who took five of the first six wickets to fall. The nineteen year old Godwin played for Montréal, but would play for Somerset after the war. He was born and died in Bristol, but had played for Montréal against a touring MCC team in 1905, so was more than just a bird of passage. At 68 for 6 America would have still had hopes of reaching Canada's score, but two run outs and no runs from number 9, 10 or 11 resulted in a first innings total of 85 all out, leaving Canada with a useful lead of 71.

Canada altered their batting line up for their second innings and their ploy of dropping Wallace down to 5 worked as he and Heygate shared a partnership of 55 for the fifth wicket, doubling the score to 110. Heygate went on to hit 55, to create a statistician's dream, as he went in when the score was 55 for 4, shared in a partnership of 55 with Wallace and scored 55 himself. Ackland was again on form, scoring 23 and WC Baber playing his last innings for Canada hit 33, batting at 9. They ensured that Canada reached an impressive 194.

America started their second innings chasing an unlikely victory target of 266. The opener JL Evans made the top score of 42, but the next highest contribution was WM Fellowes' innings of 20 and America were all out for 122. Godwin was again the pick of bowlers, taking 5 for 44 to go with his 6 for 40 in the first innings. It was Canada's loss that he only represented them in this match. His bowling performance coupled with sensible batting ensured that Canada won the game by the large margin of 143 runs. The game was scheduled for three days but finished comfortably in two. It should be noted that King was absent.

The International Series was in decline as games between clubs started to take precedence. The Philadelphia Pilgrims toured Canada following this game and played against the top Canadian teams including Ottawa, Hamilton and Toronto Zingari. The last two teams also toured America, arguably with more success than the Canadian team in the International Series.

The Canadian Cricket Association cancelled the game which was scheduled for 1910 owing to a dispute over selection. In the past Ottawa had helped to defuse rows between Hamilton and Toronto by offering an alternative venue, but on this occasion they had expected at least three of their players to be selected and only one had been chosen.

The annual meeting of the Ontario Crickets' Association held in January 1911 recommended that the International Series should cease as neither team was representative, it being a game between Toronto and Philadelphian players. It was suggested that the Series should be replaced by home and away games between provincial teams against American State and District sides[lxxxviii]. This recommendation was rejected by the Canadian Cricket Association in February and so the International Series limped on[lxxxix].

42nd Match: Rosedale, Toronto on 25-26 August 1911

The forty-second match was played on the ground of Rosedale Cricket Club in Toronto on 25 and 26 August 1911. The Canadians had organised an important domestic tournament in Toronto to coincide with the International and this ensured that the Canadian selectors were not just confined to players from the Toronto area.

Canada batted first and made an excellent start, putting on 92 for the first wicket. The opener O Wallace top scored with 55 and when the 3rd wicket went down with 139 runs on the board the Canadians looked poised for a high score, but none of the seven batsmen from number 5 downwards made double figures and Canada collapsed to 156 all out, losing their last eight wickets for 17 runs. The 42 year old Cregar[56] was the chief destroyer, taking all his five wickets in a devastating four over spell, which conceded only eight runs.

R Lee opened the batting for America and top scored with 27 and with six batsmen all making double figures; they would have been disappointed to make only 123. LG Black, who had been so effective in 1907, dominated the American batsmen again, taking 7 for 35.

Canada built on their 33 run lead, with the opener Wallace again being amongst the runs, hitting 31. AH Gibson top scored with 49, and

---

56 Marder incorrectly states that he was 43, as he was born in 1868. However, his birthday was not until December 28.

assisted by 35 from TAD Bevington, Canada were able to declare at 190 for 8, leaving America with a victory target of 224.

The American innings started badly when the opener AJ Henry was dismissed for 0. R Lee was demoted from opener to number 5, but this tactic worked as he top scored for a second time, with a match-saving 57, the highest score of the game. America reached 177 for 8, 47 runs from victory, before the stumps were drawn. Marder states that the Americans made no real attempt to win the game, but their run rate of more than three and a half runs per over compares favourably with that of the Canadians. The *New York Times* blames poor fielding for Canada's failure to force a win, although it does not elaborate. This was the first drawn game since 1894 and it is surprising it was only a two day match, as three days had been allocated to the 1909 contest. It is also a pity that the captains could not agree to extend the game, as had happened in 1904.

43rd Match: Manheim, Pennsylvania on 6-7 September 1912

SR Saunders won the toss for Canada and elected to bat first. In an all too familiar story they found themselves powerless to resist the bowling of King and Clark. No batsman reached double figures in the total of 40 and the highest score of 9 was made by LH Rathbun batting at 11. No extras were conceded in the 17.4 overs bowled. Fittingly in their last International King and Clark took 5 wickets each.

King then opened the innings and underlined his dominance by top scoring with 43. When the eighth wicket fell with the score on 104, it appeared that the lead would be kept to double figures, but Clark hit 37 batting at 8 and RL Melville made 28 at 10; together they shared a partnership of 57. America were finally bowled out for 168, a lead of 128. WL Price was the only bowler of note, taking 6 for 51. Rathbun, who had taken 80 wickets at an average of 12.08 on the Zingari tour of Britain, conceded 44 off his six overs, although he did take two wickets.

Canada would almost certainly have lost this match by an innings had the American captain not decided to rest Clark and King and give the other bowlers a go. Thus Canada managed to salvage some pride by scoring 171 in their second innings, the highest score of the match. America knocked off the 44 required for the loss of two wickets. Fittingly King was there at the crease when the winning run was struck. He and Clark had won another game for America double-handedly.

The Series was already in decline, the First World War killed it off. There had been no game in 1910 and there was no match in 1913, nor one organised for 1914. More than 50 years and two world wars would elapse before the Series was re-established in 1965. It would continue to survive for the next 30 years as an oddity: an international contest, without national pride at stake; a cricket match between neighbouring nations in a vast continent that had never really taken to cricket; a friendly in a competitive age where everything is measured and ranked. The last game was played in 1995 and although America and Canada will to continue to meet each other in qualification matches for ICC tournaments, it appears unlikely that cricket's first International Series will be revived. The world has moved on and I would not advocate that a series should be maintained or resurrected merely because of its history, but due to men like Laing, Gillespie, King and Percy Clark there is a history that should be remembered.

Chapter 8 Canadian Cricketers in the First World War

"See the soldier with his gun, who must be dead to be admired"
Gordon Lightfoot (from the song Don Quixote)

Ghosts of Vimy Ridge by William Longstaff shows the Canadian Corps' dead with their monument.

The Wisdens from 1916 to 1920 list the names of prominent cricketers who died during the First World War. A staggering 182 of these were Canadian, compared to 20 Australians; both countries lost around 60,000 men. Considering the standard of cricket played in Australia it is surprising to find so few of their cricketers listed. New Zealand did not play Test cricket until 1930 and suffered fewer than 20,000 dead, but had 19 obituaries in Wisden, only one fewer than Australia. Whilst the magazine the *American Cricketer* recorded the deaths of Canadian players, giving the Wisden editor a source to use to give his obituary list a colonial feel, there was no equivalent publication in Australia. Despite this, the number of Canadian obituaries suggests a disproportionate sacrifice from Canadian cricketers.

In August 1914 Canada was part of the British Empire and foreign policy was determined in London, not in Ottawa. So when Britain declared war on Germany and Austria-Hungry, Canada found herself at war too. The political leadership acquiesced with enthusiasm; Wilfred Laurier heading the Liberal opposition summed up the consensus, often brought about by war, by declaring Canada's response must be "ready, aye ready". War changed everything: by the end of the conflict Laurier would be a broken man of a broken party, split over the thorny issue of conscription, whilst Canada's sacrifice had earned a place at the League of Nations and inexorably the right to determine her own foreign policy.

At the outbreak of war Canada had a population of about 15 million of whom approximately 10% were males of military age. One third of these fought in Europe, with those of British descent, and in many cases of British birth, making up the majority. French Canadians had lived in Canada for generations and were less inclined to fight in a European war either for a pro-British Government, which they felt discriminated against them, or for a French nation which they felt had abandoned them. It was the *British* Canadians who were most eager to fight for the Empire and it was the *British* Canadians who played cricket in Canada. This was detrimental to Canadian cricket for two reasons. Firstly, and most obviously, it meant that many players crossed the Atlantic never to return. Secondly, the sacrifice of so many Canadians ultimately led to a more independent Canada, free to pursue her own foreign policy. Ironically the death of so many British Canadians led to a decline both in Britain's influence over Canada and of British institutions, like cricket.

Cricketers started to contribute to the war effort immediately. On 5 September 1914 a Canadian team played against a West Indian side at the Rosedale grounds in Toronto for the benefit of the war relief fund. The game enjoyed the patronage of Sir John Gibson, Lieutenant

Governor of Ontario from 1908 to 1914[xc]. These benefit games continued throughout the War. In late July 1918 a similar match was played under the auspices of Toronto District Cricketers' Association, between Old Country and The Others in front of 5,000 spectators[xci].

Inevitably the amount of domestic cricket decreased as players signed-up. The Toronto *Globe* reported on 11 September 1915 that cricket had been more affected by the war than other sports with over 300 Toronto cricketers serving overseas. The Toronto Cricket League and the Western Ontario Cricket League were disbanded. The more rural Church and Mercantile Cricket League continued but with a reduced number of divisions. The only competition which was unaffected was the Little Big Four contest between the students of the Upper Canada College, Ridley College, Trinity College School and St Andrews College. In June 1918 spectators who saw Ridley College beat St Andrews College were also entertained by some stunt flying from three former Ridley College cricketers who had since joined the RAF[xcii]. So David Gower and John Morris were not the first![57]

The majority of the Canadian cricketers to sign-up did so with the early volunteers. In August 1914 recruits flocked to Valcartier, the military camp hastily set up to assemble the Canadian Expeditionary Force, but it would be October before approximately 33,000 Canadian troops crossed the Atlantic in what would become known as the First Contingent. The possibility that the War would be over before the Canadians arrived in France was a real concern.

The Canadian soldiers camped on Salisbury Plain in Wiltshire only to endure the wettest winter in living memory. The conditions prompted Colonel JW Carson, the representative of the Canadian Minister of Militia and Defence, to complain to the British War Office, which ordered the construction of huts. Unfortunately these were poorly ventilated and infections spread: 28 Canadians died from meningitis, including the chaplain of the 3rd Battalion, Reverend Leychester Ingles. He had been a useful medium-paced bowler and a good batsman for Toronto Cricket Club and Toronto Zingari, touring America with both teams before the war. His father Archdeacon Charles L Ingles had been an Honorary President of Parkdale Cricket Club[xciii]. He asked that the Reverend Captain Ingles be buried as a priest and a soldier, at Bulford Church cemetery.

---

[57] During a tour match between England and Queensland in Australia in 1991 David Gower and John Morris hired two Tiger Moth biplanes and persuaded the pilots to fly low over the ground. The tour management were not impressed. See pp. 212-17 of Gower The Autobiography.

The Canadians landed in France in early 1915 and the first action for the Canadian troops inevitably brought about its first casualties. Captain Robert Darling had played cricket for the Upper Canada College[58] XI in 1897 and 1898 and was a graduate of the Royal Military College. This Toronto-born merchant had signed up with the 15th Battalion on 22 September 1914 with two other UCC old boys, William Marshall and Trumball Warren. These three comrades were listed second, third and fourth in the nominal roll of the 15th Battalion taken when they signed up at Valcartier. The roll was in order of rank and headed by Lieutenant-Colonel John Currie who was the only one of the four to survive the war. Darling was shot in the shoulder on 23 March 1915 near Neuve Chapelle whilst serving the 15th Battalion as adjutant. According to the Battalion's war diary, Darling was wounded when he followed another officer taking a dangerous short-cut to avoid being seen as a coward, instead of walking unhindered along the communication trench[59]. He was given "a Blighty" and invalided to a hospital in London where he died on 19 April aged 28 with his wife Phyllis, whom he had married[60] before leaving for Valcartier, by his side. His body was taken back to Canada where it was buried at Mount Pleasant Cemetery in Toronto: the first Canadian soldier to be killed overseas, but buried at home. His military funeral on 6 May allowed the whole City of Toronto to grieve over the sacrifice that he personified[xciv].

In April Canadian troops found themselves defending Ypres, which as the last Belgian city still in Allied hands was of huge symbolic importance. The allied line was in a dip in the land, putting the defenders at a strategic disadvantage. The practical solution would have been to abandon Ypres and retreat to a more easily defendable position, but this was rejected as a betrayal of the thousands of allied soldiers who had already died defending the city. When Sir Horace Smith-Dorrien, who was the Commander of the British Second Army, suggested a tactical withdrawal he was forced to resign.

A day after Robert Darling's death his friend and comrade Captain Trumball Warren, who succeeded him to the post of adjutant and had played for the UCC in 1903, was killed by a German shell that landed in the Cloth Hall Square at Ypres. Before the bombardment the old city had been left largely undamaged and Warren's 15th Battalion had been relieved that day, making his death unexpected. He was 29 years old.

---

[58] The UCC has a fine tradition of producing notable cricketers, but only five of the sixteen players who have obituaries in Wisden are recorded as having played for another team.

[59] The *Globe* of 26 March 1915 tactfully stated that the communication trench was full of water.

[60] Men wanting to sign-up in 1914 needed the permission of their wives. This veto was lost in August 1915, as demand for new recruits increased.

The wives of Captains Darling and Warren had sailed over to England to be closer to their husbands, and they returned to Canada on the same boat, the *Transylvania*.

The day after Trumball Warren's death, Corporal Evan Cameron was killed at St Julien whilst fighting for the 14th Battalion, which was relieved that night by the 13th Battalion. He was the son of Sir Edward Cameron KCMG, a man of distinguished diplomatic service. Corporal Cameron was born on Turks Island[61], presumably where his father was stationed. The young Evan was sent to be educated at Bludell's School in Tiverton, Devon. In 1912 he was made head boy and captain of the cricket team where he topped the batting averages with 40.92. This earned him selection for the Public Schools XI v MCC match, where he scored 20. He then moved to Canada to make his own start in life, as a bookkeeper according to his attestation papers. He had certainly left home as his father was the Governor of The Gambia at the time of his sign-up, a post that he would hold from April 1914 to the end of 1920. Unsurprisingly Evan Cameron played cricket in his adopted country, playing for McGill Cricket Club in domestic cricket and for Montréal against the touring Australians in 1913. He also toured Philadelphia and New York in the same year with the same team, hitting 140 against Staten Island. He signed up at Valcartier on his 21st and last birthday.

The second battle of Ypres was the first serious action seen by the Canadian troops and it would prove to be a baptism of fire. On 22 April the Germans used chlorine gas for the first time, in direct violation of the 1899 and 1907 Hague Conventions. It had a devastating effect on the Algerian and Senegalese units of the French army, who were forced to flee their trenches, opening a four-mile gap in the line. The Canadians rushed forward to stop the German advance[62]. The 10th and 16th Battalions launched a counter-attack on Kitchener's Wood on the same day, in an attempt to recover the British guns that had been abandoned there. Private Clifford Roughton of the 10th, a clerk from Alberta, was killed in the attack, which was arguably the first significant Canadian operation of the War. He was a member of St Johns Cricket Club in Calgary and the war would claim two more of his teammates.

---

[61] In 1917 Canadian Prime Minister Robert Borden suggested that Turks and Caicos Islands join Canada. He was overruled by the British Prime Minister Lloyd George.
[62] There are eyewitness accounts of the Canadians shooting the retreating French Colonials troops. See the account given by Private W. Underwood of the Canadian First Division on page 79 of *Forgotten Voices of the Great War* or p.11 of *A Rattle of Pebbles: The First World War Diaries of Two Canadian Airmen* or a letter from James Wells Ross: http://www.canadianletters.ca/letters.php?letterid=3247&warid=3&docid=1&collectioni d=202

On 24 April the Germans used gas again, this time on the Canadian front line.[63] The Canadians held the line despite the gas, which they combated by holding wet handkerchiefs over their faces and despite their inadequate Ross rifle which was totally unsuitable for trench warfare as it overheated and jammed too easily under rapid fire. The Canadians overcame this by kicking the mechanism or by finding another rifle, preferably the more suitable Lee-Enfield from fallen British comrades. The Ross rifle would not be replaced until the summer of 1916, although it would continue to be used by the Canadian snipers who had to fire accurately rather than rapidly.

The Canadian Corps lost 5,828 men at the second battle of Ypres,[xcv] most dying on 24 April. The cricketing fraternity lost four men that day including Private Reginald Lawrence and Lance Corporal Arthur Lawrence, brothers who had played for Calgary Cricket Club. Both men were from the 10th Battalion and were killed at St Julien. They were descendants of William Lillywhite the great round-arm bowler, known as The Nonpareil. He was the father of John Lillywhite who had toured Canada in 1859, producing scorecards from his portable machine wherever the team went. Arthur was the elder brother and like many of the First Contingent he had served in the Boer War. Calgary Cricket Club would lose six team members to the Great War including Private Leonard Lovell, who was from a sporting family; his brother 2nd Lieutenant John Lovell had been an international hockey player and was also killed. The youngest and last Calgary player to be killed was Private Reginald Pryce-Jones who was mentioned in dispatches and died on 18 November 1916 a month after celebrating his 20th birthday.

Corporals William Twynham and Charles Bligh had both served in the Boer War. They played for Burrand Cricket Club in Vancouver and the Free Press Cricket Club in Winnipeg respectively. Bligh died on 25 April a day later than Twynham who had captained Burrand Cricket Club in 1913. He was one of three Burrand cricketers who died in the war and one of over two hundred cricketers from British Columbia who served in total[xcvi].

The fourth cricketer to die on the 24th was the Bombay born Lance Corporal Joseph Bell who had joined Rosedale Cricket Club in 1906 and had played for them annually. He was a good enough player to represent Ontario on several occasions, which he did with some success, hitting 41 against the Gentlemen of Ireland in 1909 and scoring 84 and 87 not out against Eastern Canada. He was killed near St Julien fighting for the 3rd Battalion.

---

[63] According to Captain JW Warden's account in the 7th Battalion War Diary, the Germans dressed their front line troops in British uniforms.

The Canadian Pacific Cricket Club of Winnipeg lost two players[64] at Ypres, the brothers Private Henry Perkin and Private Leslie Perkin. They had been born in Tavistock, Devon 11 years apart but died within a month of each other fighting for the 15th Battalion. Both deaths appear unfortunate. Henry died on 25 April whilst the Battalion was in a reserve trench south of Ypres and Leslie was killed on 22 May 1915 when the Battalion was relieved. Another fatality from the 15th Battalion was Winnipeg born Private Herbert Butler who was killed on 21 May 1915 aged just 19. He was the youngest of three players from Fiveways Cricket Club of Victoria who died during the war. Wisden described him as being "one of the most promising young cricketers in Victoria".

Some Canadians transferred to British units. Lieutenant Henry Price, who had played for Québec Cricket Club, transferred to the 5th Battalion of the London Rifle Brigades and was mentioned in dispatches. He was killed at Ypres on 3 May, the day that the Canadian troops were relieved by the British.

The Canadians established themselves as a credible fighting force at Ypres and Sir John French, the Commander-in-Chief of the British Expeditionary Force, stated that the Canadians had saved the situation. Despite this it was more than a year before they were involved in another major battle.

War casualties outside of Europe added to the list of cricketing obituaries. On 7 May 1915 the passenger ship *Lusitania* was sunk by a German U-Boat. 128 Americans were amongst the dead and the world held its breath as the American government decided whether this outrage justified war with Germany. The fact that Canada was already at war meant that the 170 Canadians[xcvii] amongst the 1,201 dead[65] have been largely overlooked. The 170 included the Reverend Canon Ernest Phair who had played for St Johns Cricket Club in Winnipeg. The sinking of the *Lusitania* greatly assisted recruitment in Canada and in a reverse of what would occur 50 years later with the Vietnam War, many Americans went over the border to fight overseas. Despite the sinking of the *Lusitania*, it would be two years before America finally declared war.

Cricketers from the Canadian fee-paying schools bore a disproportionately large amount of the sacrifice. One hundred and

---

[64] 11,340 employees of the Canadian Pacific Railway enlisted, 1,116 were killed and 2,105 were wounded. (Source: P.6 Canadian Pacific Railway and the War)
[65] It is often stated that 1198 people died on the Lusitania, but this fails to include the three men arrested as German spies. Their detention gave them no chance of escape.

seventy-nine of the Upper Canada College's former students were killed in the War and Lieutenant-Colonel William Marshall was both the most experienced ex-UCC cricketer to die and also the most militarily distinguished. He was a wicket-keeper batsman, who had played for Hamilton following his graduation from the UCC, scoring 58 against the touring Phoenix XI from Ireland. In 1910 he toured Britain with Toronto Zingari and scored 155 against the same opponents. He played for Canada against the United States in the International Series in 1898 and 1911. Marshall was a veteran of the Boer War, in which he served with the Canadian Mounted Rifles. In the Great War he was mentioned in dispatches serving with the 15th Battalion. He was the second in command at the second Ypres, but the commander, Lieutenant-Colonel John Currie, remained some distance from the front line during the conflict[66], leaving Major Marshall effectively in command. When Currie was sent home, to spend the rest of his life defending himself against charges of cowardice, Marshall was promoted to Lieutenant-Colonel and commanded the Battalion. He was killed by a sniper whilst inspecting the trenches on 19 May 1916.

Highfield School in Hamilton lost nine of its cricketers to the war: one of these was Lieutenant Walter Marshall, who played for the school from 1902-4 and was William Marshall's half brother. The Marshalls had played together in at least three teams: Hamilton Cricket Club, Toronto Zingari in the 1910 tour of Britain and Canada in the International match of 1911. Walter appears to have been the more talented player, representing Canada in 1908 and scoring 101 against the MCC in the Zingari tour. Lieutenant Walter Marshall died of his wounds on 4 October 1916, whilst fighting for the 3rd Battalion at the Somme.

Mont Sorrel
In June 1916 the Canadian Corps lost and then recaptured the strategically important heights of Mont Sorrel. Major Wilfred Dobson was the most senior casualty of a successful repulse of an enemy counter-attack on 9 July. He had been born in Dulwich, South London and had played for Exeter College, Oxford. He had been captain of the Toronto Cricket Club in 1914 and Wisden states that he was the Secretary of the Club when he was killed. The War took a disproportionately high toll of the cricket clubs' secretaries, which is surprising since for many clubs this role would have been performed by someone too old for military service. Nevertheless, I have identified five Canadian cricket club secretaries[67] killed in the War. Perhaps men who

---

[66] According to the historian Desmond Morton, Colonel Creelman found Lieutenant-Colonel Currie drunk in his dugout, two miles from where his battalion was suffering heavy casualties during the second Ypres. See page 45 of *When Your Numbers Up*.

[67] The other four secretaries were Lieutenant R Buckley of the Wanderers Cricket Club of Alberta, who fought with the Manchester Regiment; Sergeant James Edmondson of the

were prepared to volunteer for the position of secretary were also prepared to volunteer for risky missions! For example Private Frederick Derbyshire, Secretary of Brantford Cricket Club, led a platoon of the 19th Battalion into battle during the struggle to take *Regina Trench* described below. By volunteering for a job that nobody else wanted to do he received a commission for bravery and efficiency[xcviii]. He survived the War.

Lynn Valley Cricket Club, Vancouver lost no fewer than six of its players to the War. The only one of Canadian birth was the Nova Scotian Lieutenant Francis Layton, who was also the highest ranked and was described by Wisden as an all round player, the only Lynn Valley member to warrant a description of his ability. He was killed near Mont Sorrel at 3:30am on 24 July 1916 by an enemy grenade attack. His 4th Canadian Mounted Rifles Battalion had just relieved the 5th Canadian Mounted Rifles Battalion. He was 28 years old.

The Somme

On the morning of 1 July 1916 a massive offensive was launched near the river Somme. Nearly 60,000 British soldiers were killed or wounded in the doomed attack, including 684 Newfoundlanders at Beaumont Hamel, who found themselves channelled into machine gun fire by uncut barbed wire. PJ Myler wrote anecdotally about cricket in Newfoundland before the war in his book *Recollections of Cricket* and it is probable that cricketers would have been among the first Newfoundland volunteers, the Blue Puttees, who crossed the Atlantic on the *SS Florizel* to fight in the War. Unfortunately I have been unable to make any satisfactory links between cricketers mentioned by Myler and the military records, with the single exception of John Munn who did not serve overseas.

On 23 February 1918 the *Florizel* ran aground off Horn Head on the east coast of Newfoundland. The Chief Engineer's family home had been badly damaged in the Halifax Explosion of 6 December 1917 and he wanted to spend the night with them. So he arranged for the ship to go slower than the Captain had ordered to ensure that they reached Halifax later than expected and would have to wait until the following morning before continuing their journey to New York. In rough seas the Captain believed his position to be south east of Cape Race and he steered the *Florizel* into the rocks[xcix]. Out of the 124 civilians on board, 80 men, women and children died including the 37 year old John Munn,

---

Point Grey Cricket Club of British Columbia who was awarded the Distinguished Conduct Medal; Private Frank Myers of the Yorkshire Society Cricket Club of Toronto who was the son of Colonel Sergeant-Major JT Myers and Private Harvey Wright who was secretary of the St Barnabas Cricket Club of Toronto.

a noted Newfoundland cricketer, whose ability had been praised by Myler. He had been sent to England for his education and honed his skills as a left-arm bowler and useful tail-end batsman by playing for Forest School[68], north east of London. He was accepted by Oxford University, who recognised his ability and selected him to play 10 games for their first XI, making Munn only one of three Newfoundlanders[69] to play first class cricket. He returned to Newfoundland without graduating, suggesting that his entry to Oxford University was not based on academic ability. When war broke out his age, marital status and impending fatherhood would all have counted against active service and instead he helped with recruitment, being treasurer of an organisation which funded the costs of sending the Newfoundland Regiment to France.

Munn died with his 3 year old daughter Betty Munn, who was ripped from his arms by a huge wave that swept the deck. When a sailor offered the barefooted Munn his boots he gallantly refused, adding that he did not care what happened to him after losing Betty. In fact Betty had not been swept overboard and was still alive, sheltering with the Chief Steward in the lee of the Captain's cabin. Had Munn obeyed the sailor's instruction to move forward towards the wireless house, where those who survived were sheltered, he could have found Betty and both could have survived[70]. Betty was also the step-granddaughter of Sir Edgar Bowring, founder of the Bowring Brothers company which owned the ship. A monument of Peter Pan was erected to Betty as this was the fairy tale she loved the most. It stands in Bowring Park, St Johns and bears the inscription "in memory of a little girl who loved the park".

The Canadian troops remained in Flanders until they were moved to the Somme in late August 1916. With the exception of the battles for Mont Sorrel the Canadians were involved in minor attritional skirmishes. One of the casualties was Private George Poile of the 27th Battalion, who played for Indian Head Cricket Club, one of the most well known cricket teams in Saskatchewan. They lost three members to the War, but Poile was the most well-known and was described in Wisden as "a good batsman and bowler and a fine field." He had also played in Winnipeg and was a member of the North Western teams

---

68 England cricket captain turned commentator Nasser Hussain, and Essex and England wicket-keeper (seven tests at time of writing) Jamie Foster were both former Forest School pupils.

69 I am indebted to David Liverman for this information, who shared with me an unpublished article that he wrote on John Munn. The other two first-class players were: Munn's step-cousin William Bowring, who represented Barbados; and George Pitts, who played twice for Middlesex.

70 This is my assumption from reading pages 125-7 of A Winter's Tale by Cassie Brown.

which visited Chicago in 1904 and 1910. He was wounded fighting for the Manitoba Regiment south of Ypres and invalided back to Britain. He died in London on 27 May 1916 at the relatively mature age of 40.

The first mainland Canadian cricketer to be killed at the Somme was William Casey who was one of four Victoria Cricket Club players lost to the war. Major Casey was the only native born Canadian of the four and was the eldest son of MP George Casey. He had signed up at Valcartier as a sergeant and had been wounded in the spring of 1915. Following his recovery he had been promoted to captain in March 1916 and then to major in August. He was one of many casualties sustained by the 7th Battalion on 8 September 1916 in trenches near the town of Albert, fighting off an enemy attack after relieving the 14th Battalion.

Trinity College School in Port Hope, Ontario lost sixteen of its former cricketers. Two were killed in the gain of Courcelette, including Captain Ernest Pinkham who played for the School in 1903. His father was the Right Reverend William Pinkham, 1st Bishop of Calgary. His death is commemorated on a plaque erected by the law society of Alberta, as he was a Calgary law student. The most senior Trinity School casualty was Major John Ross DSO who played for the college in 1911. He served in the 24th Battalion, was awarded the Military Cross and was mentioned in dispatches. He was killed on 17 September 1916 in a follow up attack after the successful offensive gained Courcelette. The gains were small, which the war diary blames on inadequate artillery fire which did little but alert the enemy.

Thiepval Ridge lay north west of Courcelette and was attacked by the Canadians under the command of Sir Julian Byng in conjunction with the British 2nd Corps on 26 September. Four cricketers were killed on this date including Captain Stanley Walker of the 5th Battalion, who was one of four players from the Hillhurst Cricket Club in Calgary to be lost to the war. Sergeant William Hunter was also killed on this day fighting for the 5th Battalion. He had played for Coquitlam Cricket Club in Vancouver and was described by Wisden as a good all-round cricketer. By the 28 September the Canadians had secured most of their objectives, although their position remained vulnerable whilst the objective they named *Regina Trench* remained in enemy hands. The Canadian troops would spend more than a month and over two thousand lives trying to take that trench. They eventually succeeded on 11 November and so secured the ridge.

Incidentally Regina Cricket Club only lost one of its players to the War; this was 2nd Lieutenant Horace Travers whom Wisden describes as having been "a very useful bowler." He was born in Hong Kong and was killed fighting for the 10th Battalion of the Loyal North Lancashire

Regiment on 8 November 1916. His gravestone is in the Thiepval Memorial cemetery in the Somme area, so although his Regiment had been in Flanders in September, it is possible that he died indirectly assisting his fellow countrymen in their ultimately successful objective of securing the trench with the same name as the cricket club for which he had played.

Major Gordon Southam of the Field Artillery of the 8th Battalion was one of those killed in an unsuccessful attempt to take *Regina Trench*. He had been a great all-round sportsman, playing rugby and hockey, as well as cricket for the UCC and Canada. He won the Varsity novice championship at tennis, represented the Ontario interprovincial golf team and was also a member of the Royal Canadian Yacht Club. He played soccer for Hamilton Tigers, scoring a last minute goal in a famous match against Montréal. After graduation he followed his father, the newspaper owner William Southam, into journalism, working for the *Hamilton Spectator*. Following the outbreak of war he went to Kingston to become an artillery officer. He arrived at the Somme in July 1916 and was killed on 15 October supervising the retreat of the 40th battery near Courcelette; his bravery led to his posthumous inclusion in dispatches. He was 30 years old. A $500 scholarship was set up in his name, presumably by his parents.

The offensive should have ended after the securing of *Regina Trench*, but Haig felt that more gains could be made. Brantford Cricket Club lost four of its players to the war, including Lance Corporal William West, who had captained the team in 1915 and then signed-up on 15 September, presumably at the end of the cricket season. He died of his wounds on 23 November 1916, a victim of a pointless attack. Two days before he died Haig gave the order to abandon all further offensives until the spring. Perhaps this eased West's passing.

Vimy Ridge

The successful assault on Vimy Ridge was of huge military and nationalistic importance: the Canadian Corps were fighting together as a unit for the first time, rather than supporting a British division, and the taking of Vimy Ridge was the most successful allied action of the war to date in terms of ground won and weapons captured. It became a source of great Canadian national pride. In the words of one veteran *"we went up Vimy Ridge as Nova Scotians and British Columbians. We came down as Canadians."* The victory came at a price, however, with approximately 3,600 Canadians killed.

The attack began on Easter Monday 9 April 1917, a day that saw the deaths of four cricketers. Lieutenant John Manley was one of twelve former Ridley College cricketers to be killed in the war, but he was the only old boy who is recorded as having played for another club[71]. He moved to British Columbia and represented Vancouver Cricket Club, before signing up with the 72nd Battalion in December 1915. He was killed on the first day of the assault with his Battalion on the left flank. His gravestone is on the western slope of Vimy Ridge above the village of Souchez, one of the fifteen special memorials erected to those believed to have been buried there.

Lieutenant George Reid was one of two members of the Coquitlam Cricket Club of Vancouver lost to the War. Wisden described him as being a useful bowler, a hard hitting batsman and the best fielder in British Columbia. He was also killed on 9 April 1917, a day after his 32nd birthday. A few days later Private Charles Lipscomb became one of at least 10 Cowichan Cricket Club members to be killed when he died of his wounds on 18 April 1917. Two days after this, the Australian-born Lieutenant Roderick Finlayson of Incogniti of Victoria also died of wounds, sustained whilst fighting for the 7th Battalion.

The other two cricketers to be killed on 9 April were both Acting Majors: Charles Gwyn, formerly of the Highfield School cricket team in Hamilton, and Walter Curry, another Upper Canada College old boy. Both men had enlisted at Valcartier. Major Gwyn was killed leading the B company of the 72nd Battalion to within fifty yards of its objective. He was mentioned in dispatches. Curry had contracted typhoid despite being vaccinated and was invalided back home to Toronto following the second Ypres. He returned to the front and was promoted to Acting-Major in the 3rd Battalion. He was killed instantly, along with his batman, by an enemy shell whilst leading A Company in the early stages of the attack. Walter Curry was the only son of J Walter Curry KC and, along with Major Gordon Southam, he was one of the sixty-one members of the Royal Canadian Yacht Club to be lost to the War.

Private Walter Cooper died on 12 April 1917, presumably of wounds as this was a day after his 4th Battalion from Ontario was relieved following the successful attack on Vimy Ridge. He had played in the intercollegiate match against the American students in 1895 and represented Canada four times in the International Series. He was also of sufficient standing to be appointed by the Canadian Cricket Association to the five man panel to oversee the arrangements for the MCC touring team in 1905. To avoid being rejected on the grounds of age, Cooper had lied about his date of birth when signing up, claiming to be 43 years old when he was actually 48. He also lied on question 10 of his attestation paper, stating that he had never served in the

---

[71] This discounts Lieutenant G Heighton who died of influenza in Toronto on 2 November 1918. He had played for Toronto Cricket Club after leaving Ridley College.

military. Presumably he felt that admitting to his prior service would have risked revealing his real age. As we saw in the previous chapter Cooper appeared on an 1893 scorecard as a corporal and he appears on the nominal role as a sergeant. I have been unable to find out why he was demoted to a private.

Hill 70
Following the success at Vimy Ridge Sir Julian Byng was given the command of the British Third Army, but his relationship with Canada was not over. He would be Governor-General from 1921-26. Sir Arthur Currie replaced Byng to become the first Canadian to command the Canadian Corps. He was given the task of taking Lens, but Currie surveyed the ground and came up with the far more sensible plan of taking Hill 70 which overlooked the enemy positions at Lens. Currie correctly predicted that the enemy would have to try and retake the Hill and as a consequence would suffer more casualties. First they had to take the Hill. Preparation was crucial and information gathered from the air was an important part of this, although this was not risk free. Flight-Lieutenant Robert Jardine, who had played for Ridley College, was killed on 20 July, his 29th birthday. The attack began on 15 August, a day that saw the death of Private Albert Burrows of the 7th Battalion, which failed to reach its objective that day and had to withdraw back to a more defendable line and wait for its relief. Albert Burrows had played for the Lynn Valley cricket club in Vancouver. His teammate Private Samuel Aspell was killed on the 21 August fighting for another British Columbia regiment, the 29th Battalion. The Canadians took the Hill and air reconnaissance had been the key to the success.

RAF
The contribution made by Canadian pilots to the war effort is legendary. They were awarded over 800 decorations, including three Victoria Crosses, which were given to Billy Bishop, Alan McLeod and William Barker. Three of the Canadian cricketers who died in 1918 were in the RAF or its equivalents. One of these was Robert Ferrie, son of the Robert Bown Ferrie who had toured Britain in 1887. Ferrie junior had captained the 1915 Highfield School team of Hamilton. He joined the 46th squadron of the Royal Flying Corps, the same squadron as Phil Tufnell's grandfather. Captain Ferrie was just 19 years old when he was killed on 3 January 1918. His damaged plane crashed as he was leading his patrol back from a dog-fight. His death was described in the book "No Parachute" by Arthur Gould Lee:

> "I'm terribly depressed this evening. Ferrie has been killed. He led his patrol out this afternoon, had a scrap, came back leading the others, then as they were flying along quite normally in formation, his right wing suddenly folded back, then the other, and the wreck plunged vertically down. A bullet must

have gone through a main spar during the fight. The others went after him and steered close to him in vertical dives. They could see him, struggling to get clear of his harness, then half standing up. They said it was terrible to watch him trying to decide whether to jump. He didn't, and the machine and he were smashed to nothingness. I can't believe it. Little Ferrie, with his cheerful grin, one of the finest chaps in the Squadron. God, imagine his last moments, seeing the ground rushing up at him, knowing he was a dead man, unable to move, unable to do anything but wait for it. A parachute could have saved him, there's no doubt about that. What is wrong with those callous dolts at home that they won't give them to us?"

Ferrie was posthumously awarded the Military Cross, presumably to placate his comrades.

Sons of players who had represented Canada

Dyce Willcocks Saunders and Robert Bown Ferrie had represented Canada and toured Britain together in 1887. They had shared many successes and trials on the cricket pitch; the War ensured that they also shared the tragic loss of their young sons. Lieutenant Thomas Saunders was the eldest son of Dyce Willcocks Saunders KC. Thomas Saunders played for Trinity College School in Port Hope from 1911-1914 and captained the side during his last two years at the School. As recorded in the next chapter he also played for Toronto Cricket Club. He served in the 13th Battalion and was killed at Mont Sorrel on 13 June 1916, nine days after his 20th birthday.

Saunders and Ferrie had another reason to grieve on 7 September 1916 when Lieutenant Colonel Coote Shanly, the Assistant Manager of the 1887 tour, died of a respiratory illness in Toronto after being invalided home in July. He had signed up at Valcartier where he was appointed the Canadian Expeditionary Force's chief field paymaster. He was 53 years old.

Another cricketer to lose a son was John E Hall, a retired Major, who co-wrote the famous book "Sixty Years of Canadian Cricket" with Robert McCulloch. Hall had also represented Canada with Saunders in July 1891 against the Ontario Association. Captain George Hall had followed his father into the Toronto Cricket Club and died of his wounds on 16 June 1917 aged 21 in the Vimy area, during a lull in the fighting.

The last year of the war

After Passchendaele the number of cricketing casualties decreased, with only sixteen cricketers dying alongside their many comrades in 1918, as the Canadian Corps were repeatedly used as "shock troops" to break the enemy lines, especially during the last hundred days of the War. Cricketers had signed-up in the early stages of the war with most serving with the first contingent. By 1918 they had little left to give.

Not all cricketers who served died in the War and Ethelbert Lionel Cross was one such cricketer. He was born in Trinidad in 1890 and was educated at Naparima College, which was founded in 1894 by Dr Kenneth J Grant a Canadian Presbyterian missionary, as one of the first schools to educate Indo-Trinidadians. Cross captained the cricket team for his last two years at the College. He went on to play for the south part of the Island, alongside cricketers who would represent the West Indies. After moving to New York and scoring a century for Gotham Cricket Club he arrived in Canada and was in Halifax, Nova Scotia when the War broke out. He signed-up in January 1916 but was initially rejected for military service due to his race[72], eventually being sent overseas in March 1917 with the No.2 Construction Battalion, a segregated unit made up entirely of non-whites. He was promoted to Sergeant and ended the War as the Company Sergeant-Major.

Not all soldiers killed, died in combat. In January 1919 Cross was stationed at Kinmel Park, a camp in north-west Wales which was set up for Canadians waiting to return home. Tensions were running high amongst the soldiers, who were frustrated by their length of stay. It was understood that those who had served the longest would be the first to return and so when conscripted men who had never seen action were returned home first to a hero's welcome, a mutiny broke out in March. There had been unrest leading up to the mutiny, including an unsavoury incident in January where white troops threw stones at black soldiers from the No.2 Construction Company in retaliation for the arrest of a white soldier by a black sergeant from this Company[c]. This was Cross' unit and so the sergeant could well have been him. Hundreds of soldiers mutinied and it was fortunate that there were only four fatalities amongst the thirty or so casualties, as gun fire was exchanged between the rioters and those defending the Camp.

Cross eventually returned to Canada in June 1919 and started playing for the local West Indian team in Halifax, scoring 121 against Windsor Cricket Club. By 1921 he was playing for the West Indians of Montréal against McGill University, taking nine of the ten wickets to fall in his team's two run victory. In the same year he was selected to play for Québec against Ontario in the prestigious inter-provincial match. When he moved to Toronto to start his own law practice he represented Ontario in the same annual fixture.

---

[72] I'm uncertain as to Cross' ethnicity but the school he attended suggest that he was probably an Indo-Trinidadian.

He joined the West Indian team of Toronto and in 1922 carried his bat for 108, playing against the West Indian team of Hamilton. In 1923 he made another undefeated century, 103 against the Kentish Society. He then joined the Albions where he contributed with bat and ball. He scored centuries against Toronto and Bell Telephones in 1925 and Rosedale in 1926. His batting led the *Toronto Star* to name him the "man of many centuries", but he was also an excellent bowler, topping the bowling averages of the Toronto and District Cricket Council in 1922, 1923 and 1925. Against St Edmunds in 1928 he took five wickets in five balls in one over. When the Albions folded he became a key member of West Toronto[ci].

Like the turn-of-the-century Canadian all-rounder John Laing, Cross graduated from Osgoode Hall[73] and became the only non-white admitted to the Law Society of Upper Canada between 1900 and 1923[cii]. He took on controversial cases such as representing Ernest V. Sterry, the editor of the Christian Enquiry, in his appeal against his jail sentence for blasphemy and he continued to the champion the rights of those outside the social elite before being disbarred in 1937, which is a story for a different book.

Impact of the War on Canadian cricket

Whilst the War was detrimental to cricket it benefited baseball, especially in Britain as, according to the Toronto *Globe* of Saturday 7 April 1917, Canadian servicemen made baseball as popular as cricket in Britain. This was built on by the Americans and 10,000 spectators saw a Canadian team beat an American side by 12 runs to 3 at Lord's![ciii] In June 1918 baseball was played at the football stadium at Highbury, with one American claiming "we're going to torpedo cricket!"[civ] More baseball was played in British battalions than cricket[cv] and at the end of the War a Baseball League was proposed for England to be made up of Canadian and American players. I argued in the previous chapter that the American Civil War had been unfairly blamed for preventing cricket from becoming a national sport in the United States and this argument is strengthened by the failure of baseball to take-off in Britain. Baseball can be more easily played in wartime, because a pitch is not required, but history has shown that the short-term increase in popularity of baseball due to a conflict has little long-term impact on the sports a nation plays.

Cricket in Canada has been sustained by the influx of cricket-playing immigrants, but it has been held back by the reluctance of the sons of immigrants to play an un-Canadian game. The War killed many

---

[73] I am grateful to the Archivist at Osgoode Hall, Paul Leatherdale, who told me about Cross when I phoned to ask him about Laing.

Canadian-born cricketers, including at least three who had fathers that had represented Canada.

The war indirectly led to a more independent, less British Canada, which inevitably contributed to the decline of cricket, as it was seen as a British game. The war also took a heavy toll on Canadian cricketers, as a disproportionate number of them signed up. Most had been born in Britain but well over a third had been born in Canada. The war killed off a generation of cricketers, many of whom could have succeeded in altering the perception of the game from a British pastime into a Canadian sport.

Chapter 8: The John Ross Robertson Trophy

"Have drowned my glory in a shallow cup" *Edmund Fitzgerald, the Rubaiyat of Omar Khayyam*

The silver trophy donated by John Ross Robertson (right) on 23 January 1911 was 68cm high with the pedestal and 28cm wide. It was decorated with two cricket bats encircled with maple leaves on the cup and a crouching beaver on the lid. It was engraved with the words "The J. Ross Robertson Challenge Trophy, emblematic of the cricket championship of the Dominion of Canada."

The John Ross Robertson Trophy was a double-edged sword for cricket. Introducing a competition to establish which was the best club team in the nation helped to modernise the sport, but by excluding professional players it restricted the development of Canadian cricket in the twentieth century.

Canadian cricket is dominated by Upper Canada College old boys. One of these, the great philanthropist John Ross Robertson, donated a silver trophy on 23rd January 1911 to be awarded to the best club team in Canada. Robertson became president of the Ontario Hockey Association in 1899, where he sought to prevent the professionalisation of the sport. This earned him the title "Father of Amateur Hockey in Ontario", but in that sport he was fighting a losing battle. In cricket, however, he helped to prevent its professionalisation in Canada. By insisting that only amateurs could compete in its premier competition he closed an avenue to incentivising the employment of professional players.

The John Ross Robertson Trophy was a challenge competition and three trustees were appointed to determine the rules. They were JW Woods, of whom I know nothing, and former international players George S Lyon and Dyce Willocks Saunders. Earlier domestic competitions had been flexible with regard to player eligibility, as many cricketers played for more than one team. On occasion this had led to controversy and bad feeling when a player chose to represent one team over another. The Trustees determined that all players in the competition either needed to be a continuous resident of the city or town they represented for at least a year before the date of the relevant match, or have played for the team in five regular games before the cup match. The following year this rule was tightened further to bar any cricketer who had played more than once for any other club, excluding college or school teams. In this respect the John Ross Robertson Trophy was a modern competition.

All challenge competitions need a holder and so it was decided that the winners of Toronto's City League in 1910 would defend the John Ross Robertson Trophy in 1911. Rosedale became the first holders of the Trophy by winning the A division and then defeating Parkdale, the B division champions. Three challenges were to be allowed every season and if there were more than three challengers, preliminary rounds would be organised. For the 1911 competition, clubs were given a deadline of 29 April to enter at a cost of $10, a nominal fee which was not altered for many years.

All Canadian teams were eligible, although in the early years the vast majority of the games were contested by sides from Ontario. Before the

First World War the challengers from outside the Toronto area were given a bye to ensure that the touring sides would not have to travel a long distance, at their own expense, just to be defeated in a preliminary round. Teams from Ontario were less likely to receive this advantage when challenging simply because they would not be the only team from the Toronto area challenging for the Trophy. Between the wars entrants came from either Montréal or Toronto areas and so it made sense to have only two challenges a season.

There were five challengers for the inaugural contest in 1911: St Albans, Hamilton, Toronto, Ottawa and Winnipeg Canadian Pacific Railway, necessitating a preliminary round. Winnipeg and Ottawa were given byes to the challenge stage of the competition, because they had further to travel than the other sides. St Albans withdrew and Toronto added themselves to the list of challengers by beating Hamilton. Toronto were given the first challenge match, which was actually a disadvantage as it meant that they would be liable to defend the Trophy against two further challenges if they defeated the holders. It is possible that the draw was random, but I think it more likely that to avoid any charges of favouritism DW Saunders, as one of the Trustees of the competition, ensured that his Toronto Cricket Club were given the most difficult draw.

Toronto defeated the holders Rosedale Cricket Club on 14-15 July 1911 by the narrow margin of 17 runs. Three former internationals made key contributions for Toronto: AA Beemer top scored in the first innings with an unbeaten 27 and JM Laing made the top score of 23 in the second innings. He was ably assisted by Toronto's captain DW Saunders who finished unbeaten on 22, thus leading his team to victory in a competition that he had helped to organise.

The John Ross Robertson Trophy established itself as the most important competition in domestic cricket in its first year. A Church and Mercantile League game had to be rearranged to accommodate the Trophy match between Rosedale and Toronto[cvi], indicating the challenge competition's premier status. The best players were expected to play in these matches and the absence of an international player from the Toronto team, Harry Lownsborough, was commented on and the hope that he would be able to play against the Winnipeg team was expressed in the press. Unfortunately Ottawa were unable to mount their challenge on 28-29 July, due to a late session of Parliament! This left the third and final challenge to Winnipeg Canadian Pacific Railway Cricket Club who had topped the Winnipeg league the year before. Their captain, HL Pratt, made a battling 43 in the second innings, but he was powerless to prevent Toronto winning the game easily by an innings and 95 runs on 18-19 August. Harry

Lownsborough made 52 in Toronto's only innings and Norman Seagram, who would play in the final International Match for 50 years in 1912, took 8 for 45 in Winnipeg's first innings to ensure that Toronto Cricket Club became the holders of the John Ross Robertson Trophy for 1911 and the first side to win it in competition.

In 1912 there were six challenges for Toronto's title and again the two clubs from outside the Toronto area were not required to play in the preliminary rounds. Lachine, now a borough of Montréal but then a separate settlement, were drawn to play the winner of the first challenge match on 5-6 August, whilst Winnipeg, who had been unbeaten the previous season[74], were drawn to contest the final challenge match on 2-3 September. The other four teams: Rosedale, Simpsons, Hamilton and Eaton had to play off against each other to win the right to challenge the holders Toronto on 19-20 July. Clearly the draw was unfair, as Winnipeg only had to win a single game to become champions, whilst say Hamilton would have to play two games in the preliminary rounds and then three challenge matches to win the trophy in 1912. For the record Rosedale won the play-offs but then lost to Toronto in the first challenge match by 120 runs with Harry Lownsborough hitting 56 and Jack Laing 38 for the victors; they put on 44 for the sixth wicket. I can find no record of the match against Lachine, but if it was played Toronto must have won, for they beat the Winnipeg Wanderers by 137 runs in the third and final challenge match to retain their trophy. Two international players bowled them to victory: LM Rathbun, who played in his first and only international match a few days later, took four for 23 in Winnipeg's second innings and his fellow opening bowler AA Beemer took three for only eight runs. He had played once for Canada against America in 1904. WL Price of Winnipeg took all ten Toronto wickets in their first innings with his left arm medium pace bowling, although Harry Lownsborough, who was captaining Toronto, had the misfortune to be caught behind off the *seventh* delivery of one of Price's overs.

Apparently all eleven Toronto players were born in Canada, whilst the Winnipeg team included ten Englishmen[cvii]. If victory over the team from Manitoba was seen as a triumph for Canadian born cricketers and a sign of the coming of age of Canadian cricket then it would be short-lived.

---

74 P.10 of the *Toronto Star* of 11 June 1912 stated that Winnipeg Wanderers had won the western championship of 1911. The Wanderers, in defiance of their name, had spent $16,000 on a new stadium in preparation for the 1913 International Match, which never happened.

This capped a fine season for the Toronto Cricket Club. They had not just retained the John Ross Robertson Trophy but they also won the City League championship and the Albany Cup, when they defeated Hamilton by 8 runs.

In 1913 the *Globe* reported that the play offs would be held in the region where the Trophy was held, which only made sense whilst the winners resided in Ontario, where most of the cricket clubs were. After defeating St Barnabas and St Albans Cricket Clubs, Toronto ensured a rematch with the Winnipeg Wanderers, who were a strong side made up of players who had learnt the game in Britain including TAD Bevington[75] who had played for Harrow and Middlesex, EC Laver who had played for Somerset and WL Price, described by the Toronto *Globe* of Monday 28 July 1913 as "the best bowler in Canada." He played for Worcestershire and for Canada in 1912, as did EC Laver, who scored an unbeaten 102 for Toronto Cricket Club against Chicago Wanderers in 1895. He then moved to Manitoba where he scored 160 not out, a record for the province. Dr Sam Smith also played for Canada in 1912 and hit 120 against the Chicago Wanderers in the same year.

In contrast Toronto were struggling. Wright was unavailable due to injury and Davidson, Rathbun, Button and Usher all made themselves unavailable due to business engagements, the perennial curse of the amateur. They were forced to draft in the seventeen year old Thomas Saunders, son of Dyce Willcocks Saunders who also played. Thomas Saunders played for Trinity College School and was their captain from 1913-14, although he was eligible to play for Toronto Cricket Club in the John Ross Robertson Trophy, as membership of college teams did not preclude representation on another team in this competition. I can find no reference to any College teams playing in the John Ross Robertson Trophy and so can only assume that they were not eligible. In the game against Winnipeg Thomas Saunders batted at 11 and did not bowl.

The game was played in an excellent spirit: when the umpire failed to spot that Dyce Saunders had played the ball onto his stumps and gave him not out, Saunders sportingly walked off the field. Bevington top scored for Winnipeg with 46 and was ably assisted by K Habershon who made 25. Captain Habershon was killed in the Great War, fighting for the 12th Battalion of the British Rifle Brigade on 12 February 1916. His opponent Lieutenant Thomas Saunders was also killed, as described in the last chapter.

---

[75] His full name was the rather pleasing Timothy Arthur Dent Bevington.

The Winnipeg team's victory came more quickly than expected as a number of Toronto batsmen were absent in the second innings. According to the Montréal Gazette, reporting 14 years after the event on 5 September 1927, Toronto Cricket Club lost the game when their second innings was declared closed, due to the absence of several batsmen, just a few runs from victory.

Winnipeg Wanderers' seizure of the Trophy at the second attempt was much celebrated, with telegrams of congratulations being sent to Toronto. One of the first to be received was from their President, Sir Hugh John MacDonald, who was the son of Sir John A. MacDonald and had been knighted just a few months before. He had moved to Winnipeg in 1882 to make a fresh start following the death of his first wife. Unsurprisingly for a man of his pedigree, Hugh MacDonald was Conservative MP for Winnipeg from 1891-93 and 1896-97, briefly serving as Minister of the Interior in Charles Tupper's short administration. MacDonald formed a law practice in Winnipeg with Tupper's son James Stewart Tupper. MacDonald became Premier of Manitoba in 1899, a post he resigned in 1900 in order to contest the seat of Brandon, against the sitting MP, Minister of the Interior Clifford Sifton. His narrow defeat signalled his retirement from politics. His Presidency of the Wanderers showed that the sport still enjoyed a cosy relationship with the political elite. This relationship would wither and die following the First Word War.

The Winnipeg captain Eddie Smith wrote to the press stating that they had not yet been presented with the Trophy, which suggests poor organising and poor form from the Toronto Cricket Club, although the Winnipeggers had been well entertained by the Torontonians at both the Royal Canadian Yacht Club and at the Albany Club. Smith did not dwell on the matter, swiftly adding that "there are lots of cricketers in Winnipeg waiting to fill it as soon as it reaches us, and we'll take good care of it till you send a team West to try and take it away from us."[cviii] The Wanderers returned back to a rousing reception at the CPR depot at Winnipeg. There were in action again by 1 September against the touring Australians.

This rounded up an excellent sporting year for Manitoba: they had won hockey's Allen Cup, soccer's Connaught Cup, their sprinter J. Army Howard held the championships for the 100 yards and 220 yards and their rowers held cups in the fours and eights[cix].

For the first time the John Ross Robertson Trophy had been won by a team from outside Ontario, which made it more difficult for some of the best teams in Canada to compete for the cup. In July 1914 the Winnipeg Wanderers faced challenges from Regina, Saskatchewan and Grace Church of Toronto. A challenge from McGill University of Montréal was scheduled for August, but was cancelled after war broke out, with players such as Evan Stuart Cameron of McGill signing-up at Valcartier.

Regina were beaten by the comfortable margin of 241 runs and Winnipeg's second innings of 278 made a third day's play necessary to complete the game. Grace Church, under the captaincy of W Paris, were the next team to challenge. I have been unable to discover any evidence of any preliminary rounds, so it is probable that Grace Church were the only team from Ontario willing to travel to Winnipeg. Certainly the Toronto Cricket Club decided not to compete for the Trophy, citing the demands of two day cricket as a reason[cx], although the cost of travel must have also been a factor. Grace Church ran an appeal in the press to raise the $500 necessary just to cover the travel costs[cxi]. It was usual for teams required to travel a great distance for the John Ross Robertson Trophy to arrange additional games as part of the tour. For example Grace Church played Chicago as part of their tour in 1914. Winnipeg defeated Grace Church by six wickets on 30-31 July and retained the Trophy.

Unsurprisingly the Trophy was not contested during the First World War[cxii], the competition would not recommence until 1920[cxiii]. The year of 1919 was a time of great upheaval and uncertainty. Winnipeg, which was Canada's third largest city, experienced a General Strike, when 96 of the 94 unions[76] decided to down tools and bring the City to a standstill. It lasted six weeks from 15 May to 25 June, with veterans of the Great War playing a key role on both sides. It all reached a head on 21 June – *Bloody Saturday* – when the Police fired into a rioting crowd. One man was killed and many were injured. Unsurprisingly not even the draw of the John Ross Robertson Trophy could convince any teams to tour Winnipeg in such circumstances.

It would take a few years for the tournament to regain its pre-War popularity and when it did, it became clear that Montréal not Winnipeg would be mounting the main challenge to Toronto's dominance. In 1920 the Yorkshire Society Cricket Club defeated Winnipeg Wanderers and brought the title back to Toronto. The Winnipeg team may only have won the competition twice but they had kept the Trophy for seven years.

---

[76] The two unions who continued to work were the typographers and the Police, who had voted in favour of industrial action but had been convinced by the Strike's leaders to remain at work to maintain law and order and avoid giving the Government an excuse to bring in the troops.

In September 1921 Yorkshire Society defeated Albion Cricket Club and retained their title. I can find no evidence of Yorkshire Society receiving any other challenges in 1921, although Albions had beaten Westmounts to win the right to challenge. If there were other games they went unreported in the press.

By 1922 the organisers received five challenges; these were from clubs: McGill, Toronto, Grace Church, St Edmunds and Albion. The rules only permitted three challenges and so preliminary rounds were organised. The McGill Cricket Club of Montréal was given a bye and the right to make the final challenge match of the year, as warranted a team from outside Ontario. Grace Church won the right to challenge Yorkshire Society by beating Toronto, ending the latter club's first challenge for the Trophy since the end of the Great War at the first hurdle, suggesting that they had still not fully recovered from the conflict's impact. St Edmunds beat Albion in the other tie, to complete the list of the three challengers. The Yorkshire Society beat their two fellow Ontarian teams, but was defeated by 62 runs by McGill Cricket Club who became the champions for 1922. Once again the teams from the Toronto area, who made up the majority of entrants for the competition, would have to travel outside their province in order to win the Trophy. It must have seemed unfair to Ontarian challengers that they always had to play in preliminary rounds, whilst sides from outside the province never had. At least the entrance fee remained at $10.

McGill's victory encouraged two sides from the Montréal area: Lachine and Westmount, to enter the competition in 1923. The contest now entered a new era, with preliminary rounds being held in Montréal and Toronto to determine who the two challengers would be. The usual convention of having three challengers was abandoned for practical reasons. Toronto Cricket Club became the challengers from Toronto when they beat Albions and so won the right to play McGill. The Toronto team were captained by Dyce Saunders and they were beaten by 17 runs by McGill, who were captained by Dyce's brother Stuart Saunders[cxiv]. McGill retained their title.

The 1924 season mirrored the 1923 session. Lachine won the right to be the challenger from the eastern section of the competition, but were beaten by McGill by 9 wickets. In the final eliminator match to decide the challenger for the western section Toronto were 107 for 6 chasing Albions' 181 when the time ran out in a match where too many overs were lost to rain. Instead of scheduling an extra day to finish the game they replayed the match, which threw out the scheduling for other matches. In recognition that amateurs had to work for a living these games were played on the weekends. Toronto beat Albions in the rescheduled match, but in a repeat of the final game of the previous year, McGill beat Toronto by 25 runs to retain the Trophy.

McGill were now the dominant club in Canada. They retained the Trophy again in 1925 when they beat the challenges from Westmount and Albions, defeating the latter by eight wickets. Albions had defeated Toronto to win the right to challenge McGill. In a demonstration of their supremacy McGill easily beat Toronto over the Labor Day weekend, scoring 138 for 4 declared against their opponents' 115.

McGill retained the trophy in 1926. They defeated the eastern challenger Westward, who had changed their name from Westmount, by seven wickets and then defeated the western challenger Bell Telephones by only a single wicket[cxv]. Bell Telephones were arguably the best team to never win the John Ross Robertson trophy.

West Indian cricketers would dominate the game in Canada in the 1960s and 1970s, but they were following in the footsteps of other players such as those from the Montréal based West Indians, who in 1927 beat three other teams to challenge McGill for the Trophy in the first year that they entered the contest. McGill might have defeated them that year, but they would be back. In November 1928 members of the West Indian team were in the Liquor Court testifying on behalf of the defendant, a Mrs H Best. They claimed that the two officers of the Québec Liquor Commission could not have bought unlicensed liquor from Mrs Best, as there were no white men there on the date in question. They were celebrating a victory in a John Ross Robertson Trophy match,[cxvi] presumably with alcohol supplied by Mrs Best. Their testimony was not helped by the fact that nobody seemed able to remember which opponent they had defeated.

In 1927 Toronto defeated Bell Telephones to win the right to play McGill in the second and final challenge match over the Labor Day weekend. Labor Day and the day after became the dates for the final challenge match of the competition, which was now the highlight of the domestic season. When McGill won the game, and the contest for a sixth successive year, the squad were awarded miniature versions of the Trophy, which were paid for by Kenneth Mappin[cxvii], who was the President of Mappin and Webb Ltd and a member of the Montréal Amateur Athletic Association.

In 1928 the West Indians were the challengers again from the eastern region, beating the Montréal Amateur Athletic Association by 18 runs. The umpiring was of a poor standard with 4 ball and 7 ball overs and appeals for a run out and a catch behind in the MAAA innings controversially declined. It is possible that latent racism was behind these decisions but this is a matter of conjecture. B Clarke did the hat-trick, which in effect won this game narrowly for the West Indians. McGill again defeated the West Indians in the first challenge match and faced Bell Telephones in the final challenge match over the Labour Day Weekend. The importance of the contest to McGill is shown by their decision not to enter the local Montréal cup in order to focus on the John Ross Robertson Trophy[cxviii].

When rain prevented any play on Labor Day in 1928 the McGill captain was asked to allow the match to continue on Wednesday but at first the College grounds were declared unavailable. When this ruling was declared at the lunch break, the Bell Telephone management appealed directly to McGill's Vice-Chancellor and Principal, Sir Arthur Currie, who had been the first Canadian commander of the Canadian Corps during the First World War. He ruled that the grounds would be available should the cricketers want it. The Bell Telephone players therefore expected that the game would continue on Wednesday and were greatly upset by the decision taken by McGill's captain[77] to refuse to continue the game[cxix]. The Torontonians had travelled about 400 miles to play in Montréal and although they were within their rights to demand a rematch, this was clearly not practical. In 1929 the Bell Telephones team declared that they would not enter in that year's competition after being "victim of last year's unprepared for denouement at Montréal." They also complained about "this incipient 'laissez faire' disease" in cricket scheduling[cxx]. The unsatisfactory termination of the game at Montréal was much discussed at the official end of season review in Toronto and one article in the press suggested that no teams from Toronto would be prepared to travel to Montréal next season[cxxi]. Fortunately this prediction proved incorrect.

Despite the controversy the year before, the competition to become the challenger from the west in 1929 was well contested with Toronto Cricket Club facing West Toronto Cricket Club in one semi-final and Yorkshire Society Cricket Club beating St Clair in the other. It had been agreed that the match between Toronto and West Toronto should continue after the result, but rather unsportingly the vanquished West Toronto team abandoned the game within an hour of stumps. Toronto beat the Yorkshire Society to win the right to travel to Montréal to challenge for the Trophy.

---

[77] Stuart Saunders, who had captained McGill's successful defence of the Trophy from 1923-6, had a letter published in the Toronto Star of Tuesday 11 September 1928 on page 11, stating that McGill's captain would have continued had Bell Telephones been in a winning position at the end of Tuesday's play. Through their writer ES Jackson, the Toronto Star published the letter but rejected the claim.

In the eastern half of the competition McGill faced the West Indians again and once again the University team were victorious. The final challenge game between the best of the east and west was played over the Labor Day weekend as usual. Toronto were in fine form: although they had lost against Hamilton, Ridley College and St Andrews College early in the season, they had then gone undefeated for the rest of the year[cxxii]. To the delight of all Toronto teams the Toronto Cricket Club thrashed McGill by an innings and 213 runs to ensure that after seven years of having all their Trophy games in their city, the Montréal clubs would now have to travel to Toronto in order to challenge the holders. Bell Telephones ended their one-year boycott of the competition and entered again in 1930.

The 1930 competition took another step towards modernisation when the organisers decided that umpires would be appointed by the Umpiring Authority, thus abandoning the age-old practice of the two competing teams choosing an umpire each. Both the West Indians and Bell Telephones protested against this innovation, which could have put the umpire Fred Heather in an awkward position as he was a former player for Bell Telephones, but by 1930 had just embarked on his illustrious career as an umpire.

By 1932 Heather was considered one of Canada's top umpires and he was chosen to officiate in Eastern Canada's game against Don Bradman's touring Australians. There were over 8,000 spectators, which was a record for cricket in Canada. He would umpire in games involving Sir Julien Cahn's touring team in 1933 and in the MCC tours of 1937, 1951 and 1959. On 8-10 September 1951 Heather officiated in the inaugural first-class game played in Canada when the touring MCC team played against Canada at the grounds of Toronto Cricket Club. In these auspicious circumstances it would have been understandable for an umpire to shy away from controversy, but Heather had the courage to no ball the Canadian Padmore six times in his first four overs. In 1967 Heather crossed the Atlantic and umpired in the game between the Canadian Colts and the Highgate School. He retired in the same year and the High Commissioner for Canada recognised his services to the game by requesting his attendance at Westminster Abbey to commemorate Canada's Centennial Year. Heather became the first Life Member of the Toronto Cricket Umpire's Association on 12 January 1970. He died on 22 February 1976 in Toronto.

In 2009 Cricket Canada gave Heather the Jack Kyle Development Award for his lifelong contribution to the growth and development of cricket in Canada, making him only the ninth person to receive this honour. In April 2010 Heather was given the Syl Apps Special Achievement Award for his lifetime contribution to Canadian cricket.

Unfortunately the Canadian Sports Hall of Fame selection Committee decided not to induct Heather into their select list of Canadian sportsmen. To date no Canadian cricketer has received this honour.

Dyce Willocks Saunders was also a legend of the game, albeit from a previous era. He died on 12 June 1930 in London. His body was bought back to Canada, to be buried in Toronto, where the competition that he had helped to create was in full swing.

Toronto defeated Bell Telephones and so faced the West Indians, who had beat Westward of Montréal, in the final challenge match of the season. I can find no evidence that McGill entered in the 1930 competition. After seven seasons of playing challenge matches without having to leave Montréal, the prospect of having to travel to Toronto may not have appealed.

Toronto's second and final defence of the 1930 season was a competitive match against the West Indians from Montréal. If we accept the sentiment: "never believe anything unless it has been officially denied", then there was some bad feeling between the two teams, which resulted in the following being issued in the press: "The Indians wish to refute any statement which had been made to the contrary and the cordiality shown at the luncheon held at the conclusion of the match is ample proof of the good feeling and respect shown between both the teams concerned.[cxxiii]"

The Toronto team conceded a single run lead in the first innings, managing only 99 in response to the West Indians' 100, so when the Montréal team compiled 110[78] in their second innings they would have been favourites to lift the Trophy for the first time. The run chase was competitive, with the Toronto batsman Carlton being struck on the cheekbone by one of Jemmott's deliveries. This was in fact the seventh delivery of the over, perhaps suggesting that the Umpiring authority did not yet have the most qualified umpires. Jemmott and Carlton played together in the victorious RC Matthews XI, which beat the touring MCC side on 6 August 1937 by 10 wickets. Jemmott was the only black player selected.

Carlton was out hit wicket shortly after receiving the blow to the face, dismissed by Jemmott who took six wickets for 46 in the Toronto innings. Unfortunately for the West Indians, Jemmott was the only bowler to take any wickets and the Toronto team won the game by four

---

[78] According to the Montréal Gazette of 3 September 1930 the West Indian score was increased by two when it was realised that the scorer had not noticed two of the wides signalled by the umpire.

wickets and retained the Trophy. The West Indians would not have long to wait for their first title.

Seven local Montréal teams entered the 1931 contest: Sun Life, Lachine, McGill, MAAA, Westward, West Indians and CP Recreation. The West Indians ran out the eventual winners. Toronto Cricket Club defeated Bell Telephones in the first challenge match by 9 wickets, with E Carlton top scoring with 70. This set up the final challenge match against the West Indians in Toronto on Labor Day and the day after.

The West Indian captain Holder won the toss and opted to bat first. The batsmen justified their captain's decision by amassing 313. When Toronto collapsed from an overnight 100 for 6 to 118 all-out, to follow-on 195 runs behind, an easy victory for the West Indians appeared inevitable, but the Toronto Cricket Club did not surrender the Trophy without a fight. They rallied in their second innings scoring 303 to set an awkward victory target of 109. When the West Indians were reduced to 20 for 3 the game was in the balance, but the Montréalers avoided any further losses to win the game by 7 wickets. The game was terminated at 7:15pm; sensibly the decision was taken to allow the two-day match to continue to its inevitable conclusion. The West Indians had finally won the Trophy after being the challenger from the east five years in a row since they had first entered the contest in 1927.

In recognition of their achievement, the officers of the Canadian Pacific Railway received the West Indians as their guests of honour at their official dinner at Windsor station in Montréal. Press reports of 1933 stated that the West Indians were all porters from Windsor station[cxxiv] and there must have been mixed feelings when their employers sought to honour them in their national victory whilst still denying them employment in other positions due to their race. At least cricket gave them a chance to compete on equal terms.

In 1932 McGill were again defeated in the pre-challenge stage, as Lachine beat them by 194 runs to 73, with the McGill batsman Crissen being run out with his bat above and not grounded[cxxv]. Since losing the Trophy in 1929 McGill had failed to challenge the holders for the Trophy, suggesting that their star had faded. Westward became the challengers from the east, but were defeated by the West Indians to set up a rematch of the previous year's final challenge match.

The West Indian squad was announced in the press with the rider that one of the players would have to make way for B Clarke who was travelling from New York to play the game. This caused controversy as the rules of the competition prohibited the selection of players who had competed for another club or were not either a resident of the club's city or had played five regular games for the club. Presumably the West Indians considered that Clarke, who had played against Toronto in the previous year's contest and played in the West Indians' last league game, was eligible as he had played for an American club, which obviously could not compete for the Trophy. Two trust officials travelled to the Westward Cricket Club grounds in Montréal to ensure that the contest's rules were complied with.

Without B Clarke the West Indians were forced to follow-on after making only 67 in reply to Toronto's 178. In a reverse of the previous year's contest the West Indians rallied in their second innings to make 220 and leave Toronto 110 to make for victory. The West Indians dropped at least seven chances[79] in Toronto's second innings of 114 for 6, which was enough to win the match by four wickets to regain the Trophy. The Toronto batsman Biggar top scored with 29, but was given not out for an appeal for a catch behind the wicket, which apparently surprised the batsman as well as the fielders[80]. Clearly players did not routinely walk when they knew they were out.

Unsurprisingly the West Indians were back as the challengers from the east in 1933, beating McGill in the final eliminator match by 145 runs, with Jemmott taking 8 for 37 in McGill's second innings. For the third successive year the final challenge match was played between the West Indians and the Toronto Cricket Club.

The eccentric Englishman Julien Cahn toured North America and Bermuda with his team in 1933. All the tourists were first-class cricketers and four of them had played Test cricket. They played 10 games in Canada, including two matches against Montréal and three games in Toronto, with their itinerary taking them into America when the final challenge of the Trophy match was played on Labor Day and the following day. The West Indian Jemmott played both games for the 15 men of Montréal, but 12 men of the Toronto Cricket Club were given their own match against the tourists, with many of them also playing for the team simply called Toronto. I suppose that it would have more difficult for the tourists, who were being entertained at Canada's most exclusive clubs, to play against the Montréal West Indians, a team made up of black porters.

Toronto Cricket Club scored a record 473 in their only innings to successfully defend their Trophy. The West Indians were described as

---

[79] The Toronto *Globe* of 7 Sep 1932 stated that JAK Rutherford finished undefeated but was missed off three successive balls and Biggar was dropped four times.
[80] This is according to the account of the *Montréal Gazette* of 7 September 1932. It is unclear if the West Indians always received fair decisions. In this match the redoubtable Fred Heather was one of the umpires, PJ Richards was the other.

being a shadow of their former selves, missing many of their key players, including Clarke who caused such controversy the previous year. Toronto won the game by an innings and 195 runs and were now the dominant team in Canada.

For the first time since their entry into the competition in 1927 the West Indians failed to qualify for the challenge stage in 1934. The Montréal Amateur Athletic Association beat Westward by five wickets to become the challengers from the east. In the west, Toronto ruthlessly dismissed the challenge from Rosedale, who could only make 97 in response to Toronto's huge 448, which included 197 from EF "Derby" Loney, so called because he had played first-class cricket for Derbyshire.

Unsurprisingly the Toronto Cricket Club retained the Trophy by comfortably defeating the Montréal Amateur Athletic Association by an innings and 162 runs, with LC Bell making 142 in Toronto's only innings of 275.

In 1935 McGill qualified for the challenge stage of the Trophy for the first time since losing the Trophy to the Toronto Cricket Club in 1929. It made no difference to the overall result of the competition with Toronto Cricket Club easily defeating Rosedale in their first challenge and then beating McGill by an innings and 82 runs in a single day. EF Loney took 4 for 20 and 8 for 27.

In 1936 Westmount were the challenger from the east (having presumably changed their name back again from Westward) and once again Rosedale were the challenger from the west. The two challenge matches were fitted into a tight schedule with Toronto playing Rosedale, rather unconventionally, on Wednesday 2 September and Saturday 5, before then taking on Westmount on Labor Day 7 September and Tuesday 8 September. Theoretically this put Toronto Cricket Club at a disadvantage, having to play two matches in quick succession. The players would have had little time to recover and would also have needed an understanding employer to permit the time off. It made no difference as Toronto Cricket Club won both games to retain the Trophy.

For the first time in decades the holders were obliged to make three defences of the Trophy in 1938, as St George's Society Cricket Club of Winnipeg made a challenge. The Montréal teams and Toronto teams were obliged to beat all other entrants in order to reach the challenge stage as usual, whilst for practical reasons the Winnipeggers were given a bye. They were also given the first challenge match against Toronto Cricket Club on the weekend of 15-6 July. They sensibly managed to arrange a warm-up game against a United Colleges XI the weekend before. It was to no avail as Toronto Cricket Club retained the Trophy, beating St George's Cricket Club, Broadview of Toronto and finally McGill on Labor Day and the day after.

The eliminator matches were played in the 1939 season, with Dentonia Park beating St George's of Hamilton and Grace Church beating Lincoln County in early July. The Canadian Government led by McKenzie-King asserted its independence by not declaring war on Germany until 10 September, a week after Britain. There would have been sufficient time to complete the 1939 competition before war was declared, but I can find no evidence of the challenge matches, though it is clear that Toronto Cricket Club retained the Trophy.

The Trophy was not contested from 1940-44, although Lieutenant Clarke Bell of the Canadian Active Service Force was quoted in the Ottawa Citizen of 19 September 1940 as having an average of 70.04 in 12 John Ross Robertson Trophy matches. Bell was killed on 19 August 1942 during the ill-fated raid on Dieppe. On 27 July 1945 the Toronto Globe reported that West Toronto Cricket Club had challenged Toronto Cricket Club for the John Ross Robertson Trophy. After a five year hiatus caused by the War, Canada's premier domestic cricket club competition was back in business.

The trophy continues to be played for today, although since 1982 the contest has been divided into two divisions: east and west, with the Manitoba-Ontario border being the dividing line. For a full list of winners see appendix 1.

Chapter 10: Canadian Cricket Since the War

"Cricket? Some East Indians play that here!"
Winnipeg Librarian

Don Bradman described the Brockton Oval ground in Vancouver as the most beautiful he had ever played on. The picture on the top is from the MCC tour in 1951, whilst the picture below shows a Tomalin Cup game in progress in September 2004 (photo from Howard Martin).

Cricket in Canada has been a fringe sport since the Second World War, sustained by immigrants from cricket playing nations. What steps can be taken to develop cricket in Canada into a national sport? The odds are stacked against it.

Following the Second World War, Canadian cricket was at a low ebb. Immigration from Britain increased as many Britons crossed the Atlantic to escape their ravaged homeland and, in many cases, to start a new life with a Canadian bride. Unfortunately, their arrival did not appear to reverse the decline of cricket in Canada and the game remained in the doldrums. That said, William Weighton, the renowned administrator of Canadian cricket, was one of these immigrants and he did more than most to rage against the dying of the light. Weighton was born in Glasgow in 1924 and trained as a navigator in the RAF in Manitoba. Like me, he had the good fortune to marry a Winnipegger and he settled there after the War. He became a tireless supporter of Manitoban and Canadian cricket, writing *Cricket our Weakness*, an account of the Provincial Tournaments after the War and the often quoted *The Story of 100 Years of Cricket in Manitoba* that was published in the *Manitoba Pageant* of Autumn 1974. Weighton also wrote a letter that was published in *The Cricketer* magazine of February 1974, correcting a wildly inaccurate editorial of the *Cricketer* Winter Annual. I replicate the letter in its entirety, as it is a wonderful example of how to allow a publication to correct an embarrassing mistake without losing face:

> *Sir,–Winnipeg cricketers were mortified to have been responsible for inflicting a nasty injury upon England's new skipper in the course of the Kent match here, and none more than this writer, a Scottish compatriot in whose home Mike and Molly Denness were at once welcome and charming visitors.*
>
> *To read in the Editor's news column in the Cricketer Winter Annual that the incident had cost Mike 'several teeth' was even more mortifying, especially since my recollection of the day's unfortunate events was that Mike had, indeed, had one tooth broken but had been assured by a specialist at the Manitoba Dental College that the damage was susceptible of repair and that the tooth could be salvaged. Mike, characteristically, refused to blame anyone but himself, although certainly the state of the pitch – which, incidentally, we hope to have replaced by a shale wicket next year – contributed to the injury sustained.*
>
> *But 'several teeth' missing to mar the friendly smile of this most engaging personality? Please say it isn't so! Manitoba cricket needs publicity, but not this kind of publicity!*

WILLIAM WEIGHTON
    Winnipeg, Canada

To this the editor could only respond as follows:

Another of the (fortunately rare) instances where we were quite unable to verify the accuracy of a news agency cable until some time after going to press. – Ed.

It should be noted that Weighton described himself as a "Scottish compatriot" and not a Canadian. Mike Denness, a Scottish captain of England, had a similar circle to square. When William Weighton died in August 2007 his obituary notice stated: "when an old person dies, a library is lost." I hope I have managed to preserve a small part of it.

In an attempt to revitalise the game, an MCC tour of Canada was organised in 1951. Unfortunately, this team was not of as high a quality as touring sides of the past. The captain was former England player and Middlesex skipper Walter Robins, but at the age of 45 his best years were behind him. In a newspaper interview Robins warned that his team were no better than an average county side and that Canadians should not expect the high standard of past tours.

The Canadian Cricket Association paid the costs of the tour, possibly explaining why each tourist had only $75 each spending money for the 40 days away[cxxvi]. Robins was reported in the press as stating: "I want my team to play the game in a way that will interest the most rabid baseball fan."

Baseball had surpassed cricket in popularity at the end of the nineteenth century and by the 1950s there were no players left who could remember when cricket had once challenged baseball as the nation's premier bat and ball game. The tourist Arthur Brodhurst wrote an account of the tour for the 1951 *Cricketer* Annual, where he stated that the Englishmen were surprised by the standard of the fielding, which he attributed to the cricketers playing baseball in their youth.

A game called Tippy, a hybrid of baseball and cricket, was played in Waterloo County, west of Toronto after the Second World War. The game had no stumps but involved two batters who had to swap ends to score. Perhaps the gap between the two games is not as wide as many people think[81]. At Lord's, the real tennis club used to encourage talented young cricketers on the ground staff to take up real tennis in the knowledge that many of them would not make the grade at cricket

---

[81] On page 224 of *Our Second American Adventure* Sir Arthur Conan Doyle stated that "I have all the prejudices of an old cricketer, and yet I cannot get away from the fact that baseball is the better game." There is a photograph of Doyle playing baseball at Jasper Park in 1914 and in 1923 he took his family to a game in Winnipeg. He was reported as supporting the introduction of baseball to Britain in the *New York Times* of 24 October 1924.

but had the potential to excel at real tennis, a fringe sport with only a few thousand players and fewer than 50 courts worldwide. Those running Canadian cricket should encourage young baseball players to take up cricket as a second string to their bow. Their fielding would be world class before they donned flannels for the first time. The great Barton King started off as a baseball player: his rare ability to be able to swing the ball both ways came from his experience as a baseball pitcher.

Montréal-based Scotsman Angus Bell, who wrote *Batting on the Bosphorus* – an account of seeking out cricketers in eastern and central Europe, suggests that now might be an opportune time to convert baseball players to cricket. He informed me that: "Baseball is dying in Canada, leaving a large number of empty fields and thousands of sporty people with skills and interest in a bat-ball game. The best fielders in our club have come from baseball/softball. They all prefer cricket. Youth clubs would do well to make a deal with the city authorities and baseball association to convert baseball fields to cricket."[cxxvii] If baseball is in decline, then Cricket Canada must seize the initiative and ensure that cricket fills the void. Angus also organises and plays cricket for the multi-national *Pirates of the St Lawrence*. All power to his elbow!

The highlight of the 1951 tour was the game the tourists played against a Canadian XI at Toronto on 8-9 September. As described in the previous chapter this was the inaugural first-class match played in Canada and was watched by a record 8,000 people. After matching the tourists 270 with a score of 260 in the first innings, the Canadians required 218 to win with only two sessions left. The English bowlers were too wily to allow the local batsmen to score at the requisite rate. They went for the win anyway and were bowled out for 76.

Three years later Hal Robinson led a Canadian tour to Britain. Their playing record of won 4, lost 3 and drawn 11 was comparable to other tours, although comparing the standard of the opposition with those of previous tours is practically impossible. Robinson was a former Oxford Blue and he recruited players that had recently emigrated from Britain, West Indies and Australia. Unlike the 1887 tour, the 1954 venture could not be said to reflect the standard of domestic cricket in Canada.

1947 saw the inaugural Interprovincial Tournament, which was contested again in 1948, 1949 and 1950, but after that only sporadically. The early tournaments involved Alberta, British Columbia, Manitoba, Ontario and Québec and they give gave an indication of the different strengths of domestic cricket in the provinces of Canada at that time. The first contest was won jointly by Ontario and British

Columbia and a list of winners can be found at appendix 2. Ontario would win the tournament 11 times, British Columbia and Québec three times each, and twice by Alberta. Manitoba was the weakest team, winning no games in the competition until 1950, when the tournament was held in Winnipeg and Manitoba defeated British Columbia by 5 wickets. Manitoba beat British Columbia again in 1952, but this time in contrived fashion: if British Columbia had beaten Manitoba they would have had to travel over a hundred miles to London to face Alberta. By deliberately losing to Manitoba the British Columbians ensured that they would face this team again in a semi-final in Toronto. The result stood, despite the clear disapproval of officials from the Canadian Cricket Association, indicating the weakness of this organisation. Ontario beat British Columbia in the final.

In 1959 the MCC toured Canada again under the leadership of Dennis Silk. This commemorated the centenary of the first international tour led by George Parr (see Chapter 4). It is regrettable that the 150th anniversary of this tour went unnoticed.

Cricket in Canada enjoyed something of a renaissance in the 1960s and 70s and at the heart of this was the administrator Donald King. In 1974 he received the MBE for services to Anglo-Canadian sport, illustrating the problem with Canadian cricket. It was a British game played by immigrants from Britain. Their children would play ice hockey or Canadian football. There was a lack of Canadian-born players and so cricket remained an un-Canadian game. Touring teams played against ex-pats who had learned the game in Britain or other Commonwealth countries. In the nineteenth century Canada may have been less independent of Britain, but its leading cricketers had been born in Canada. Following the Second World War, the nation may have been freer of British influence, but its cricketers were not.

The *Britishness* of the sport received a further challenge from the number of cricket-playing immigrants from the West Indies and Asia. The quality of these players was reflected in both the Canadian and American teams that squared off against each other in the oldest International cricket series, which was restarted in 1963 after a gap of over 50 years. As related in a previous chapter, the International Series continued to be played irregularly until 1995 but, fifteen years later, seems to be gone for good.

Canadian cricket had benefited from the tours from England, but it was clear that they were unsustainable for two reasons. Firstly, in an age where touring sides no longer play matches against local teams of a superior number, Canada did not have the players to provide enough of a challenge to professional cricketers from a Test-playing nation.

Secondly Canada's links with the mother country were loosening with the adoption of the national flag in 1965, the centennial celebrations of 1967 and perhaps more importantly the great increase in immigration from countries other than Britain. Canadian cricket mirrored this change by becoming more dependent on immigrants, firstly from the West Indies and then from Asia. This caused a great evolutionary change to cricket in Canada, which had always been synonymous with English culture. Now it became something different. Nothing illustrated this change more clearly than the anti-apartheid protests which dogged the Derrick Robins tour of 1976. Canada became a less attractive tour option for English players.

The Derrick Robins tour of 1976 should have been a great boon for Canadian cricket. A glance at the squad shows that it was the equivalent of an England A tour today, as it included the following young players on the threshold of their international careers: Bill Athey, Paul Downton, Mike Gatting, David Gower, Vic Marks and Chris Tavaré. The uneasy relationship between those British-born immigrants who ran the game and the increasing number of West Indian and Asian immigrant players was exposed, as many of the most talented players refused to play the tourists due to Robins' links to South Africa. An article written by the CCA President in the establishment-run *Canadian Cricketer* magazine condemned many Canadian cricketers' political reaction to the tour: this would hardly have helped to build bridges on an issue that was ripping the sport apart[82]. The tour also attracted protests from those who had no interest in cricket, the worst example being at Edmonton where 62 protesters were arrested.

Canada was awarded ICC Associate status in 1968 and, in 1979, travelled to Britain to take part in the ICC Trophy tournament in the knowledge that progression to the final would mean qualification for the second World Cup. When the first World Cup had been organised in 1974 the 11 Associate ICC nations were invited to select two teams from their ranks to compete with the six full members of Australia, England, India, New Zealand, Pakistan and the West Indies. The competition was a great success and so, when the next tournament was organised for 1979, there was enough interest from the Associate ICC nations to have their own competition to decide which two countries would compete in the main tournament.

There were 17 Associate countries at this time but the Hong Kong team was unable to meet the ICC player qualification due to its transient

---

[82] The President lamented that the 1976 season had been a "disaster" for Canadian cricket with leagues being threatened by the politicisation of the sport. See page 6 of *Canadian Cricketer* magazine October 1976.

population, West Africa failed to complete the entry form in time, and Gibraltar had to pull out at short notice as they were unable to raise a team. Gibraltar's place was taken by Wales, the only non-associate country taking part.[cxxviii] No sponsor could be found for the event, so all nations had to pay their own expenses, with the ICC paying the administrative costs.[83] A Trophy and accompanying medals were donated by JR Gardiner, Chairman and Secretary of the ICC Associate members' World Cup management Committee.

The ICC Trophy required 33 different grounds and 90 practise matches in addition to the 32 games played in the competition. The Midland Cricket Club Conference made the necessary arrangements and the Tournament commenced on 22 May, ending a little over a fortnight later to ensure that the two finalists could compete in the World Cup starting on 9 June. To help with the scheduling, the final of the ICC Trophy would be played on 21 June, a day after the final of the World Cup between the West Indies and England.

The 15 teams who played in the ICC Trophy were divided into three groups of five for the first round. The teams were of varied ability and some form of seeding must have taken place to ensure that all the best teams did not end up in the same group. Argentina, Fiji, Israel and Malaysia lost all their games, discounting those matches which were abandoned due to the weather. Argentina's cricketers appear to have been either British citizens working for British companies and Embassies or the descendants of British or Commonwealth settlers. Teams from England had visited Argentina in 1911, 1926, 1930, 1938, 1959 and 1965: presumably this sporting link was severed after the Falklands conflict and Argentine cricket went into decline. Fiji's cricketers travelled 12,000 miles to play in the tournament only to be defeated in all the games they played – and to read a patronising article in the press declaring disappointment that they did not play in grass skirts. Israeli cricket was dependent on immigrants from cricketing countries and, due to the lack of open spaces in Israel, cricket was played in football stadia on matting wickets. Israeli cricketers had toured England and Ireland in 1970 and 1974, but they lost all the games they played in the Tournament, although they were awarded the game against Sri Lanka, as their opponents refused to play them for political reasons. The separation of Malaysia and Singapore in 1965 appears to have spread their talent too thinly: the Malaysian team lost all its completed matches and Singapore only

---

[83] p.15 of the Victoria and District Cricket Association 1979 Handbook states that the ICC offered a grant to help cover the expenses, whilst the *Guardian* of 22 May 1979 states that all expenses were met by the nations themselves.

managed one victory, by a single wicket against Argentina, who, as already mentioned, lost all its games.

The two best teams in Group 1 were Bermuda and East Africa. The Bermuda cricket club was formed in 1845 and Bermuda had been toured by teams from Australia, England, New Zealand, Pakistan and the West Indies. East Africa consisted of Kenya, Tanzania, Uganda and Zambia and became an Associate ICC member in 1966. The presence of the East African team at the first World Cup in 1975 was its only appearance. Bermuda beat East Africa by 9 wickets to progress to the semi-finals.

Group 1

	ARG	BER	EAFR	PNG	SING	Points
Argentina	-	Lost 9 wkts	Lost 5 wkts	Draw	Lost 1 wkt	2
Bermuda	Won 9 wkts	-	Won 9 wkts	Won 7 wkts	Draw	14
East Africa	Won 5 wkts	Lost 9 wkts	-	Draw	Won 5 wkts	10
Papua New	Draw	Lost 7 wkts	Draw	-	Won 87 runs	8
Singapore	Won 1 wkt	Draw	Lost 5 wkts	Lost 87 runs	-	6

Group 2 had three teams with realistic ambitions of qualification for the World Cup: Bangladesh, Canada and Denmark. Bangladesh came into being as a country in 1971 and was awarded ICC Associate status in 1977. Before independence New Zealand (1955-6), the West Indies (1958-9), Australia (1959-60) and England (1961-2 & 1968-9) had all played in Dacca. In 1979 the team clearly was not yet the force it would later become. The success of Sri Lanka presumably helped to spur them on towards full ICC membership. Denmark's first official national cricket team played its inaugural game in 1954 against Oxford University and they became an Associate member of the ICC in 1966. Denmark's cricketers beat Holland for the first time in 1972 and appear to have punched above their weight in the Tournament, winning all their group matches easily to qualify for the semi-finals. In 1975 Eastern Canada had beaten the touring Australians, who were en route to the inaugural World Cup. Franklyn Dennis top scored with an unbeaten 58 and he was part of the Canadian team in the 1979 competition. The *Observer* of 10 June 1979 estimated that 70% of cricket in Canada was played by those of West Indian descent, 15% Indian or Pakistani and only 15% English. Canada defeated Bangladesh by 49 runs and qualified for the semi-finals as the best runner-up of the three groups. This would not be the last time that Canada beat Bangladesh.

Group 2

	BAN	CAN	DEN	FIJ	MAL	Points
Bangladesh	-	Lst 49 runs	Lst 10 runs	Won 22 runs	Won 7 wkts	8
Canada	Won 49 runs	-	Lst 46 runs	Won 56 runs	Won 44 runs	12
Denmark	Won 10 runs	Won 46 runs	-	Won 8 wkts	Won 7 wkts	16
Fiji	Lst 22 runs	Lst 56 runs	Lost 8 wkts	-	Draw	2
Malaysia	Lost 7 wkts	Lst 44 runs	Lst 7 wkts	Draw	-	2

The ICC Trophy became a regular event and Gibraltar hold the current record of having played 33, won 6 and lost 27 in all competitions. Gibraltar's replacement by a talented Welsh team was unfair to the other sides in Group 3. Strictly speaking Wales was not allowed to accumulate any points in the competition, as it was not a member of the ICC, and so could not have qualified for the semi-finals. However, its presence made it more difficult for the teams of Group 3 to qualify as the best runner-up. Wales never has become a member of the ICC. Ireland became an ICC Association Member in 1993 and Scotland joined in 1994. The best Irish and Scottish players can play for England as well, making a nonsense of the name "England" and creating an anomaly: if Scottish and Northern Irish cricketers can play for a team which is Britain in all but name, then surely it is unfair to have Scotland and Ireland competing as separate entities. The solution is to rename England as England & Wales and restrict the team to English and Welsh players. If Ireland had the services of players like Ed Joyce and Eoin Morgan their case for full ICC membership would be greatly strengthened.

Holland had beaten the Australians in a one day game at The Hague in 1964 and had an experienced South African coach in Dik Abed. He had played for many years as a professional in the Lancashire League and would represent Holland four times in the 1982 ICC Trophy. Holland's hopes of qualification for the World Cup were all but ended in its first game against Wales where the Dutch limped to 59 for 2 off 30 overs, chasing 171 for victory, before rain intervened. Holland lost the game, and all realistic chances of progressing to the semi-finals, due to a slower run rate.

Most of the best cricket played in America was played on the east coast around Philadelphia and New York. The Americans had beaten Canada by 22 runs in the International match the previous year and would have felt that their chances of qualification were at least as good as that of Canada's. They were unfortunate to be in such a strong Group.

The Sri Lankan team was the clear favourites to win the tournament. Its national side regularly played against teams who were either going to or returning from playing Test cricket on the sub-continent, but the Sri Lankan Government's decision not to permit their team to play against Israel almost cost their cricketers dear. Sri Lanka managed to progress from the group stage only due to a better run rate than the United States. The game between the US and the Dutch was drawn due to the weather, but if the Americans had won, which would have been the most likely result, Sri Lanka would have been eliminated despite comfortably winning all the games it played.

Group 3

	HOL	ISR	SRI	US	WAL	Points
Holland	-	Won 8 wkts	Lost 45 runs	Draw	Lost RR	6
Israel	Lost 8 wkts	-	Won*	Lost 41 runs	Lost 91 runs	4
Sri Lanka	Won 45 runs	Lost*	-	Won 6 wkts	Draw	10
United States	Draw	Won 41 runs	Lost 6 wkts	-	Won 8 runs	10
Wales	Won RR	Won 91 runs	Draw	Lst 8 runs	-	10

RR = Run Rate *Game forfeited by Sri Lanka

Presumably the draw for the semi-final was done on merit to ensure that the two unbeaten teams, Denmark and Bermuda, avoided each other. Sri Lanka's decision to forfeit the game against Israel meant that Canada did not have to beat the best side in the competition to qualify for the World Cup. Canada's semi-final match against Bermuda was keenly contested and Canada managed to bowl out the islanders for 181. JN Valentine was the key bowler, taking only one wicket, but delivering his 12 overs for a miserly 13 runs. In reply Canada slumped to 62 for 5 before a 111 run partnership between the wicket-keeper and captain BM Mauricette(72) and Tariq Javed(47*) brought them to within 9 runs of victory, which was duly achieved by 4 wickets in the penultimate over. Bermuda would not qualify for its first World Cup until 2003. Inevitably Sri Lanka beat Denmark in the other semi-final, by the huge margin of 208 runs. To date Denmark has never qualified for the World Cup and finished bottom of the tournament to determine qualification for the 2011 competition.

As already stated, the two finalists, Canada and Sri Lanka, did not actually contest the final until after the main event – the World Cup – was over. The expectations of the two teams were very different. Sri Lanka was playing in its second consecutive World Cup and its players were aiming to prove themselves worthy of full ICC membership. Canada, on the other hand, gave the appearance of amateur players who were delighted to be there. The *Montréal Gazette* of 18 June 1979 stated that the Canadian cricketers had "made numerous friends with their positive approach and the exuberant manner in which they enjoyed the experience of playing against the world's top test cricket countries." The realistic expectations of the Canadians were summed up by their opening bowler John Valentine. The summer had been wet and, unusually for an opening bowler, Valentine hoped that the wickets remained soft, reasoning: "It's our batsmen I'm thinking of. There are a lot of bowlers a lot faster than me in some of the other teams, and I want my buddies to stay alive."

Being able to select the best players is a constant challenge for amateur teams, as the older cricketers are likely to have responsibilities that will prevent them from taking an extended unpaid holiday just to play cricket, even for their national team. Robert Calendar was one such player. He had played in Eastern Canada's victory over Australia in 1975, taking 4 for 39 in 10 overs and on merit alone would have been a certain selection for the ICC Trophy. However, he could not get the five weeks necessary off from work so had not been included in the original squad. When Canada qualified for the World Cup he was sent for, as two weeks off was acceptable to his employer. He missed the first game against Pakistan, but played in the matches against England and Australia.

John Arlott declared in the *Guardian* of 9 June 1979 that the Canadian team was "hardly the quality of Sri Lanka" and mentioned its odds of winning the tournament as 1,000-1. The assessment was a fair one, as Sri Lanka made an excellent case for full member status by defeating India by 47 runs. Canada, on the other hand, was soundly beaten by Pakistan, England and Australia. Canada's total of 45 was the lowest ever score in a World Cup, until Canada beat this in 2003. Despite the soft pitches John Valentine succeeded in taking a wicket in every match, finishing with a tournament average of 22 and an economy rate of 3.47, an impressive performance considering the standard of the opposition, as demonstrated by the tournament averages of his teammates.

Sri Lanka's efforts were rewarded with full ICC membership in 1981 and suddenly Canadian entry into the game's elite group did not look so far away. This was an illusion. In the mid-twentieth century the standards were lower as there were fewer professionals, thus making it easier to develop a team that could compete at international level, especially against sides below the top tier, but the Packer revolution in the late 70s meant that more cricketers could make a living from the game and those at the very top could earn the amounts we now expect sport stars to be awarded. Playing standards improved and the gulf grew between the top tier which had professional players and the second rung which did not. In 2009, Cricket Canada, the new name for the Canadian Cricket Association, made the national captain Ashish Bagai the first cricketer to be given a central contract by the Board. If Canadian cricket is to compete at the highest level more such contracts must be awarded.

To attempt to compete on the international stage, the Canadian Cricket Association started employing players who lived in a full ICC member nation, but happened to qualify for Canada. All national teams select the best team that the rules allow and had the Canadian Cricket Association not followed suit they could not have hoped to compete amongst the second tier teams. Those questioning the commitment of such players should examine the example of John Davison who was born in Vancouver Island, where his Australian parents were teaching, before going home to Australia when he was only five weeks old. He played state cricket for Victoria but was never likely to play for the Australian national team. In 1999 the Canadian Cricket Association managed to secure his services as a coach and he was soon playing for Canada. Davison sacrificed time and income to represent his adopted country and was rewarded with participation in the 2003 and 2007 World Cups. He hit the fastest century in World Cup history in 2003, taking just 67 deliveries to bring up his ton against the West Indies. At the age of 39 he once again donned the red of Canada to travel to South Africa in 2009 to help them qualify for the 2011 World Cup. He smashed 131 off just 99 balls against Namibia and few would have complained had he returned home when an injury ended his participation in the tournament before the super eight stage. He remained to cheer on his teammates who finished runners-up in the tournament, behind Ireland. More importantly they became one of the four teams, out of the twelve competitors, to qualify for the 2011 World Cup.

The 2003 World Cup was marred by politics, in particular the belated decision taken by England not to play in Zimbabwe. In August 2002 Aeneas Chigwedere, Zimbabwe's Education, Sports and Culture Minister accused Australia, England and Canada of trying to persuade countries not to play against Zimbabwe in the forthcoming World Cup. Unlike Australia and England, Canada had not been drawn in the same group as Zimbabwe so, assuming that Chigwedere's allegations were true, Canada's participation in the proposed boycott is intriguing. Australia decided to play against Zimbabwe and went on to win the tournament.

On the whole Canada had a good tournament. For the first time in its history Canada beat a Test-playing nation in a meaningful competition. In a repetition of the victory in the ICC Trophy competition of 1979, Canada beat Bangladesh by 60 runs. Bookmakers were offering odds of only 1-7 on a Bangladesh victory[cxxix], so the result was a major upset. Associate members need to beat those in the top tier to achieve full ICC membership themselves, so this victory was seen by some as step towards the game's elite. A 9-wicket humiliation at the hand of Sri Lanka shattered this illusion, as Canada was bowled out for 36, the lowest score made by any team in the World Cup.

The ICC does not determine whether a country is worthy of full ICC membership by merit alone: if it did, Ireland would already be part of that exclusive club. It is very unlikely that full membership will ever be awarded to a country where cricket is not a national sport. The results on the international stage should be seen as a means to encourage the growth of the sport in Canada. There is no denying that participation in the World Cup helps promote the game, generating funding and sponsorship opportunities[84], but good results on their own will not achieve promotion to the sport's elite. For Test-playing nations, the performance of the national team is the be all and end all, but for Canada it can only be a means to an end: this is what made the defeat by Sri Lanka so frustrating. The momentum gained following the victory against Bangladesh was totally lost and the status of "minnows" reaffirmed.

When Canada qualified for the 2007 World Cup, the CCA was awarded funding which had to be spent on employing a new coach, in this case the former Nottinghamshire bowler Andy Pick. This unfortunately meant that the existing coach, who had achieved qualification, lost his position.[cxxx] Canada was comfortably beaten in all three of its matches and the seven-wicket defeat by fellow Associate members Kenya would have been the most disappointing. Whilst Canada's bowlers let themselves down, scores of 198 all out against Kenya, 228-7 against England and 249-9 against New Zealand showed a promising

---

[84] But these opportunities need to be taken. Somehow Canada failed to find a sponsor for the 2003 World Cup, which made it difficult for the team to pay its flight costs and living expenses.

consistency of batting. The fact that Canada has qualified for its third World Cup in a row also shows a consistency matched only by Kenya and the Netherlands, amongst the ICC Associate nations. Cricket Canada needs to exploit this success and media coverage is crucial to this. If the national team can spring an upset then cricket may move from its niche pay per view market into national coverage.

*   *   *   *   *   *   *   *   *

I cannot, indeed I feel a must not, end my book without referring to women's cricket in Canada. The earliest reference that I have found of women playing organised cricket in Canada is of a match in August 1889. The game was played in London on the Asylum Grounds between a women's side and the local men's team[cxxxi]. The men had to play left-handed and both teams ended up scoring 70 runs each, suggesting that the result was contrived. The captain of the women's team was Louise Shanly, the younger sister of Cuthbert and Coote Shanly who played for Toronto Cricket Club. Coote was also the assistant manager, umpire and emergency player on the 1887 tour of Britain. One of Louise's fellow bowlers was a Miss Bethune, presumably related to HJ Bethune, also of Toronto Cricket Club. In 1896 a similar game was played between a team made up of nurses and doctors' daughters and the London Asylum Cricket Club one of the leading clubs of the time. The men had to bat with broomsticks and the women's team was victorious.

The earliest reference that I have found of a competitive game between two women's teams is June 1891 between East Toronto and West Toronto. There was a similar fixture played between men's team with eligibility dependent on whether the player lived east or west of Yonge Street. This was a serious two innings match that was played on the Toronto Cricket Club's ground on Bloor Street and the well known cricketer WJ Fleury umpired for West Toronto, who were represented by no fewer that three women by the name of Shanly. Louise Shanly was one of them and her sister Frances was probably another, although the press report only gives her initials making it impossible to be certain. West Toronto won the game by seven runs.

In June 1901 Havergal Ladies College beat Rosedale Ladies College by 40 runs to 30. This game was reported in both the *Globe* and the *Toronto Star* and although the reporting of the match was minimal, at least there were no comments of this as an oddity, suggesting that other games were played that went unreported.

The Women's Cricket Association was set up in England in 1926 and in a few years presided over a thriving movement with hundreds of members and several teams. The *Toronto Star* of 15 October 1929 stated that women's cricket lagged behind their English counterparts, but women of the Toronto Cricket Club played alongside men. No mention was made of any clubs and so it must be assumed that to play any cricket, female players were required to play in a man's team. In 1934-5 a women's team from England toured Australia and New Zealand and not for the first time Canadian cricket was lagging behind its Commonwealth counter-parts.

In 1994 Andrena Baksh and Ave Mogan first established a women's cricket programme in Canada, with the intention of participating in the 1997 Women's World Cup. Unfortunately Canada has not yet competed at this level. Ave Mogan remains at the forefront of women's cricket in Canada and re-started the women's programme in 2004.

Ave Mogan was the Vice-Captain of a combined Canada and United States team which competed in the 2003 West Indies Ladies[85] Championships held in Grenada. Sisters Jeanine and Maryse Barrate of Virden, Manitoba ensured that Canadians from outside Ontario were represented. The combined North American XI competed against St. Lucia, Guyana, Trinidad & Tobago, Grenada, Jamaica and St. Vincent & the Grenadines.

In 2007 Canada, captained by the 55 year old wicket-keeper Janet John-Dorrie, won the inaugural ICC Americas women's championship when they defeated Bermuda by five wickets on 22 August. The other teams in the tournament were Argentina and Trinidad & Tobago. Canada won the 2009 Americas Regional Championship, which earned them the right to compete against the United States for a place in the Women's World Cup qualifier tournament in 2012. The Americans won the series.

This year a women's team called Kaisoca took part in the fourth division of the Toronto and District Men's league and in 2011 the same league is planning a women's division with at least five competing teams. All power to their elbows!

*   *   *   *   *   *   *   *   *

The odds are against cricket becoming a national sport in Canada. The fact that the Canadian cricket season takes place at the same time as England's has made Canada a less attractive destination for English players and coaches. It has also denied talented Canadian players an

---

[85] The word "ladies" is as dated as the term "gentlemen" and has a patronising air to it. I prefer the word "women's".

English venue in the Canadian off-season. Perhaps Cricket Canada can send some of their young talent to countries such as India, Australia or South Africa, where cricket is played during the Canadian winter.

Canada's extreme climate means that the sport is forced to compete with all other outdoor games, such as Canadian football, which in a temperate climate would be played in winter. A glance at the figures below, showing the funding that Canadian sports associations receive from the Government, indicates the challenge facing Cricket Canada:

	Funding in 06/07	Funding in 07/08	Funding in 08/09	Funding in 09/10
Cricket Canada	$ 40,000	$ 77,000	$80,550	$128,500
Canadian Rugby Union	$816,958	$613,500	$633,500 + $49,999 hosting programme	$603,500 + $49,999
Canadian Soccer Association	$1,430,008	$3,355,271	$1,476,000	$2,162,070

Rugby and soccer are both fringe sports with a similar status to cricket in Canada, but receive far more funding from the Government.

Theodore Roosevelt stated that "There is no room in this country for hyphenated Americanism", but the opposite is true north of the border. Canadians are unable to fill out just "Canadian" on their census form; they must enter their ancestral roots. On my first visit to Winnipeg I was surprised to find a Belgian war memorial on Provencher Boulevard. It is truly amazing that a Canadian city has a Belgian quarter. If America has a melting pot, Canada has a tossed salad where each person retains his or her ancestral identity. This characteristic has ensured the survival of cricket in Canada, as immigrants retain their national identity and their sports. The challenge is to make cricket break out from these enclaves by convincing other Canadians to play the game.

In describing the current state of cricket in Canada, Angus Bell states that: "Sadly, most clubs are drawn along racial lines, so if you're not from the country or region, you're not welcome."[cxxxii]: this does nothing to encourage the wider public to get involved. This is not just a Canadian problem, as a glance at the Bradford leagues in England indicates, but if any country can encourage integration without loss of identity, it is multi-cultural Canada.

The solution is to develop cricket amongst the young, because unlike adults, children do not care who they play with. I understand that the Royal Bank of Canada has supported cricket by giving equipment to thousands of schools across the country. This form of sponsorship is necessary, especially given the lack of Government support, but much work still needs to be done to ensure that school kids are able to make the next step and start playing club cricket.

Another issue is that of residents supporting the national team of their ancestral roots, instead of the team where they live. In Canada this phenomenon arguably helped cricket, as it made Toronto a suitable venue for India versus Pakistan matches. Encouraging support for the Canadian national team amongst these cricket fans ought to be encouraged by everyone, because Canada is rarely in direct competition with these teams. Asian cricket fans in England, who support the Indian, Pakistan or Sri Lankan teams, have found themselves criticised by those arguing that they should support England. This attitude - that these supporters are un-British - is epitomised in the infamous Norman Tebbit's cricket test. I have no desire to open that particular can of worms, only to note that in Canada this should not be an issue, as contests are rare between the Canadian national team and those Asian teams in the top tier. Canadians generally view these things as a less of threat anyway.

Canada's size, climate and immigration from non-cricket playing nations have all combined to prevent cricket from reaching the same level of national importance enjoyed in other Commonwealth nations. Cricket is a complicated game and, like learning a language, much easier taught to children than to adults. If the game can be taught not just in schools but also in local clubs throughout the nation, then the dream of turning cricket from a sport that is played by small groups of first generation immigrants to a national pastime can be realised.

Appendix 1: Winners of the Ross Robertson Trophy

Date	Holders	Notes
1910	Rosedale Cricket Club	Became the first holders by virtue of winning Toronto's City League in 1910
1911	Toronto Cricket Club	Beat Rosedale and then had to defend the Trophy twice in order to be crowned champions for 1911.
1912	Toronto Cricket Club	Defeated Rosedale and Winnipeg
1913	Winnipeg Wanderers	Defeated Toronto Cricket Club in the final challenge match of the season.
1914	Winnipeg Wanderers	Beat Grace Church. The War meant they avoided having to face Montréal's McGill University
1915-19	Winnipeg Wanderers	Uncontested due to the First World War
1920	Yorkshire Society Cricket Club	Beat Winnipeg Wanderers.
1921	Yorkshire Society Cricket Club	Beat Albions Cricket Club
1922	McGill Cricket Club	Beat Yorkshire Society CC in final challenge match of the season
1923	McGill Cricket Club	
1924	McGill Cricket Club	By beating Toronto in the final challenge match McGill became the first club to successfully defend the Trophy two years in a row
1925	McGill Cricket Club	Beat Albions Cricket Club by 8 wickets
1926	McGill Cricket Club	
1927	McGill Cricket Club	
1928	McGill Cricket Club	Final challenge match against Bell Telephones not completed, who refused to enter 1929 competition
1929	Toronto Cricket Club	Beat McGill by an innings and 213 runs
1930	Toronto Cricket Club	Beat West Indians of Montréal by 4 wickets
1931	West Indians Cricket Club	Beat Toronto by 7 wickets
1932	Toronto Cricket Club	Beat West Indians by 4 wickets
1933	Toronto Cricket Club	Beat West Indians by an innings and 195 runs, after scoring a record 473.

Year	Club	Notes
1934	Toronto Cricket Club	
1935	Toronto Cricket Club	Beat McGill
1936	Toronto Cricket Club	Beat Rosedale by an innings and 58 runs with EF "Derby" Loney taking 7 for 35
1939-1944	Toronto Cricket Club	Uncontested
1945	Toronto Cricket Club	West Toronto challenged for the Trophy
1946	Toronto Cricket Club	
1947	Toronto Cricket Club	
1948	Yorkshire Society Cricket Club	Beat Toronto by 70 runs
1949	Yorkshire Society Cricket Club	
1950	Yorkshire Society Cricket Club	
1951	East Toronto Cricket Club	
1952	East Toronto Cricket Club	
1953	Yorkshire Society Cricket Club	
1954	Yorkshire Society Cricket Club	
1955	Toronto Cricket Club	Beat Yorkshire by 144 runs, with Alan Percival making 120*
1956	Toronto Cricket Club	
1957	Toronto Cricket Club	
1958	Yorkshire Cricket Club	
1959	Adastrians Cricket Club	From Montréal
1960	Yorkshire Cricket Club	
1961	Yorkshire Cricket Club	
1962	West Indian Cricket Club	From Toronto
1963	West Indian Cricket Club	From Toronto
1964	West Indian Cricket Club	From Toronto
1965-67	West Indian Cricket Club	Uncontested
1968	Toronto Cricket Club	
1969	Toronto Cricket Club	
1970	Toronto Cricket Club	

1971	Toronto Cricket Club	
1972	Toronto Cricket Club	
1973	West Indian Cricket Club	From Toronto
1974	West Indian Cricket Club	From Toronto
1975	West Indian Cricket Club	From Toronto
1976	Toronto Cricket Club	Beat Vancouver Island
1977	West Indian Cricket Club	From Toronto
1978	Vancouver Cricket Club	First Club from British Columbia to win the Trophy
1979	West Indian Cricket Club	From Toronto
1980	Toronto Cricket Club	
1981	Sportsman's CC	From Edmonton
1982(E)	Yorkshire Cricket Club	From Toronto
1982(W)	Regina Cricket Club	First team from Saskatchewan to win the Trophy
1983(E)	Defence Cricket Club	From Ottawa
1983(W)	Antilles Cricket Club	From Edmonton
1984(E)	Commonwealth Cricket Club	From Toronto
1984(W)	Lions Cricket Club	From Winnipeg
1985(E)	Overseas Cricket Club	From Toronto
1985(W)	Incogs Cricket Club	From Toronto
1986(E)	Cambridge Cricket Club	From Ontario?
1986(W)	Cosmos Cricket Club	From Winnipeg
1987(E)	Grace Church Cricket Club	From Toronto
1987(W)	Brockton Point CC (Vancouver) & Cosmos CC	Shared the title
1988(E)	Guelph Cricket Club	From Ontario
1988(W)	Brockton Point CC	From Vancouver
1989(E)	Guelph Cricket Club	
1989(W)	Cosmos Cricket Club	
1990(E)	Guelph Cricket Club	
1990(W)	Lions Cricket Club	
1991(E)	Vikings Cricket Club	From Toronto
1991(W)	Strathcona Cricket Club	From Edmonton
1992(E)	Vikings Cricket Club	From Toronto

1992(W)	Meralomas Cricket Club	From Vancouver
1993(E)	Verdun-Montréal Cricket Club	
1993(W)	Meralomas Cricket Club	
1994(E)	Kaiteur Cricket Club	From Kitchener, Ontario
1994(W)	Queen City Cricket Club	From Regina, Sask.
1995(E)	Cavaliers Cricket Club	From Toronto
1995(W)	Meralomas Cricket Club	From Vancouver
1996(E)	Grace Church Cricket Club	From Toronto
1996(W)	Gujarat Cricket Club	From Edmonton
1997(E)	Cavaliers Cricket Club	From Toronto
1997(W)	Ismaili Cricket Club	From Vancouver
1998(E)	Kaiteur Cricket Club	
1998(W)	Ismaili Cricket Club	
1999(E)	Victoria Park Cricket Club	From Toronto
1999(W)	Ismaili Cricket Club	
2000(E)	Victoria Park Cricket Club	From Toronto
2000(W)	Victoria Park Cricket Club	From Edmonton

In 1982 the Trophy was divided into an east and a west division.
Information taken from:
http://www.canadiancricket.org/images/glawards.pdf

Appendix 2: Winners of Canada's Interprovincial Tournament

Date	Venue	Winner
1947	Toronto	Ontario and British Columbia
1948	Vancouver	Ontario
1949	Calgary & Edmonton	Alberta
1950	Winnipeg	Ontario
1952	Toronto	Ontario
1955	Vancouver	Ontario
1961	Calgary	British Columbia
1964	Montréal	Ontario
1967	Ottawa	Québec
1971	Toronto	Ontario
1975	Calgary	Ontario
1977	Toronto	Ontario
1978	Winnipeg	Québec
1981	Edmonton	Alberta
1983	Vancouver	Ontario
1986	Winnipeg	Ontario
1990	Ottawa	Québec
1994	Vancouver	British Columbia

From 1947 to 1981 it was known as the Hiram Walker Trophy. From 1983 it became known as the Bracht Trophy, after Ed Bracht.

Appendix 3: Time Line For Canadian Cricket

Date	Event
1785	Reference to cricket in Montréal
1827	York Cricket Club set up, renamed Toronto Cricket Club in 1834
1828	St Johns Cricket Club founded in Newfoundland
1829	Two garrison teams place at Montréal
	Upper Canada College (UCC) founded
1834	Guelph play Toronto Cricket Club at Hamilton
1836	Upper Canada College Cricket Club founded
1840	New York's St George's Cricket Club play Toronto Cricket Club
1844	International Series starts
1846	International Series suspended after an on-field dispute
1853	The International Series resumes
1859	George Parr's professionals tour North America
1868	Ed Willsher's team tour North America
1872	Fitzgerald's MCC team, including WG Grace, tour North America
1874	Halifax Tournament is won by Philadelphia
1879	Daft's team tour North America
1879	Ireland tour North America
1879	International Series resumes, first match since 1865
1880	First Canadian cricket tour of Britain
1887	Second Canadian cricket tour of Britain
1888	Ireland tour North America
1892	Canadian Cricket Association set-up
1892	Ireland tour North America
1898	PF Warner's XI tour Canada
1909	Ireland tour North America
1912	Last international match played until 1963
1922	Norman Seagram's Canadians tour Britain
1932	Australians, including Don Bradman, tour Canada
1936	RC Matthews XI tour Britain
1951	MCC Tour Canada
1957	Toronto Cricket Club merges with the Skating and Curling Club
1959	MCC Tour Canada to mark the 100th anniversary of the 1859 tour
1967	MCC Tour Canada as part of the 100th anniversary of confederation
1968	Canada awarded ICC Associate status
1973	Ireland tour North America

1975	Australians tour Canada, losing to Eastern Canada
1976	DH Robins tour of Canada, marred by protests
1979	Canada reach the ICC Trophy final and so qualify for World Cup in the same year
2003	Canada play in their second World Cup
2007	Canada play in their third World Cup
2008	Scotiabank agree to sponsor domestic cricket
2009	Canada qualify for the 2011 World Cup

Appendix 4: Who's Who of Canadian Cricket

Name	Notes
ACKLAND, Henry	Played in six International matches against the United States from 1896 to 1909, with an average of 14.10 and a top score of 54. He kept wicket in the games that Saunders did not play in. He scored 109 for Rideau against Ottawa in August 1896.
BABER, Walter Crosbie	Played in five International matches against the United States from 1899 to 1909. He could only manage an average of 12.8 in his ten innings, with a top score of 33, but he secured 12 wickets with best figures of 5 for 44. Baber was a witness at the wedding of Hugh Cyril Hill, his Canadian teammate in 1899 and 1903. He signed-up for the First World War in December 1915, enlisting with the 148th Battalion.
BARBER, George Anthony	Known as the father of Canadian cricket for his involvement in the setting up of both the Toronto Cricket Club and the Upper Canada College Cricket Club. Many of the notable Canadian cricketers in the nineteenth century played for one or even both of these two institutions. In the 1830s Barber played in many of the earliest matches in Canada for which scorecards exist. He played in the first International match in 1844 and then umpired in two International matches in 1846 and 1853.
BARRON, F W	Joined the staff of Upper Canada College in 1834 and would later become Principal. He played for the UCC against Toronto in their first match in 1836, with two other masters, George Barber and John Kent.
BELL, Benjamin Taylor A	Played once in the International Series in 1886 where he only managed to make eight runs. Domestically he was more successful, making a total of 1,036 runs in the 1886 season at an average of 35.21. Wisden called him a "splendid field at cover point".
BOULTON, Reverend William	Taught cricket at Upper Canada College. Uncle of WH Boulton below. Died of typhoid fever in 1834 aged just 28.
BOULTON, William Henry	Played for Toronto Cricket Club in the 1830s. His public support of the Canadian cricket team in the International Series furthered his political ambitions. He served two terms as Mayor of Toronto.

BOYD, Mossom Martin	Played ten times for Canada in the International Series from 1882-95, but could only manage a disappointing average of 8.06 in his 19 innings, with a top score of 58. He scored 113 not out for Canadian Zingari v Pittsburg in August 1885. His father was also a cricketer and was also called Mossom and played for the Upper Canada College
COOPER, Walter Henry	Played four times for Canada in the International Series from 1896 to 1901, he averaged 21.63 with a top score of 40. He played for a variety of clubs, scoring centuries for Toronto in 1896, Trinity Rovers in 1897, Moinico Asylum in 1899 and Rosedale in 1901. He did not bowl in the Series, but he took four wickets against the visiting Australians in 1893, opening the bowling with JM Laing. He was killed in WW1 at Vimy Ridge.
COUNSELL, Jack L	Played four times in the International Series from 1898 to 1904, achieving a disappointing average of 10.88. He was an occasional bowler and took a total of three wickets, bowling in three matches in the Series. He scored two centuries in domestic cricket, one for a Canadian XI against Chatham in July 1898 and one for Hamilton v Guelph in August 1900.
FERRIE, Robert Bown	A fine opening bowler, with a fast round-arm action, who overcame injury to enjoy a good tour of Britain in 1887. He played in six International matches from 1881-90, taking 29 wickets for a miserly average of 8.14. He usually opened the bowling with Alec Gillespie in these matches.
FLEURY, William James	Played in nine matches during the 1887 tour of Britain. His average of 17.17 placed him sixth in the batting averages with a top score of 56 not out against Staffordshire. He played twice in the International Series in 1890 and 1892, where he bagged a pair. His average in the Series was a disappointing 2. He scored a century for Toronto against Rosedale in July 1888 and another for Ontario v Québec. He toured Britain again in 1910 as captain of Toronto Zingari. This was the first tour of the UK by a Canadian cricket club.
GILBERT, Walter Raleigh	Cousin of WG Grace. According to www.cricketarchive.com he played for Canada in one of their games during their first tour of Britain in 1880. He emigrated to Canada in 1886 to avoid a scandal involving charges of theft from his

	teammates' dressing room. He scored a century for Halifax Wanderers in July 1887 and two centuries for Montréal in June 1897 and September 1900.
GILLESPIE, Alexander	Played in a record 14 matches in the International Series from 1881-1901, where he took 48 wickets at an average of 11.04. He also toured Britain in 1887, visiting Scotland to trace his ancestral roots at the end of tour. Gillespie was educated at the UCC, but he didn't start bowling until his last year at the College; his bowling style was medium pace. He scored two centuries for Hamilton against Toronto; the first in July 1881 and the second in August 1892. Like his father, George H Gillespie, Alexander was a keen curler and played for Toronto Curling Club.
GOLDINGHAM, Percy Clarke	Played eight times in the International Series from 1891 to 1899. He averaged 14.21 with a top score of 50. He scored four centuries for Toronto.
HALL, John E	Secretary of the Canadian Cricket Association and co-author of the 1895 book "Sixty Years of Canadian Cricket with RO McCulloch.
HANSARD, Hugh H	He played once in the International Series in 1893 and though he failed he arguably would have represented Canada more times had he not lived in St John, New Brunswick. He scored the first century made in the Maritimes in July 1892 for St John v HMS Magicienne. In June 1893 against Courtney Bay he hit another century, also for St John. In 1894 he toured Toronto with the Maritime Provinces.
HARDINGE, Samuel	Played in three matches in the International Series from 1856-60, where he took 17 wickets at an average of 8.06.
HEATHER, Frederick James	Played for the St George's Cricket Club who won the Toronto City Championship in 1922 and the Bell Telephone Cricket Club, who contested the final of the John Ross Robertson Trophy competition in 1927. However, it is as an umpire that Heather is best remembered. He served his umpiring apprenticeship in the Toronto leagues in the late 1920s and then went on to become Canada's most notable umpire. He officiated in games involving the 1932 Australian tourists, Sir Julien Cahn's team of 1933 and the MCC tours of 1937, 1951 and 1959. He retired in 1967 and was made a Life Member of the Toronto Cricket Umpire's Association on 12

	January 1970.
HEWARD, John O'Brien	A Canadian cricketer of notable longevity. He played in six matches in the International Series from 1846 to 1859. He was still topping his club's averages in 1873. He was elected the President of Toronto Cricket Club for ten consecutive years.
HILL, Hugh Cyril	Played in five International matches from 1897 to 1903. He averaged 17.44 in nine innings with a top score of 57. He was also a useful bowler taking 15 wickets at an average of 14.53, with the best figures of 7 for 58. Domestically Hill scored a century for McGill University in Montréal in 1901.
JOHNSON, Francis Godschall	Governor of Assiniboia from November 1855 to 1858, when he returned back to his law practice in Montréal, where he stated that cricket had been played at the Red River settlement with homemade cricket equipment.
KAISER, FA	Played only once in the International Series in 1891, but without success. He had a better record in domestic cricket, scoring three centuries for Halifax teams, two against visiting Navy teams and one against Northwest. He shared an partnership of 252 with FAW Taylor for Halifax Wanderers v Navy in July 1889, at the time a Canadian record. He played in the 1892 Halifax International Tournament and toured Toronto with the Maritime Provinces in 1894.
KENT, John	He joined the Upper Canada College as the Head of the Preparatory School in 1829, its founding year. He became the master of the Boarding House and more importantly the first President of the Upper Canada College Cricket Club in 1836. He also played in the inaugural match between the UCC Cricket Club and Toronto Cricket Club in 1936.
KING, Donald	Administrator most responsible for the renaissance in Canadian cricket following the Second World War. The Canadian Encyclopaedia states that cricket "was well served by the untiring administrative efforts of Donald King during the 1960s and 1970s, when teams from several countries toured Canada."
KIRCHHOFFER, John Nesbitt	Born in Cork, Ireland in 1848 and came to Canada in 1864. He studied law and was called to the Bar in Ontario in 1871. He played against Daft's 1879 tourists and represented Canada in one

	international match in 1880, without success. He became a Senator in 1892, a post he held until his death in 1914.
LAING, John Mellville	Canada's finest ever all-rounder. He played eight times for Canada in the International Series from 1892 to 1901, where he attempted to be Canada's answer to Bart King. Whilst his bowling did rival that of the great Philadelphian, he failed to do himself justice with the bat, averaging a surprisingly poor 7.19 in his 16 innings. Domestically he scored nine centuries between 1893 and 1901. He played his last international aged 28, before dedicating himself to a notable legal career. He continued to play for Toronto for 10 years or so after his last International. TC Patteson questions the legality of Laing's actions in his "reminiscences" in *Sixty Years of Canadian Cricket.*
LITTLE, William Carruthers	Played five times in the International Series from 1886 to 1902, without any success, hitting a top score of 4 in his 10 innings. Domestically he hit a century in Ottawa in May 1886. He toured Britain in 1887, playing in all 19 matches, but only managing seventh in the batting averages.
LOGAN, CJ	Played in three International matches between 1880 and 1883, taking six wickets for 70 runs in his first match, where he also opened the batting. The Toronto *Globe* of 4 May 1880 described him as the "best acknowledged bowler in Canada." He played for Trinity College, Port Hope and Carlton. In 1881 he took 178 wickets in the season, which was the first recorded incident of 100 wickets being taken in a season in Canada.
LYON, George Seymour	Played in eight International matches between 1880 to 1899, but could only manage a disappointing average of 14.07 in his 16 innings with a highest score of 34. Domestically it was a different story. Lyon hit four centuries in the mid-1890s, including an undefeated 238 for Rosedale v Peterborough on 24 August 1894, which was the highest score hit in Canada, eclipsing the 204 made by Mr Browning for Montréal. He won an Olympic gold medal in 1904 for golf. He was one of the original trustees of the competition for the John Ross Robertson Trophy.
McCULLOCH, Robert Osborne	Co-author of *Sixty Years of Canadian Cricket,* published in 1895. He hit a century for Galt v Brantford on 25 July 1900.

McGIVERIN, Harold Buchanan	A fast bowler who represented Canada in eight matches in the International Series from 1890 to 1903. He usually batted at 11 in these games, which was clearly too low for a player who averaged 29.67 in the Series, albeit with 10 not outs. Like his contemporaries Saunders and Laing he was a barrister. He was well travelled and came over to Britain in 1893 and played for St Neots Cricket Club. Outside cricket he had a notable political career, representing Ottawa as a Liberal MP before and after the First World War, becoming a Minister without Portfolio in 1924.
MORRISON, George N	Scottish born cricketer who played for Canada four times from 1881 to 1885 in the Series. He was a failure, averaging only 5.63 in eight innings with a top score of 10. He hit two centuries for Toronto Cricket Club in 1882.
MUNN, John Shannon	He played for Oxford University in 1900 and 1901, making him one of only three Newfoundlanders to play first-class cricket. He died with his three year old daughter Betty when the SS Florizel sank in February 1918.
OGDEN, Edward Russell	Captained Canada in the International Series and on the 1887 tour of Britain. He played in six Internationals from 1880 to 1888, but could only average 12.1 with a top score of 49 in his 12 innings. He scored two centuries for Chicago in the 1890s. Ogden was an UCC old boy, making his debut for the 1st XI in 1876 and being captain from 1877 to 1880. He played in the Western Association team of 1882, as a Chicago player. He missed much of the 1885 season due to poor health. He was a left-handed player and a round-arm bowler.
OTTAWAY, Cuthbert John	Toured Canada in 1872. Scored 102 for Hamilton against Montréal in August 1876. A great all-round sportsman, he was the first captain of the England football team. He attended Oxford University earning blues in rackets, real tennis and athletics as well as cricket and football. He a married a Canadian called Marion Stinson.
PARSONS, Benjamin	Played in eight consecutive matches for Canada in the International Series from 1853 to 1865.
PATTESON, Thomas Charles	Invited the MCC Secretary RA Fitzgerald to tour Canada. Tour took place in 1872 and included WG Grace.
PHILLIPPS,	Taught cricket by George Barber at the Upper

Reverend Thomas Dowell	Canada College and rivals him for the title "Father of Canadian cricket". The Reverend Phillipps edited three editions of the Canadian Cricketer's Guide in 1858, 1876 and 1877. He played four times for Canada in the International Series, the first time in 1858 and the final time in 1879. He excelled in the Halifax Tournament of 1874 where he made 197 runs at an average of 39.40, winning an award for the highest aggregate of runs made in the Tournament. He was a member of the ill-fated 1880 tour of Britain, stepping in to captain the side following the arrest of Thomas Dale, the original skipper. Phillipps proved his longevity when he hit a century for Chicago 2nd XI against St George's 2nd XI on 4 July 1896, aged 63.
PICKERING, William Percival	A Cambridge Blue and captain of Eton, who went on to represent the Gentlemen against the Players. He was one of the original members of Surrey County Cricket Club and I Zingari. He emigrated to Canada and represented his new country in the International Series in four consecutive matches from 1853 to 1857, without much success, his top score being 18 not out in 1857. According to Wisden, Pickering was chiefly responsible for ensuring that George Parr's 1859 tour went ahead. A nephew, FPU Pickering, was a member of Fitzgerald's 1872 tour.
RAY, S	Played in four Internationals from 1879 to 1883 without much success. He had a batting average of 7.00 and a top score of 20. Domestically he hit two centuries for Peterborough in 1884 and 1888.
ROBERTSON, John Ross	Philanthropist who donated the John Ross Robertson Trophy in 1910 for the best domestic Canadian cricket team.
ROBINSON, John Beverly	Played for Toronto and the Upper Canada College in the 1830s and for Canada in the first International match in 1844. He umpired in the 1856 International and was elected Mayor of Toronto in the same year.
SAUNDERS, Dyce Willcocks	Fine wicket-keeper batsman who played 12 times for Canada in the International Series from 1881 to 1901. He was captain for five of these matches and in four of those games he opened the batting as well as kept wicket. He averaged a disappointing 9.73 in the Series, but hit an impressive eight centuries in the 1880s and 1890s for Guelph,

	Toronto and Trinity. Saunders played for Trinity College School in 1877 and was made captain the following year. He then went on to play for Guelph, before moving to Toronto to study law and play for Toronto Cricket Club. He had a successful tour of Britain in 1887, prompting *Cricket: A Weekly Record of the* Game to favourably compare his glove work "with some of the very best of our amateur wicket-keepers." He toured again with Seagram's team in 1922. Like JM Laing, Saunders had a notable legal career and became a KC. He was one of the original trustees for the competition for the John Ross Robertson Trophy.
SEAGRAM, Norman	Played once in the International Series in 1912. Captained, selected and finance the Canadian team that toured Britain in 1922.
TERRY, Francis William	The Reverend Terry played in eight Internationals from 1891 to 1907, where he averaged 22.38 with the bat, scoring the first century for Canada in 1893. He hit eight other centuries in the 1890s, six for London Asylum, where he may well have been a patient. He was born in Wells, Somerset and played for that county before emigrating to Canada.
VALENTINE, John	Played in Canada's first World Cup in 1979, being one of two Manitobans selected for the squad. Canada were outplayed by Pakistan, England and Australia, but Valentine took a wicket in every match and was never dismissed, although he batted at 11. His father played for Cambridge University and became the Bishop of Rupertsland.
WALLACE, Nesbit Willoughby	Captain in the 1st Battalion of the 60th Rifles, based at Halifax, Nova Scotia. He was born in Halifax, but educated in England, playing cricket for Rugby School. He designed and organised the 1874 Tournament in Halifax. He played for Gloucestershire in 1871 and then again for Hampshire in 1884 after returning to Britain.
WEIGHTON, William	Head of the Manitoba Cricket Association in the 1960s and 1970s. Helped to organise the western half of the MCC 1959 tour to Canada.
WENHAM, Walter **Reg**inald Gower	Born in Souris Manitoba in August 1903. Hit five centuries for the province of British Columbia and played against the touring teams of Australia (1933) and the MCC (1937 & 1951). In 1951, aged 48 he top-scored with 24 and took 4 for 36 against the visiting MCC team.

WILSON, Herbert G	One of the finest players to come out of Winnipeg. Geographical location restricted him to just one International match in 1895, but he scored no fewer than four centuries in the 1890s playing for Winnipeg and W Bannatyne's XI. On 7 August 1888 he took a hat-trick against an American team, whilst on tour with Winnipeg Cricket Club. In a tournament hosted by Winnipeg Cricket Club in 1894, which involved five clubs, Wilson averaged 95. He was an adventurer who was a member of the 1884 expedition sent to relieve General Gordon in Khartoum and in 1897 he took part in the Klondike gold rush. He then returned to Winnipeg and became Commissioner of the Workmen's Compensation Board. He was suspended from this post in January 1925. He committed suicide in December of the same year.

Index

References

i P.124 *Sixty years of Canadian cricket* by JE Hall and RO McCulloch

ii P.30 "The British Protestant Pioneers and the Establishment of Manly Sports in Manitoba, 1870-1886" in Journal of Sport, Vol. 7 No.3 (Winter 1980) by Morris Mott

iii P.68 *Bastards & Boneheads: Canada's Glorious Leaders Past and Present*

iv P.7 Whimpress B. and Hart N. "Great Ashes Battles" Andre Deutsch, London 2005

v P.2 Bowen, Roland North America in International Cricket.

vi p.13 Marder J.I. The International Series

vii Chapter 35, Third paragraph of J. B. Mansfield, ed., History of the Great Lakes. Volume I, Chicago: J. H. Beers & Co., 1899. See http://www.linkstothepast.com/marine/chapt35.html

viii P.22 Marder J.I. The International Series

ix A letter to the paper, 15 August 1853, *New York Times*

x See Weekly Herald of 27 August 1853 and Milwaukee Sentinel of 30 August 1853.

xi 24 August 1853, *New York Times*

xii 4 August 1858, *New York Times*

xiii *New York Times* 3 August 1858

xiv *New York Times* 5th August 1858

xv *New York Times* 8 August 1858

xvi *New York Times* 7 August 1860

xvii Toronto *Globe* 30 August 1865

xviii P.188 Major, J More than a Game

xix P.36 Marder, J.I. The International Series

xx P.38-9 Marder, J.I. The International Series

xxi P.392 Hutchinson, HG Cricket

xxii P. 10 "Keeping in Touch" by Ruth M. Buck pp.4-10 in The Beaver magazine Oct/Nov 1986

xxiii *New York Herald* 24 October 1859

xxiv *New York Herald* 27 October 1859

xxv p.78 Sixty Years of Canadian Cricket

xxvi *New York Herald* 7 October 1859

xxvii p.9 Fitzgerald, RA *Wickets in the West*

xxviii p.172-3 Fitzgerald, RA *Wickets in the West*

xxix pp 42-3 Fitzgerald, RA *Wickets in the West*

xxx P.39 Fitzgerald, RA *Wickets in the West*

xxxi P.55 "*Wickets in the West*: Cricket, Culture and Constructed Images of Nineteenth Century Canada" by Greg Gillespie in Journal of Sport History Vol. 27 No.1 Spring 2000

xxxii P.78 Fitzgerald, RA *Wickets in the West*

xxxiii p. 71 Fitzgerald, RA *Wickets in the West*

xxxiv P.76 Fitzgerald, RA *Wickets in the West*

xxxv 3 September 1872 *Toronto Globe*

xxxvi p.94 Fitzgerald, RA *Wickets in the West*

xxxvii p.136 Fitzgerald, RA *Wickets in the West*

xxxviii p.156 Fitzgerald, RA *Wickets in the West*

xxxix pp.142-3 Fitzgerald, RA *Wickets in the West*

xl p.152 Fitzgerald, RA *Wickets in the West*

xli P.151 Fitzgerald, RA *Wickets in the West*

xlii Toronto *Globe* 11 September 1878

xliii p.191 Fitzgerald, RA *Wickets in the West*

xliv P.176 Fitzgerald, RA *Wickets in the West*

xlv P.180 Fitzgerald, RA *Wickets in the West*
xlvi p. 220 Fitzgerald, RA *Wickets in the West*
xlvii Philadelphia Inquirer 25 September 1872
xlviii p. 289 Fitzgerald, RA *Wickets in the West*
xlix Toronto *Globe* 23 Sept 1878
l p.349 Sixty Years of Canadian Cricket
li Toronto *Globe* 12 Sep
lii P.350 Sixty Years of Canadian Cricket
liii Toronto *Globe* 13 September 1879
liv Toronto *Globe* 15 September 1879
lv Toronto *Globe* 23 September 1879
lvi p.9 Cricket Across the Sea
lvii p. 153 Cricket Across the Sea
lviii p.151 Cricket Across the Sea
lix p.144 Cricket Across the Sea
lx P.157 Cricket Across the Sea
lxi 16 July 1888, Toronto *Globe*
lxii p.174 Cricket Across the Sea
lxiii p.175 Cricket Across the Sea
lxiv 4 August 1887, Toronto *Globe*
lxv *Globe* 14 August 1886
lxvi *New York Times* 13 July 1868
lxvii P.97 Bowen Rowland, *Cricket: A History of its Growth and Development Throughout the World* (London, Eyre and Spottiswade, 1970)
lxviii Toronto *Globe* 2 August 1879
lxix http://www.cricketarchive.com/Archive/Scorecards/120/120646.html
lxx P.433, Cricket: A Weekly Record of the Game 1883
lxxi Philadelphia Enquirer 17 September 1884
lxxii *New York Times* 15 August 1886
lxxiii *New York Times* 17 September 1892
lxxiv *New York Times* 16 September 1893
lxxv *Globe* 13 September 1893
lxxvi *Globe* 12 August 1895
lxxvii *New York Times* of 5 September 1896
lxxviii *New York Times* 28 July 1897
lxxix *New York Times* 8 September 1897
lxxx Minneapolis Journal 8 September 1897
lxxxi *New York Times* 9 August 1899
lxxxii *New York Times* 9 August 1899
lxxxiii *Globe* 9 August 1899 & Maryland Sun 9 August 1899
lxxxiv http://www.cricinfo.com/england/content/player/9158.html quoting 1925 Wisden
lxxxv *Toronto Star* 22 July 1905
lxxxvi *Toronto Star* 21 March 1905
lxxxvii *Toronto Star* 31 July 1905
lxxxviii *Globe* 31 January 1911
lxxxix *Globe* 1 March 1911
xc Toronto *Globe* 31 August 1914
xci Toronto *Globe* 31 July 1918
xcii Toronto *Globe* 10 June 1918
xciii Toronto *Globe* 5 May 1911
xciv P.42 Miller, Ian Hugh McClenan, Our Glory and Our Grief

xcv P. 45, Granatstein JL & Morton D, *Canada and the Two World Wars*

xcvi 2 November 1915 *Toronto Star*

xcvii P.104 Madley M & Sarty RF, *Tin Pots and Pirate Ships: Canadian Naval Forces and German Sea Raiders*

xcviii Toronto *Globe* 14 October 1916

xcix P.253 Brown, Cassie, *A Winter's Tale: The Wreck of the Florizel*

c Pp13-4 Putkowski, Julian *The Kinmel Park Camp Riots 1919*

ci *Toronto Star* Wednesday 20 February 1929

cii P.7 of *Gender and Race in the Construction of "Legal Professionalism": Historical Perspectives* by Constance Backhouse.

ciii Toronto *Globe* 11 August 1917

civ Toronto *Globe* 12 June 1918

cv Toronto *Globe* 12 November 1918

cvi The Toronto *Globe* of Monday 10 July 1911

cvii Toronto *Globe* of Friday 6 Sep 1912

cviii *Toronto Star* p.13 Monday 18 August 1913

cix 24 November 1913 *The Toronto World*

cx P.22 Sat 28 March 1914 *Toronto Star*

cxi 10 July 1914 *Toronto World*

cxii 2 October 1918 *Toronto World*

cxiii 21 August 1925 *Montréal Gazette*

cxiv Mon 28 July 1924, Toronto *Globe*

cxv 8 September 1926 *New York Times*

cxvi 29 November 1928 *Montréal Gazette*

cxvii 26 November 1927 *Montréal Gazette*

cxviii 19 July 1928 Montréal Gazette

cxix p.11 Thu 6 Sep 1928 Toronto Star

cxx p.13 Fri 19 Oct 1928 Toronto Star

cxxi p.11 Thu 6 Sep 1928 Toronto Star

cxxii Fri 30 August 1929 *Montréal Gazette*

cxxiii 3 September 1930 *Montréal Gazette*

cxxiv 26 Aug 1933 *Montréal Gazette*

cxxv 20 June 1932 *Montréal Gazette*

cxxvi *Montreal Gazette* 1 August 1951

cxxvii E-mail from Angus Bell, received on Thursday 11 December 2008

cxxviii 22 May 1979 The Guardian

cxxix 11 February 2003 Racing Post

cxxx Phone conversation with Manitoba Cricket Association.

cxxxi *Globe* Friday 23 August 1889

cxxxii E-mail from Angus Bell, received on Thursday 11 December 2008

1336530R0

Printed in Great Britain by
Amazon.co.uk, Ltd.,
Marston Gate.